P9-AFZ-487

DATE DUE

FE 12 '96			
MR 18 '97			
RENEW			
AP 14 '97			
DE 19 '97			
AG 10			

DEMCO 38-296

The Culture of Food

THE MAKING OF EUROPE
Series Editor: Jacques Le Goff

The Making of Europe series is the result of a unique collaboration between five European publishers – Beck in Germany, Blackwell in Great Britain and the United States, Critica in Spain, Laterza in Italy and le Seuil in France. Each book will be published in all five languages. The scope of the series is broad, encompassing the history of ideas as well as and including their interaction with the history of societies, nations and states, to produce informative, readable and provocative treatments of central themes in the history of the European peoples and their cultures.

The Culture of Food

Massimo Montanari

Translated by Carl Ipsen

BLACKWELL
Oxford UK & Cambridge USA

Riverside Community College
Library
4800 Magnolia Avenue
Riverside, California 92506

Copyright © Massimo Montanari 1994

English translation copyright © Basil Blackwell Ltd 1994

First published in 1994 by Blackwell Publishers and by four other
publishers: © 1993 Beck, Munich (German); © 1994 Critica, Barcelona
(Spanish);
© 1994 Editions du Seuil, Paris (French); © 1993 Laterza, Rome and Bari
(Italian).

Blackwell Publishers, the publishing imprint of Basil Blackwell Ltd
108 Cowley Road
Oxford OX4 1JF, UK

Basil Blackwell Inc.
238 Main Street
Cambridge, Massachusetts 02142
USA

All rights reserved. Except for the quotation of short passages for the
purposes of criticism and review, no part of this publication may be
reproduced, stored in a retrieval system, or transmitted, in any form or by
any means, electronic, mechanical, photocopying, recording or otherwise,
without the prior permission of the publisher.

Except in the United States of America, this book is sold subject to the
condition that it shall not, by way of trade or otherwise, be lent, re-sold, hired
out, or otherwise circulated without the publisher's prior consent in any form
of binding or cover other than that in which it is published and without a
similar condition including this condition being imposed on the subsequent
purchaser.

British Library Cataloguing in Publication Data
A CIP catalogue record for this book is available from the British Library.

Library of Congress Cataloging-in-Publication Data

sh]
simo Montanari; translated by Carl Ipsen.
Europe)
rences (p.   ) and index.

d habits—Europe.   3. Europe—Social life
Series.

93–39915
CIP

TX 353 .M7213 1994

MONTANARI, MASSIMO, 1949-

THE CULTURE OF FOOD

Typeset in 12 on 13.5 pt Garamond 3 by
Pure Tech Corporation, Pondicherry, India
Printed in Great Britain by T. J. Press Ltd, Padstow, Cornwall
This book is printed on acid-free paper

To Marina (finally)

Contents

Series Editor's Preface

Europe is in the making. This is both a great challenge and one that can be met only by taking the past into account – a Europe without history would be orphaned and unhappy. Yesterday conditions today; today's actions will be felt tomorrow. The memory of the past should not paralyse the present: when based on understanding it can help us to forge new friendships, and guide us towards progress.

Europe is bordered by the Atlantic, Asia and Africa, its history and geography inextricably entwined, and its past comprehensible only within the context of the world at large. The territory retains the name given it by the ancient Greeks, and the roots of its heritage may be traced far into prehistory. It is on this foundation – rich and creative, united yet diverse – that Europe's future will be built.

The Making of Europe is the joint initiative of five publishers of different languages and nationalities: Beck in Munich; Blackwell in Oxford; Critica in Barcelona; Laterza in Rome; and le Seuil in Paris. Its aim is to describe the evolution of Europe, presenting the triumphs but not concealing the difficulties. In their efforts to achieve accord and unity the nations of Europe have faced discord, division and conflict. It is no purpose of this series to conceal these problems: those committed to the European enterprise will not succeed if their view of the future is unencumbered by an understanding of the past.

The title of the series is thus an active one: the time is yet to come when a synthetic history of Europe will be possible. The books we shall publish will be the work of leading historians, by no means all European. They will address crucial aspects of European history in every field – political, economic, social, religious and cultural. They will draw on that long historiographical tradition which stretches back to Herodotus, as well as on those conceptions and ideas which have transformed historical inquiry in the recent decades of the twentieth century. They will write readably for a wide public.

Our aim is to consider the key questions confronting those involved in Europe's making, and at the same time to satisfy the curiosity of the world at large: in short, who are the Europeans? where have they come from? whither are they bound?

Jacques Le Goff

A Proposal

The plan of this book is an ambitious one. It is a study of food, its production systems and consumption models, which aspires to be something more, perhaps the entire history of our civilization, a civilization the many faces (economic, social, political and cultural) of which have always had a direct and important relationship with the problem of nutrition. Nor could it be otherwise, as daily survival is man's first and unavoidable need. Yet food represents pleasure as well, and between these two poles there exists a difficult and complex history, strongly conditioned by the relationships of power and social inequality. It is a history of famine and plenty in which cultural images also play a decisive role, a history which is by no means 'alternative' (a point worth emphasizing). By virtue of its centrality, the history of food proceeds in step with the 'other' histories – it determines and is determined by these – even though its strong anthropological implications make simple chronological comparisons difficult.

I am a medievalist and have devoted many of these pages to the Middle Ages. This fact has not, however, prevented me from extending my gaze to less familiar periods. Going back to the third century and forward to the nineteenth and twentieth, I have tried to identify the essential characteristics of the history and culture of food in Europe, to reconstruct the origins, development and results. In sketching this history, I have become

ever more convinced of the uselessness of 'medieval' as a traditional chronological category (a conviction shared by many scholars); it is a false entity of little interpretative worth. The events
and values it presumes to contain are too varied and even contra-
dictory to permit the attribution of a uniform historical significance. Why then do we persist in using that unifying term
invented by fifteenth-century humanists to describe a vacuum,
an *absence* of history and culture?

The chronology I have chosen to use in this book ignores
academic periodization and as a result banishes the medieval
altogether, dismantling and reassembling it in diverse parts. I
have simply eliminated the 'Middle Ages' from both my vocabulary and mental horizon. This was not an easy challenge for
me: it made me realize that even a 'professional medievalist' can
occasionally make use of the category in order to simplify and to
economize his discussion, thus avoiding the need to discover the
essence of history and to compare himself with the people and
ordinary daily activities of a past time. In the end, I felt freed as
from a restrictive and artificial scaffolding that had prevented
me from working and thinking freely. Needless to say, anti-
quity, the modern age and other such constructs also disappeared. There remain people, things and ideas.

Imola, September 1992

1

The Basis for a Common Language

The Age of Famine

'In these times of misery and misfortune we cannot seek fame in poetry because we must tend to the famine which afflicts our homes.'[1] Such was the lament of Fabius Fulgentius at the end of the fifth century AD, though he managed to incorporate a play on words (eternal *fama* and daily *fames*) and so highlight the literary and rhetorical nature of his position. The apparent levity of the passage should not, however, lead us to disregard its content. The years in which Fulgentius wrote were difficult ones, both for individuals and for public institutions. Signs of a state of emergency abounded: the Roman Empire was in the process of dissolution and out of its ruin there emerged only with difficulty new political and administrative systems; peoples and cultures were thrown together; the productive infrastructure was in a state of crisis which had begun in the third century with the decline of agriculture, the depopulation of the countryside and the weakening of the cities' redistributional function; war and disaster were frequent; epidemics regularly followed periods of want; plague broke out periodically.[2]

But was this really an emergency? Perhaps not. A state of emergency might last a few months or years, at most a few decades, but not several centuries – the duration usually assigned to Europe's difficult period. The crisis began in the third century; it worsened in the fourth and fifth and, in certain

regions such as Italy, reached its peak in the sixth, period of the
bloodiest conflicts and most devastating famines and epidemics.
This 'emergency' seems then to have been the day-to-day state
of affairs to which men and women had to accustom themselves
for several centuries, over at least ten generations. Perhaps those
generations had no concept of a different sort of life, and gradually they must have developed survival techniques adapted to
difficult times. The progressive decline in European population
from the third through to the end of the sixth century might
suggest an inability to adapt sufficiently to adversity. Yet the
link between population decline and nutritional hardship is by
no means so direct: many indices suggest that it was during
phases of reduced population pressure that individual levels of
consumption were most secure, while phases of rapid population
growth were not necessarily linked to an abundance of food – a
situation with which we are familiar today. Let us not then be
too hasty in characterizing the nutritional situation of the fifth
and sixth centuries as catastrophic. The lists of famines, epidemics and wars which historians have carefully reconstructed
with the help of literary sources and chronicles should not lead to
the oversimplified picture of a Europe on the verge of disaster.[3]

There was of course no shortage of tragedies, for example when
flood, freezing temperatures or drought wiped out a harvest,
when bands of armed marauders roamed the countryside plunder-
ing whatever they came upon, or when disease carried off livestock, bringing loss of food and draught animals. In such times of
want, alternative forms of nutrition were sought – unusual plants
and roots, invented breads, meat of all sorts – much as has
occurred in recent times during the direst periods of war. Referring to events from the late sixth century, Gregory of Tours wrote:

> During that year a great famine afflicted almost the whole
> of Gaul. Many used grape seeds or hazelnut blossoms to
> make bread while others used fern roots which they
> pressed, dried, powdered and mixed with a little flour.
> Others tried a similar operation but used weeds cleared

from the fields. There were even some who, completely
without flour, were reduced to the gathering and consumption of various grasses; they however wasted away and
became swollen.[4]

Procopius describes peasants in central Italy during the worst
years of the Graeco-Gothic war not even managing the miserable diet described by Gregory: 'Famine had so overcome them
at that point that if they saw a little grass they rushed to it
eagerly, bending over in order to tear it from the ground but
unable to do so because they utterly lacked strength. There they
fell upon the grass, hands clenched, and died.' Procopius's account abounds in horrifying images: 'emaciated and yellow of
face', their skin dried up and 'became like leather'; the hungry
collapsed to the ground 'wearing an astonished expression and a
shocked and crazed gaze'. Some died of starvation, others were
poisoned by the food they did manage to eat: 'They had lost all
their natural heat, and it became necessary to feed them small
amounts of food at a time, as with newborn babies; otherwise
they would die because of their inability to digest the food they
were given.' There was even report of some who, 'threatened by
starvation, ate human flesh'.[5]

These accounts leave a strong and frightening impression, as
do the lists of unclean foods – meat taken from corpses, soups
contaminated by rats or insects – included in the penitential
books, a sort of handbook used by confessors which originated
in the sixth century and abounding in directives on behaviour
(including diet) that the good Christian should avoid.[6] However, only a morbid preference for the horrible could make us
believe that such repasts were normal. Indeed, one can easily
find similarly disgusting anecdotes in all ages, including our
own. And why should we be fascinated only by unusual, exaggerated and extreme cases? Normality may not be the stuff of
headlines; none the less we should not ignore the simple day-to-
day aspects of survival, and perhaps hunger. Nor is it superfluous
to recall the obvious fact that hunger does not generally lead to

death, but only in rare cases of extreme and prolonged famine. It was far more normal to live with hunger, withstanding and combating it on a daily basis. The extraordinary ability that *Homo sapiens* has developed over time to resist and cope with hunger must derive in part from this situation (and also the reverse, namely the ability to consume huge, and at times excessive, amounts of food which can be stored for use in periods of want).

The European of the fifth and sixth centuries (and we shall attempt a better definition below) was not, then, simply a desperate devourer of grasses and wild roots, or perhaps when necessary a fierce cannibal, but also – and certainly more often – a normal consumer of food who even used a table, and occasionally a tablecloth. With good reason he feared that from one day to the next he might find himself without food, and so sought to differentiate the full range of nutritional sources available to him. *Differentiation* may in fact be the central concept necessary to understand the mechanisms regarding the procurement and preparation of food in the centuries during which the imperial Roman political frame of reference was in decline and a new institutional, economic and cultural order was emerging.

Environmental and demographic factors allowed and encouraged a solution of this sort: low population density, half-empty regions, deserted countryside. Describing the pestilence that struck Italy in the second half of the sixth century, the Lombard historian Paul the Deacon wrote: 'Though harvest time had passed, the crops awaited the reaper and grapes still hung on the vines.'[7] Theoretically resources were plentiful; it only required that the survivors organize themselves in order to take advantage, in particular, of the vast stretches of forest, natural fields and swamp which had since the third century taken over previously cultivated areas and come to dominate the landscape. Exploitation of these possibilities required the invention of necessary practical methods and the overcoming of that cultural prejudice – widespread in the ancient world – which excluded the *saltus*, the untilled, from productive activity, seeing it as a sort of antithesis to the human and civilized world. Progressive modification of this attitude proceeded in tandem with the establishment between the fifth and sixth centuries of a new productive and cultural model, a model that began to open the way to, and to a degree combine, choices and options that had until then been at odds and strongly opposed. It is to this process, decisive for the creation of a common 'nutritional language' comprehensible to the majority of Europeans, that we shall now turn our attention.

Barbarians and Romans[8]

The Romans – like the Greeks – did not show great appreciation of nature in its wild state, and the uncultivated had little or no place in the value systems of Greek and Roman intellectuals. It was in fact the antithesis of *civilitas* – itself a concept linked etymologically and otherwise to that of *civitas*, the city – an artificial order created by man in order to distinguish and separate him from nature. For Graeco-Roman culture, the ideal productive space consisted of rural areas carefully organized around cities; the Romans called this space *ager*, the sum of cultivated lands, and strictly distinguished it from the *saltus* or virgin, non-human, uncivilized and unproductive nature.[9] None the less, there did exist marginal methods for extracting resources from uncultivated regions, and economic activity related to the forests and swamps was certainly more widespread than the sources would lead us to believe.[10] This perception, however, testifies to the marginal and in a way 'submerged' nature of these activities, hidden by a literature ideologically inclined to emphasize other values: civilization, the city, agriculture undertaken for the city (for urban markets and consumers). The notion of the uncultivated in Roman culture was clearly negative. The forest was synonymous with marginality and exclusion; and only marginal or excluded individuals resorted to it for obtaining food, like the hunter in Dio Chrysostom's *Euboicus*.[11]

Agricultural cultivation then clearly dominated other methods of acquiring food and was the basis of Graeco-Roman economy and culture (at least with regard to the dominant models). Wheat, grapes and olives were the most important crops, a triad which took on productive and cultural significance as a representative symbol of classical civilization itself. The words of Anius, king and priest of Delos, as reported by Ovid in the *Metamorphoses*, reveal much regarding the nutritional habits and desires of the period (and the myth of Anius must surely also be Utopian): 'For at my daughters' touch all things were turned to corn and wine and the oil of grey-green Minerva.'[12] Plutarch reports that young Athenians, on reaching maturity, were led to the sanctuary of Agraulos in order to 'take oath that they will regard wheat, barley, the vine, and the olive as the natural boundaries of Attica'.[13] Those three elements were necessary and sufficient for its identification. In addition to the harvesting of field, vine and tree, horticulture played an important if secondary role, as did to a lesser extent the pasturing of sheep, the only use of natural resources for which Greek and Latin writers showed serious attention;[14] fishing was important only in coastal regions. Out of this productive system there developed a diet, which we may call 'Mediterranean', characterized by a dominant vegetable component – grain preparations and bread, wine, oil and greens – complemented by a little meat and especially cheese; goats and sheep were raised principally for the production of milk and wool.

The modes of production and cultural values of the 'barbarians' – as the Greeks and Romans called them – were entirely different. Celtic and Germanic populations had for centuries criss-crossed the great forests of central and northern Europe and had developed a strong preference for the products of virgin nature and uncultivated spaces. Hunting and fishing, the gathering of wild fruits, and the free pasturing of livestock in the woods (especially swine, but also horses and cows) were central to their way of life. Meat, rather than bread or polenta, was the most important element of their diet. Instead of wine (known only in the areas bordering the empire), they drank mare's milk and its acidic liquid derivatives, or cider (made by fermenting wild fruits), or beer in those areas where grains were grown in small plots carved out of the forest. Instead of oil (the only fat mentioned in the Roman cooking manuals attributed to Apicius), butter or lard was used for greasing and cooking.

The picture was not of course so clear-cut. The Germanic peoples also ate grains, oatmeal and a baked barley preparation, though not bread made from wheat, true symbol of the Mediterranean diet. The Romans also ate pork (which the Emperors had ordered to be distributed to the population of the capital together with bread).[15] The question here, however, is not to verify whether or not certain foods were eaten – we would find that everyone ate more or less the same thing – but rather to evaluate the role of specific foods in the nutritional regime, their place and importance within systems organized in very different ways. Taking the latter approach it is the differences that stand out, differences which served at the time to establish cultural identity and distinguish one group from another. In keeping with Homer's definition of men as 'bread eaters' – taking this practice as a synthetic emblem of civilization – the Greek and Roman writers described with amazement, and perhaps also satisfaction as the 'other' always serves to confirm our own convictions, the habits of strange peoples who were unfamiliar with bread and wine. Caesar wrote of the Germans: 'For agriculture they have no zeal, and the greater part of their food consists of milk, cheese, and flesh.'[16] Tacitus informs us that at the beginning of the second century they also bought wine (at least those living near the banks of the Rhine). Their usual drink, however, was 'a liquor . . . made out of barley or other grain and fermented into a certain resemblance to wine', namely beer, or perhaps we should call it *cervisia* to distinguish this dense, full-bodied liquid from the lighter and transparent beer produced beginning 1,000 years later by the addition of hops. For the rest 'their food is of a simple kind, consisting of wild-fruit, fresh game, and curdled milk'.[17] Several centuries later, after the

Germanic peoples had established by force of arms their own power and firmly set foot in the regions of the empire, similar descriptions were applied to other populations living 'on the edges of the world'. In the sixth century, Procopius wrote of the Lapps: 'They do not drink wine nor do they extract any food from the earth . . . men and women alike engage only in hunting.'[18] Jordanes, also in the sixth century, instead assures us that the lesser Goths were familiar with wine because of trade carried out with nearby peoples, but none the less continued to prefer milk. He also describes Scandinavians 'who live entirely off meat', Huns whose sole activity is hunting, and Lapps who 'do not get their food from the grains of the earth, but live on wild meats and birds' eggs'; in the eighth century, Paul the Deacon would specify that these meats were eaten raw, yet another sign of nutritional barbarism.[19] Agricultural practices, however, were not in themselves sufficient to qualify a people as possessing *civilitas*. Procopius wrote of the Moors that they did in fact eat grains (wheat and barley), but 'without cooking them or making them into flour'; ignorant of the art of bread-making, they ate them 'in the same way that animals do'.[20] And here lay the fundamental qualification: the active intervention in the preparation of food and its artificial creation and 'invention', rather than the simple acceptance of that which nature (even encouraged by man) offered.

Pride in one's own nutritional, and in a larger sense cultural, identity did not of course characterize the Romans alone. Celts and Germans were also strongly tied to their own traditions. Yet we should search in vain among those groups for a 'plant of civilization' (to use the well-known phrase of Braudel)[21] that played a role similar to that of wheat in the Greek and Latin worlds, or of corn in the Americas, or rice in Asia. We might find instead an 'animal of civilization', namely the pig, omnipresent in the Celtic world and perhaps the only symbol to express and embody the cultural and productive values of that civilization. Celtic mythology, for example, is replete with episodes in which the pig, indispensable sustenance of man, plays a central role, as for example in the poem *The Story of Mac Dathos' Pig*, in which a gigantic swine is fed for seven years with the milk of sixty cows and then served with forty oxen stretched over its back.[22]

Similarly, Germanic mythology depicted an other-worldly paradise in which heroes fallen in battle ate the never-ending supply of meat provided by Saehrimnir, the great pig, symbol of the origin of life and the essence of food and nutrition: according to Snorri's *Edda*, 'each day he is boiled and by evening he is once again whole'. The creation myths recounted by Snorri also give a special place to the cow Audhumla 'from whose teats spring four rivers of milk', once again an animal, once again the economy of forest and pasture.[23]

Greek and Latin writers on the other hand had a clear vision of a happily vegetarian Golden Age; from a nutritional point of view their culture valued above all the fruits of the earth. Hesiod wrote that in the time of Chronos mortals 'lived as if they were gods . . . The fruitful grainland yielded its harvest to them of its own accord; this was great and abundant.'[24] Democritus, Dicaearchus and Plato made similar statements, as did Lucretius, Virgil and many others.[25] The image repeated was always the same: an earth which at first gave spontaneously (as in the biblical Eden) and then as a result of human labour, all accompanied by the myths of wheat, wine and oil. As far as animals were concerned, Varro writes that the first to be domesticated and used by man were sheep.[26] In any case 'it is from [bread] that the whole world begins' according to Pythagoras.[27] And as we read in the *Epic of Gilgamesh*, one of the oldest testimonies to Mediterranean culture, it was bread that, together with wine, allowed the savage man to become civilized.[28]

During the first half of the third century, the confrontation between these different cultures reached a critical point. New social forces and new peoples made their appearance on the edges of the empire, and it even came to pass that individuals of 'barbarian' origin managed to conquer the throne in the rapid succession of emperors precipitated by profound institutional crisis. The biographies collected in the so-called *Historia Augusta*, probably compiled in the fourth century, well demonstrate just that conflict of values (of nutritional values as well) that we have been discussing. The 'Roman' nature of the emperor's diet, solidly founded on traditional ideological values, is often stressed in these texts, especially when presenting an individual in a positive light:

> The usual slanderers spread the word that Didius Julianus had on the first day of his reign scorned the frugality of Pertinax (his predecessor) by ordering the preparation of a sumptuous banquet including oysters, poultry and fish. This rumour was, however, totally false: Julianus was so sober in his habits that if someone gave him a roasted suckling pig or a hare, he would make it last for three days; otherwise he was content to eat greens and legumes without meat, though no religious precept required it.

This excerpt well highlights the positive light in which the culture of this author (here Elius Spartianus) viewed vegetarian fare; one could do without meat, and indeed it was preferable to do so (it is no accident that Greek and Roman traditions are replete with vegetarian philosophies). A few more examples: Gordian II, though not very interested in food, 'was particularly fond of greens and fresh fruit'. Septimius Severus, another emperor of sober and frugal habits, 'was partial to greens from his own land and occasionally enjoyed drinking wine; often he did not even bother to sample the meat that was served'. It was even the case that certain individuals, judged immoral and excessive in their eating habits, concentrated their gluttony on one particular category, fruit, and so did not stray from the ideological framework of vegetarianism. Clodius Albinus 'was an incredible glutton, especially with regard to fruit: on an empty stomach he was able to consume 500 figs, a basket of peaches, 10 melons and 20 pounds of grapes', as well as 100 garden warblers and

400 oysters. Gallienus' 'lamentable refinement' was exemplified by the fact that 'he built castles of fruit, preserved grapes for three years and served melons in the middle of winter'.

Maximinus the Thracian embodied the 'barbarian' cultural model long and vainly resisted by many Roman intellectuals. He was the first emperor–soldier, 'born of barbarian parents, one a Goth and the other from the Alani'. His biographer, Julius Capitolinus, wrote with disapproval that he drank as much as an amphora of wine a day (which must have been about 20 litres), and 'ate as much as 40 or even 60 lb of meat'; it seems even to have been the case   impossible for a true Roman – that 'he had never sampled vegetables'. His son, Maximinus the younger, was no different: 'excessively fond of food and especially wild game, he ate nothing but boar, duck, crane, and every sort of game'. Firmus too was a great drinker and 'a great eater of meat'; it was written that 'he ate an ostrich a day'. These depictions are clearly to be taken with a grain of salt. The point, however, is not to identify them as true, but rather to recognize in them the cultural tension of a period that was critical – from the point of view of nutritional models as well – to the history of Europe.[29]

An abyss separated the 'Roman' world from that of the 'barbarians'. Values, ideologies and systems of production all distinguished the one from the other. It must have seemed impossible to bridge the divide, and in fact two millennia of common history have not been enough to erase all differences; Europe is still profoundly marked by them. None the less, a degree of rapprochement did take place thanks to a two-way process of cultural blending that began during the fifth and sixth centuries and developed during those that followed.

The Meat of the Strong

A driving force behind this process of blending was, simply put, power. The political and social predominance of the Germanic tribes, who had gradually and at a rate that varied from region to region become the ruling class of the new Europe, resulted in the general spread of Germanic culture and mental outlook. As compared to the Graeco-Roman tradition, the Germans established a new way of looking at uncultivated space and nature in its wild state: no longer a cumbersome presence or a limit to human productive activity, it was instead a space to be *used*.[30] Nothing better exemplified this change than the custom – current from the seventh and eighth centuries in the regions most strongly influenced by Germanic culture (England, Germany, France, northern Italy) – of measuring the size of a forest not in abstract terms of surface area but in terms of the number of swine that could be fed and fattened on the available acorns, beechnuts and other edible plants: *silva ad saginandum porcos* . . . . This was the principal measure used for forests and the one considered most useful; it bore an analogy to the productive notions applied to fields (measured in terms of wheat production), vineyards (wine production) and pasture (hay). A conception of this sort would have been impossible a few centuries earlier. To one brought up in the Graeco-Roman cultural tradition, the raising of swine may have been the last thing that a grove of oak trees brought to mind. Plutarch wrote that 'the oak, in truth, is the tree which bears the most and the prettiest fruit of any that grow wild, and is the strongest of all that are under cultivation; its acorns were the principal diet of the first mortals, and the honey found in it gave them drink' – up to this point a purely vegetarian interpretation. Furthermore, our author continues, 'it furnished fowl and other creatures' – and here we seem to arrive at a qualification. The explanation that follows, however, is surprising: the oak provides these creatures 'in producing mistletoe for bird-lime to ensnare them'.[31] The great distance between the two cultures is revealed by comparing the observations of Plutarch with the production model established in Europe between the fifth and eighth centuries, which reserved a central role for the free pasturing of swine in the forests (*measured* now in terms of that animal). Nor was this distance ascribable, at least not primarily, to the relative frequency of oak groves, though it is true that the decline of cultivation after the third century did lead to the considerable spread of wilderness, including forests, not to mention natural pastures and swamps. However, modes of production have, in addition to their material aspects, a psychological dimension: they depend upon both the physical configuration of the environment and man's attitude to it. Neither the existence of an oak grove nor the fact of a sounder of swine rooting around underneath it is sufficient to cause men to measure that grove in terms of pigs. The latter event requires a cultural leap of exactly the sort that took place in western Europe as a result of the spread of the productive models and mentality of 'barbarian' culture.

Meanwhile meat became the most valued element of human nutrition. While a Roman physician such as Cornelius Celsus maintained that bread was unquestionably the 'the strongest kind of food (I call strongest that which has most nourishment)',[32] the nutritional handbooks that appeared after the fifth century gave clear priority to meat. Such, for example, was the opinion expressed by the physician Anthimus – who though of Greek origin had lived at the court of Theodoric, king of the Goths, in Ravenna – in his epistle *De observatione ciborum* sent to another Theodoric, king of the Franks (to whom he was ambassador). Though Anthimus owed a great debt to numerous Greek and Latin *auctores*, whom he cited explicitly in the preface to this work, there is none the less a basic originality there or at least an adaptation of the Greek tradition – source of his own professional formation – to the different culture in which he himself moved. The special attention which he devotes to the preparation of pork comes then as no surprise (it is the only meat given such thorough treatment: roasted, boiled, baked, stewed); nor does the fact that the longest chapter of the work is dedicated to lard 'which it is pointless to recall is a delicacy among the Franks'. It can be roasted, explains Anthimus, like any other piece of meat, but it will in that case become too dry; better to boil it and keep it cool. It is harmful to eat it fried, but serves well as a condiment for greens and other foods 'when oil is lacking'. This last observation of our physician reveals his Mediterranean origins, not entirely wiped out by the continental nutritional models he had assimilated. 'With regard to raw lard', he continues, 'rumour has it that the Franks eat it regularly, and I am surprised to note that for them it represents such a fine remedy as to eliminate the need for other medicines.' Anthimus does recommend that raw meats be avoided, as foods are more easily digested when well cooked, though he recognizes that at times − during a military campaign or a long voyage, for example − consumption of this sort may be necessary. In these cases he stresses the need for moderation; one should eat only the bare minimum necessary. These last comments suggest that Anthimus' public had no distaste for raw meat and perhaps even enjoyed it (in which case the scandalized testimonies of Greek and Latin authors regarding the eating habits of the 'barbarians' can be considered with rather less scepticism). What follows is something of a confirmation: anticipating possible objections from his readers or listeners, Anthimus asks how it is that 'some peoples eat raw and bloody meats and yet remain healthy'. He responds with some difficulty, suggesting that, 'like wolves', they eat only one type of food. We instead, he continues, 'stuff ourselves with all sorts of foods and delicacies', and so we must control our consumption in order to remain healthy, using moderation and all the available precautions. Anthimus then considers the various foods, their nutritional values and the best ways to use them, emphasizing, as already mentioned, meats: ox, cow, mutton, lamb, goat, deer, roe, fawn, boar, hare, pheasant, partridge, pigeon, peacock, chicken and goose, as well as pork.[33]

The first place of meat among foods was particularly stressed among the ruling classes. In their eyes it was a symbol of power, a tool for generating vigour, physical energy and the ability to do combat, qualities which constituted the primary legitimation of power.[34] On the other hand, the non-consumption of meat was a sign of humility and of marginalization (more or less voluntary, more or less a result of chance) from the society of the strong; this image is reinforced by the comparison made in the Frankish capitularies between the rendering up of arms and the forsaking of meat. In the first half of the ninth century, Lothair prescribed both punishments for those guilty of killing a bishop. The seriousness of the first – which implied a complete change of life and livelihood for individuals who had made a profession of war – helps us to understand that of the second which accompanied it.[35]

This general conception, however, did not apply only to the few and the powerful; scientific and popular opinion agreed that meat was the food best suited to man, that it was his 'natural nutrient'. For was not man himself made of meat? Other foods – for those who could not or would not consume meat – took on connotations of surrogacy and substitution. The place of bread as the nutritional symbol of 'civilization' was itself questioned. Or rather it would have been had Europe not embarked upon a process of Christianization, the result of conviction, force and at times calculation. Within this new faith, bread, together with wine and oil, held an absolutely central symbolic place.

The Bread (and the Wine) of God

In the fourth century, Christianity became the official religion of the empire, and from that time forward it took on in many ways the role of heir and interpreter of Greek and Latin, as well as Jewish, culture. Born and bred in a Mediterranean environment, Christianity easily incorporated the products which constituted the material and ideological basis of that civilization as nutritional symbols and tools of worship: bread and wine became – following considerable controversy – quintessentially sacred foods as symbols of the miracle of the Eucharist, and oil too became indispensable for the liturgy (for the administration of sacraments and above all the lighting of the *luminaria* in holy places).[36] These choices implied on the one hand a break with the Jewish tradition, which excluded both bread (in so far as it was leavened and so somehow 'corrupt') and wine (in so far as it was a source of inebriation) from the sphere of ritual;[37] on the other hand, they facilitated the insertion of the new faith into the value system of the Roman world. We might also turn this discussion around and recognize that the ritual exaltation of these three foods, symbols of Roman culture, is representative of the imprint which that culture left on many aspects of the new and developing Christianity. Whether through the prestige of the Roman tradition or the spread of the new faith, the reputation of bread, wine and oil was much enhanced.[38] As Christianity spread through Europe, displacing – sometimes violently – other religions, those products, already well known in the more Romanized areas, established themselves as symbols of the new faith.

The symbolic emphasis attached to bread, wine and oil by the Christian writers of the fourth and fifth centuries was particularly intense. Augustine wrote of Ambrose that 'his eloquence valiantly ministered to your people "the abundance of your sustenance" and "the gladness of oil", and the sober intoxication of your wine.'[39] A sermon of Augustine explained in careful detail the metaphorical analogy between the making of bread and the formation of a new Christian:

This bread retells your history. It began as a seed in the fields. The earth bore it and the rain nourished it and made it grow into a shoot. The work of man brought it to the threshing floor, beat it, winnowed it, put it in the granary, brought it to the mill, ground it, kneaded it and baked it in the oven. Remember that this is also your history. You did not exist and were created; you were brought to the threshing floor of the Lord and were threshed by the work of oxen (so shall I call the preachers of the Gospel). While awaiting catechism, you were like the grain kept in the granary. Then you were lined up for baptism. You underwent fasting and exorcism. You came to the baptismal fount. You were kneaded into a single dough. You were cooked in the oven of the Holy Ghost and became the true bread of God.[40]

The essence of bread was, however, Jesus Christ himself, 'planted in the Virgin, fermented in the flesh, kneaded in the Passion, baked in the oven of the sepulchre, and seasoned in the churches where every day the holy Host is served to the faithful'.[41]

One encounters similar metaphorical acrobatics used for the description of wine and oil, which were even more precious and sought after than bread, especially – and understandably – in central and northern Europe, where they were harder to come by. The *Vitae* of the saints – a literary genre which rapidly gained curency – are filled with individuals who in order to promote the Christian faith took care especially to plant vines and cultivate wheat, the indispensable tools of their trade. Biographies of bishops and abbots show them intent on working the fields; and archival documents reveal that churches and monasteries were important players in the progressive expansion of viticulture and grain cultivation, to the point that grapes were harvested during the following centuries in unimaginable climates and latitudes, reaching even central England.[42] Moreover, we should keep in mind that when the hagiographic texts attribute apparently evangelical miracles, like the multiplication of the loaves or the transformation of water into wine, to the various saints, these miracles were often really achieved – by dint of human labour.

Those peoples, such as the Franks, who adhered to orthodox Christianity fairly early (recognizing that such a move aided them both in settling in the territories of the empire and overcoming their enemies) were primarily responsible for the spread of the Romano-Christian dietary models in northern Europe. In those accounts which report the consolidation of their power and the contemporary victory of the 'true' faith over Arian heresy, wine occupies a strategically central role of political and cultural legitimation. According to the Life of St Remigius (written by Hincmar of Reims in the ninth century), as Clovis, defender of the Roman faith and founder of Frankish power, was about to launch the decisive battle against the Arian Alaric, king of the Visigoths, Remigius, the bishop of Reims – who had converted Clovis to Christianity and baptized him – gave Clovis a flask of wine 'as a blessing' from which (as long as it lasted) he would garner strength and enthusiasm to do battle. As if by magic, 'the king and all the royal family drank their fill of the wine and also a great multitude of people, yet its level never fell and wine continued to pour out of the bottle as if from a spring' – leading him of course to victory. Nor did Hincmar neglect to corroborate his story recalling an episode from the first book of Kings, in which are described other containers overflowing with – of all things – flour and oil: 'And the barrel of meal wasted not, neither did the cruse of oil fail.'[43]

The culture of wine was not established without resistance. When King Childebert, a successor to Clovis who lived in the sixth century, ordered the monk Carilephus to leave the wooded area that he had improperly inhabited and cultivated, the latter offered in response a cup of wine made from the few vines that he had planted there. The king refused this gesture of peace, scorning the 'vulgar juice' – might he have been more accustomed to drink beer or perhaps have preferred only fine wines? He was forced, in any case, to repent: on the return journey, his horse at a certain point came to a halt and refused to move, as if enchanted; the king recognized his error, asked Carilephus forgiveness and begged that he bless him with the wine he had refused. As a sign of friendship, the king drank an entire goblet.[44] Elsewhere opposition to the culture of beer is explicit, or rather the *cult* of beer in the role of sacred beverage, an alternative to that of wine in the Christian liturgy for certain pagan populations of northern Europe. At the beginning of the seventh century the blessed Columban, while staying with the Swabians,

came to know that they were planning a profane sacrifice

and that they had placed in their midst a large pot containing about 20 *modii* [i.e. about 180 litres] of *cervisia*. He approached them and asked what they intended to do. They responded that it was for a sacrifice in honour of the god Wotan. Columban then blew into the pot and it broke apart with a horrible crash into a thousand pieces, and together with the *cervisia* out came the evil spirit, for in that pot was hidden the devil who by means of the sacrilegious liquid hoped to possess the souls of those participating in the sacrifice.

However, the possibility for the peaceful coexistence of good Christians and the 'sacrilegious beverage' (used of course only to quench thirst) is none the less implicit in the Life of St Columban, the text which provides the preceding dramatic episode. Its author Jonas (himself a disciple of Columban), explained that it was made by fermenting wheat or barley, 'and used by all the peoples of the earth, except the Scordisci and the Dardani, but especially by those who lived near to the ocean, namely in Gaul, Britain, Ireland and Germany, and by those who shared similar customs'. In the monastery of Luxeuil, founded by Columban on the remains of the ancient spa city and today part of Burgundy, beer was initially the usual drink of the monks who daily received at table a pre-established amount. Columban himself, so Jonas reported, was forced once to intervene and save a barrel of *cervisia* that the brother in charge of the cellar had left open while the liquid poured into a jar. Remembering his unpardonable error, the brother rushed to the cellar prepared for the worst, but not a single drop of liquid had been lost, and 'it looked as if the jar had doubled in height', such was the foam which had gathered on top. The cellar-master was quick to make out the miraculous hand of his abbot. Indeed, in the Life of St Columban, an episode regarding the multiplication of the loaves and the *cervisia* is reported, a feat which bestowed upon the northern beverage an unexpected evangelical dignity. 'Father we have nought but two loaves of bread and a little *cervisia*, yet all drink and eat till they are full, and the baskets and jars fill up rather than empty.'[45]

The culture of wine then came to be intertwined with that of beer. In the ninth century, the Council of Aix established a sort of 'table of proportions' setting out the allowable daily consumption of beer or wine for the regular clergy: 'Each day they should be given five pounds of wine, providing a sufficient quantity has been produced in the region; if production is scant, they should be given three pounds of wine and three of *cervisia*; if production is non-existent, they should be given one pound of wine [apparently bought or somehow brought in from elsewhere] and five of *cervisia*.'[46] This text reveals as well that wine was both the principal beverage and that held to be the most nutritious. One reads elsewhere that the monks of Fulda did penitence by abstaining from wine and drinking only water or *cervisia*.[47]

The coexistence of these two traditions marked in particular the nutritional regimes of central Europe (France, Germany); the British Isles were also affected, and as late as the twelfth century the son of Henry II Plantagenet refused to drink wine, which he considered a 'foreign drink' (and we know that in the ninth century at the table of Ilispon, lord of the Bretons, milk was drunk).[48] For their part, the Mediterranean countries were strongly influenced by the cultural contributions of the 'barbarians': one need only recall the importance – even today – of beer in the Spanish diet.

After the barbarian invasions, an analogous and unprecedented intermingling of the dietary regimes of meat and bread took place as well, with the result that both came to enjoy the status (ideological as well as material) of primary and indispensable foods. As we shall see, tension and opposition continued to exist between the two, but also considerable harmony and reciprocal solidarity. In the second half of the eleventh century, Abbot Hugh of Cluny – so reports his biographer – strove to provide the necessities of life to the poor, namely *panes et carnes* which he had brought to the monastery from both property holdings and the market: 'and mounds of bread and meat piled up around him'.[49] Can we perhaps, borrowing a term from the history of institutions, speak of a 'Romano-barbarian' dietary model?

Feasting and Fasting

The overall attitude towards food was also profoundly changed. For Graeco-Roman culture, moderation had been the highest virtue: food was to be approached with joy but not voracity, to be offered generously but not ostentatiously.[50] In the process of identifying those worthy of public admiration, the literature of the period reinforced this model of behaviour. The Emperor Severus Alexander's biographer wrote that 'his banquets were neither too sumptuous nor too modest, but marked by excellent taste', and that 'following his instructions moderate portions of each dish were served'.[51] For every Severus Alexander who comported himself as described above, there were of course one or two Trimalchios who exhibited just the opposite sort of behaviour. Indeed, gluttony and waste are historical constants, just as are stinginess and indifference to earthly pleasure. It is clear, however, that classical culture identified a sense of balance as the highest value and judged negatively any sort of behaviour that did not conform to this ideal: excessive consumption of food – like its excessive renunciation – is described with disapproval and suspicion by those whose works have come down to us. When Aeschines and Philocrates 'commended Philip for his able speaking, his beautiful person, nay, and also for his good companionship in drinking, Demosthenes could not refrain from cavilling at these praises; the first, he said, was a quality which might well enough become a rhetorician, the second a woman, and the last was only the property of a sponge; no one of them was the proper commendation of a prince'.[52] One could cite, in addition to Plutarch, Xenophanes, who described moderate eating as 'the most important aspect of the education of men and women' and Suetonius, who criticized Tiberius for having promoted to the quaestorship an individual who had revealed his basic character by gulping down an amphora of wine during a banquet; and many others besides.[53]

By contrast, Germanic and Celtic culture viewed the 'great eater' in a positive light, and indeed it was just this sort of behaviour – prodigious eating and drinking – which gave one a sort of animal superiority over one's peers.[54] It was no coincidence that so many given names were taken from the animal kingdom – and in particular names of ferocious and aggressive animals – in those societies: the many Bears and Wolfs that dotted the European map from the fifth century on.[55] The ideal of moderation did not enjoy much currency in those societies dominating the new Europe, especially in the regions of strongest barbarian imprint. Literature favoured the heroic, voracious and insatiable eater and one encounters in Germanic mythology and chivalric poetry the image of the brave warrior who was also capable of ingesting enormous quantities of food and drink. In the Icelandic saga of *Edda*, Loki proclaimed, 'I know in which art I am ready to be tested; no one here can eat faster than I', and he proceeded to challenge those present to compete with him over a platter piled high with meat. Logi accepted the challenge and defeated Loki, eating 'all the meat and the bones and even the platter itself'.[56] Thorr followed, engaging in a drinking contest in which horns were used as cups. These were exhibitions of animal strength, of an entirely physical and muscular energy, and they would appear repeatedly in European literature.

When Charlemagne saw a man at his table strip the meat off a huge quantity of bones and then break the bones themselves into bits, sucking out the marrow and piling them in a heap beneath the table, he quickly recognized that here must be a 'heartily strong soldier' and guessed that he was Adelchis, son of the king of the Lombards. It was said of Adelchis that 'he ate like a lion devouring his prey', and the undisguised admiration of those present testifies to what was then understood by 'virility'.[57] It seems that Artistophanes was right when he stated that 'the barbarians judge you to be a man only if you are able to eat a mountain'.[58]

The lifestyle of the Frankish aristocracy appears to have been especially characterized by values of this sort, values which took on the character of true social mores. The biographer of Abbot Odo of Cluny reports that Odo was characterized by an unusual degree of frugality from infancy, behaviour that was 'in conflict with Frankish nature'.[59] In the year 888, when the Carolingian dynasty died out, an Italian nobleman, Guido, Duke of Spoleto, was invited by the bishop of Metz as a possible candidate to the French throne. There, 'following the custom of the Franks', many foods were prepared for him; it became apparent, however, that Guido was content with a modest repast and for that very reason – so a writer of the tenth century, Liutprand of Cremona, assures us – he was refused the throne. The electors held that a hearty appetite was among the necessary attributes of a king.[60] According to this same author, the 'king of the Greeks' Nicephorus Phocas (the Byzantine emperor) was contemptible because he loved greens and moderation; Otto of Saxony, 'king of the Franks', 'was never frugal and despised common foods', and was instead a great man.[61]

Within the ecclesiastical world, similarly contrasting eating habits could be found in the Mediterranean and continental areas, between the 'Roman' and the 'Germanic'. The ecclesiastical circles of northern Europe were particularly sensitive to the question of abundant eating, so much so that the 'normal' dietary prescriptions of the northern clergy were described by the Roman curia as Cyclopic: the Lateran Synod of May 1059 described the food and drink rations established at Aachen in 816 for canons as 'better suited to the gluttony of Cyclops than to Christian moderation'.[62] On the other hand, the monastic regulations of northern Europe (for example, those of the Irish Columban) were the strictest and most severe in establishing fasts, penitence and excluded foods; these were clearly conceived as reactions or 'negative' references to the prevailing dietary models. They represented the repudiation of a society that placed eating first among worldly values; so among spiritual values it was the refusal of food that held pride of place. Monastic regulations established in Mediterranean areas (for example, those called 'of the Master' and also the famous regulations of Benedict of Nursia) were instead characterized by a greater sense of moderation, of individual *discretion*, that great Benedictine virtue in which we can almost discern a Christian 'translation' of the Graeco-Roman concept of *measure*.[63]

On the whole, however, one cannot claim that Christian culture was characterized by a sense of measure. The documents available to us reveal strong resistance to that ideal, and often a preference for strict practices of asceticism, privation and renunciation. More important still, these practices were considered among the highest Christian goals, features of a perfect life which for a few might lead to holiness and for the many stood as models to be admired. The first and fundamental rule of monastic life (certainly not the only one, but long held to be the most important of all for salvation) was the rejection of meat, a choice all the more strict and obsessive as meat became firmly established as the most valued element of the ruling-class diet. Most monks came from this class and it was to the negative expression of its values that monastic culture aspired.

As for the world of peasants and 'poverty', which the monks claimed to take as a model for their lifestyle, we can be sure that it shared the values of the nobility rather than of the monks. The peasants might well have been happy with rather less poverty. In contrast to the nobility, they lacked the means necessary to enjoy copious eating, but this is not to say that they preferred such a state of affairs. The feast for them may have been simply a dream (literature would later supply us with an extraordinary testimony of popular imagination in the mythical lands of Cuccagna),[64] or perhaps a rare treat to be enjoyed only on certain holidays or special occasions. The cultural and psychological perspective was the same, however: that of a world certainly not always in the grips of famine, but always in fear of it; it was this fear which led people to eat copiously when they could. The monks themselves, when they were not fasting, ate 'irrationally and excessively'. M. Rouche has calculated that in the richest monasteries daily rations rarely fell below 5,000–6,000 calories,[65] further evidence of the 'obsession with food, the importance of eating, and, by way of contrast, the suffering (and merits) of dietary mortification'.[66]

Competing models of consumption and dietary behaviour characterized European society at the dawn of its own history; there existed, however, a common logic which connected these models, a sort of circularity according to which one followed the other. The polarity between the 'Roman' and 'barbarian' models was replaced by that between 'monastic' and 'aristocratic'. The difficult contest waged between them had cultural hegemony as its prize. It was a many-faceted contest in which the values of social ethics came up against those of religious morality, and the arguments of poverty against those of power (though we should not forget other variables such as pleasure or health – to which we shall return below).

The question becomes more complicated when a Germanic sovereign, profoundly rooted in the culture of his people and class, is forced by circumstances to don a new uniform, namely that of the Roman emperor, which brings with it the baggage of balance and moderation – annoying for a 'barbarian' – that form part of the imperial image. Such was the situation of Charlemagne – king of the Franks, Roman emperor, and Christian to boot – whose dietary habits (or at least the image we have received of them) reveal signs of profound tension, of a contradiction between two different and not easily reconciled temperaments. His biographer, the faithful Einhard, begins with the observation that Charlemagne 'ate and drank moderately'; nor could he have written otherwise, in part because such was the behaviour appropriate to the Christian sovereign, and in part because Suetonius, his principal literary model, had written similarly of Augustus. Einhard, however, quickly qualified this statement: Charlemagne ate and drank moderately, 'but was more moderate in drinking . . . and did not manage the same restraint in eating, often complaining that fasting was harmful to his constitution'. The opposition between the Christian ethic of moderation and the warrior image of abundant feasting characterizes the description of Charlemagne's daily meal as well. Einhard tells us, for example, that the emperor's dinner 'consisted of only four courses', though the number of courses (four) contrasts conspicuously with the adverb Einhard uses to describe them (*tantum*, only). Even more conspicuous, the count does not include – as though it should be obvious – the roasted meats 'which the hunters usually skewered and which he [Charlemagne] ate with greater pleasure than any other food'. So if from a formal point of view the descriptive canons of Christian moderation are maintained, the image of the powerful meat-eater emerges none the less in its fullness. It was not a coincidence that Charlemagne, like many of his ilk, suffered from gout in old age, 'and even then [Einhard assures us] he was more likely to do as he liked rather than follow the advice of the physicians, a group he particularly detested because they urged him to stop eating the roasted meats to which he was accustomed and get used to boiled ones'. They dared not suggest further measures, and were in fact unsuccessful even in encouraging this first precaution.[67]

Charlemagne's preference was of course a question of taste, but anthropologists have taught us that the image of roasted food cooked directly over the open flame is associated with cultural notions that differ markedly from those attached to water boiling in a pot: notions of violence, vehemence and belligerence, and of a closer tie to an untamed image of nature.

Terra et Silva

From the sixth to at least the tenth century, the European economy was characterized by a combination of agriculture and the extraction of resources from untilled nature. The phrase *terra et silva* appears frequently in the documents of the period, a sort of productive hendiadys that represented a vast interplay of cultivated and uncultivated spaces. The alternation, mixture and co-penetration of these spaces formed an environmental mosaic and corresponding panoply of productive activities: grain cultivation, horticulture, hunting, fishing, free pasturing, and gathering. This diversity in turn fostered an equally diverse (and well organized) dietary system which regularly combined vegetable (grains, legumes, garden vegetables) and animal products (meat, fish, cheeses, eggs). We should note as well that, through a combination of environmental and social factors, this system spread to all social levels. In the first place, a favourable balance between population and resources enabled the former to maintain a level of consumption above subsistence in spite of a low-yield productive system which utilized uncultivated nature extensively. In the second place, the relation between property and production did not forbid the use of open spaces, even when they belonged to a king, a lord or an ecclesiastical institution. The abundance of woods and pastures was such that access was generally unlimited. Germanic laws drafted between the sixth and eighth centuries reveal greater concern with overcrowding of the forests than with the definition of agricultural boundaries. Questions regarding the removal of felled game, for example, appear to have been no less important than the protection of cultivated plots. There were of course differences: the laws of the Spanish Visigoths, which were more closely tied to Roman culture as well as to a purely Mediterranean environment, paid more attention than many others to the working and products of the fields. None the less, a general reversal of emphasis characterized European culture and economy in the period.[68]

Given that the possibility of being short of food was linked to the production of several different economic sectors and so to different seasonal rhythms, this dietary diversity conditioned the notion of famine in the period. 'Forest famine' was depicted as no less serious than 'agricultural famine', and indeed it was not. Good weather for the spawning of fish or for acorn production (that assured the fattening of pigs) were as important as a good harvest and vintage.[69] These multiple concerns are revealed in Gregory of Tours's account of the crisis of 591: 'There was a great drought which destroyed the grass of the pastures. As a result a severe epidemic spread through the herds of large and small livestock alike, sparing few. The drought brought ruin not only to domestic animals, but to many species of wild animals as well. A large number of deer and other animals had fallen in the thickest parts of the forest.' Great rains followed that flooded the rivers and rotted the hay. The grain harvest was small, while the vintage was abundant. As for the acorns, 'although buds appeared on the oaks, they did not mature'. Elsewhere Gregory wrote that the winter of 548 was so harsh that 'slowed by cold and hunger, the birds could be caught without traps, using only bare hands'.[70] Freezing weather too was 'interpreted' – so to speak – in terms of the forest economy and its effect on hunting.

Other writers demonstrate similar concerns. Andrea da Bergamo wrote that in 872 a frost attacked all vegetation, 'drying up the new leaves in the forest'.[71] According to the *Annales Fuldenses*, snow fell uninterruptedly in 874 from early November until the vernal equinox, 'making it impossible to enter the forest'.[72]

Private documents also reveal attention to these problems. An Italian inventory of the eighth century listing the profits of a property agency included the observation that the estimates given were dependent upon fine weather, namely that which allowed grains and grape to grow well, acorns to mature on the trees, and fish to multiply in the streams and ponds. These last (the freshwater fish) received special attention, revealing a primary concern for home consumption rather than market considerations.[73] Food was sought in loco, and fishing figured larger in the swamp (or river or lake) economy than in that of the sea, another significant difference from the Roman economy. The poet Sidonius Apollinaris, for example, eulogized the pike, a fish little appreciated by the Romans.[74] Gregory of Tours celebrated the trout of the Lake of Geneva, 'weighing up to 100 lb', while those from the Lake of

Garda were noted in the inventory of the Italian monastery of Bobbio. Other freshwater fish mentioned in the period include the English and Po river sturgeons, eels (which seem to have been the most highly prized fish in many regions; indeed, Salic law mentions no other), salmon, lampreys, carps, tenches, gobies, barbels and crayfish.[75]

It was a period when all could count on a varied diet. Meat, fish, cheese and eggs graced every table, together with bread, porridges and greens. Dietary diversity was encouraged by ecclesiastical directives as well which prohibited the consumption of meat, and in some cases all animal products, on certain days of the week and during certain times of the year; it has been calculated that between short and long fasts these added up to more than 150 days a year. Difficult to explain in any but a markedly carnivorous culture, this state of affairs encouraged the appearance of different foods on any given table, with the periodic substitution of fish or cheese (or, better still, legumes) for meat, and of vegetable oils for animal fats. In this way the liturgical calendar had an important influence on dietary habits and fostered a degree of homogeneity between different areas of Europe.

None the less, within this common culture an irreconcilable division remained and important social differences developed. The 'fashion' – and it really was just that – of bread, wine and oil took hold in northern central Europe, especially among the lay and ecclesiastical upper classes, both in consumption habits and for liturgical uses, while the lower classes remained more strongly attached to their own dietary traditions, often connected – as we have seen was the case with beer – to important elements of religious ritual. Alternatively, in those areas that came later under the sway of Germanic power and culture the upper classes were more likely to reorient their lifestyles and eating habits towards a passion for the hunt and copious meat consumption, while the lower classes again stuck to a more traditional model. The image of the 'poor' consumer of greens handed down to us by many literary texts of the era is not simply an ideological construction. We should also distinguish between regions that witnessed a rapid fusion of the newly dominant groups with what remained of the old (as in France), and others (for example, Italy) where the encounter was long and bitter. The latter situation resulted primarily in rifts and conflicts, the former in the solid construction of a new political reality. Cultural (including dietary) development followed a similar course. It was none the less the case – even in southern Europe and even among the lowest classes – that more meat was eaten than before, while bread conquered the tables of the north. But there are different breads and different meats.

The Colour of Bread

In response to urban market demand (which determined in large part agricultural planning), Roman grain cultivation was dominated by wheat. After the crisis of the third century, the situation gradually changed as the role of the market declined relative to that of home production and consumption. Wheat – a labour-intensive and relatively low-yield crop (and lower still given the technological stagnation in agriculture) – gradually gave way to lesser but hardier and more dependable grains: rye, barley, oats, emmer, spelt, millet, Italian millet and sorghum.[76] Most of these had been known for centuries and formed a marginal part of the human diet as well as being fed to animals. Others, however, had only recently been discovered; rye, for example, which Roman farmers considered a weed. According to Pliny rye is 'a very poor food and only serves to avert starvation'; he disparaged its use by the inhabitants of the western Alps. Yet in the centuries that followed, this 'poor' plant enjoyed extraordinary good fortune throughout Europe. Indeed, until the tenth or eleventh century it was cultivated more widely than any other grain, and for a simple reason which Pliny himself recognized: 'it grows in any sort of soil with a hundred-fold yield, and serves of itself to enrich the land'.[77] Rye's tremendous yield was legendary, but the reasons for its being preferred

to wheat were clearly its hardiness and ability to grow anywhere. Today rye is grown at the highest altitudes; between the
sixth and tenth century it was also cultivated in the plains and
on hillsides in order to minimize the risks of a poor harvest.
Either side by side or mixed together with rye, other grains were
also planted. Mixed farming of this sort was characteristic of the
period and widespread; it constituted another strategy for reducing the dangers posed by inclement weather as each different
crop matured at a different rate. Wheat was planted as well, but
in small quantities generally intended for the upper classes.[78]

The contrast between the two types of bread, which had defin-
ite social connotations, manifested itself chromatically as well:
that made from wheat was white, from rye and other grains
black. The former was prepared for the upper classes and was
decidedly a luxury item. Black bread was for peasants and
servants, whether made from rye, spelt or *mixtura*. A complex
typology characterized the relationship between the type of
bread and the status of the consumer, whether it was a question
of social rank (rulers versus ruled) or a moral desire for penitence
or the humbling of self. This relationship explained the symbolic importance of certain behaviour, like that of Gregory,
bishop of Langres, who did penance by eating bread made from
barley (unanimously agreed to be the worst of all). However, in
order not to vaunt his sacrifice, he hid the fact by holding the
barley bread underneath a piece of the wheat bread which he
gave to others and which he himself pretended to eat (in keeping with the dignity of his office). Opinions of course varied
from region to region so that, for example, rye bread could be
described as a vile concoction in a French cultural and geo-
graphic setting, while in a German environment it enjoyed the
adjective *pulcher* (beautiful). In any case, the praise of 'black'
breads encountered in northern central Europe (and as far south
as northern Italy) rapidly disappeared further south, where the
persistence of wheat cultivation (and the general Roman economic model) assured that product a greater social range.[79]

Equally important were the distinctions between fresh and

stale bread, between more or less leavened breads, and between the various methods of cooking: fresh bread was the privilege of a select few, the large monasteries and the courts; barley bread *did not grow* (because the flour made from that grain contains little starch); and those without access to an oven cooked their bread either in a pan or else inserted among the ashes. These were really flat breads (*focaccia*) rather than proper breads: Rabanus Maurus wrote that 'the bread cooked by being turned among the ashes is a flat bread'.[80] None the less, it was still called 'bread' as were the incredible concoctions devised in times of famine. It was a name which evoked lofty images, a sacred name, perhaps even magical.

In many homes bread was lacking, or at best rare. The great success which the miracle of the multiplication of the loaves enjoyed in Christian Europe — stubbornly repeated by a mass of aspiring saints — was also a sign of a too often frustrated demand. The dominant role of lesser grains in the general production system meant that polentas, porridges and soups played a central role in the dietary regime of most people. Barley, oats and millet — boiling grains in general — were particularly suited to this sort of preparation, to the making of *pulmenta*, a key term in the gastronomic vocabulary of the period and one which evokes the image of a pot suspended by a chain over the fire. Grains, legumes and vegetables, flavoured with meat and fat, were constantly stirred in that pot. In addition to the primary distinction between wheat bread and that made from other grains, there existed — and would continue to exist for a long time — the equally important distinction between bread on the one hand and soups and polentas on the other.

Meat consumption was socially differentiated as well and few were able to eat fresh meat. Newly hunted game arrived at the table of Charlemagne every day (according to his biographer Einhard) and similar practices must have characterized other princely tables. Peasants on the other hand, whose first concern was to maintain sufficient stores, depended on preserved meats: pork and mutton primarily (as swine and sheep were the only animals raised in large quantities), but also that of larger livestock, especially in the north, including beef, horse and buffalo. Wild game received similar treatment, and deer and boar meats were dried with smoke and preserved in salt. This miraculous product – salt – was practically indispensable for daily survival; in the seventh century Isidore of Seville, following Pliny, called it 'as useful as the sun'.[81] Only from time to time did fresh meat – in the form of domestic fowl (chickens, geese, ducks) – grace the peasants' table, and then only on feast days.

Using Nature

The *Vitae Patrum* includes the story of a Syrian hermit who went into the desert for the purpose of solitary meditation and chose to live, as others like him, only on greens and roots. This particular hermit, however, did not know the difference between the good and bad plants; they all seemed equally sweet to him, though some were deadly poison. He began as a result to feel pains in his stomach and to retch; he lost all strength and was near death. All those things which appeared edible now filled him with horror and he no longer dared eat anything. After seven days of fasting, a wild goat approached him and took the bunch of greens that the hermit had gathered but not dared touch. The goat began to separate with his mouth the good herbs from the bad and in this way the holy man learned what to eat and what to avoid, and was able to slake his hunger without running further risk.[82]

This story is revealing on several counts. In the first place, it reveals the hermit's preference – and that of the culture from which he sprang – for a 'natural' diet, one based on the vegetation naturally available to him. One encounters this choice repeatedly in the biographies of the fourth- and fifth-century eastern ascetics. It would be repeated soon afterwards in the West where the spatial role of the 'desert' was fulfilled by a different environment, one more familiar to the daily experience of Europeans: the forest.[83] As the solitude of the forest lent itself more readily to the gathering of food offered by nature, the model was confirmed and reinforced. The list of pious individuals who in the sixth and seventh centuries went into the dense European forests in search of God, eating greens, roots, bulbs, berries, and fruit and nuts from the trees, is certainly a long one.

In contrast to the situation in the Syrian desert, the 'wild' diet of the European hermit was only one aspect of a more widespread practice; given the importance that the uncultivated had assumed in the production system, it was a solitary retreat well rooted (and this is no paradox) in the social and economic context of the period. Here our tale of the hermit provides a second important lesson: the use of naturally available foods is not a casual affair, but requires a hard apprenticeship, a learning process that incorporates knowledge of the territory and information provided by its inhabitants. In our specific case, the teacher was an animal, but this was due to the voluntary withdrawal of the hermit from human society. Elsewhere this role was filled by hunters and by animal herders, the keepers of swine and goats who pointed the way or acted as guides. The hagiographies report as much, but we also find in trial reports (a fair number are to be found among the documents from the eighth and ninth centuries) that judges frequently had recourse to these individuals in order to know more about the limits and make-up of the forests. Their depiction as somehow naive seems far from the mark. The use of nature (and the *concept* itself of nature, as Lévi-Strauss has taught us) is an eminently cultural phenomenon, and the contrast between nature and culture, when it arises, is more the product of an ideological choice than of a real opposition.

The border between agriculture and the use of uncultivated nature, between a 'domesticated' and a 'wild' economy was less rigid than we might imagine. It was a shifting border which came and went, advanced and retreated.[84] The conquest of newly tilled space and the progress of agriculture did not occur without second thoughts or setbacks. The domestication of the landscape, of plants and of animals did not rule out intermediate, nuanced and ambivalent stages. Many plants existed both in the wild and domesticated state. The garden, a productive sector of vital importance from the point of view of both nutrition and pharmacology, derived from a long tradition of collecting wild plants and herbs.[85] Some of the edible grains as well were the result of recent selection and grafting among naturally occurring species (we have already discussed rye, but the genealogy of oats was similar). The wild–domestic ambivalence held also for fruit and nut trees: apple, pear, chestnut and so on. It was a world in transition, an economy and culture of food midway between gathering and agriculture.

The same held for animals. Species which today we consider domestic still existed in a wild state: the wild ox (the famous *urus*) was caught in European forests until at least the ninth or tenth century. Other species which we consider exclusively wild were kept domestically: the Lombards kept deer around their houses, and during the mating season their bellowing upset the tranquillity of the villages; as a result, the seventh-century laws of Rotari sought to regulate their presence.[86] And what of the domestic swine? Free-pastured in the forest, they were distinguished, but only barely (by their shape, colour and presumably flavour) from the wild boars.[87]

Fishing practices were also in an intermediate state between the natural and the artificial. Planted fish ponds were generally established along the rivers and in swamps and *piscariae et paludes* (fishponds and marshes) is a combination frequently encountered in the documents of the period.[88]

As the centuries passed, the importance of cultivated plants and domesticated animals increased while that of the 'wild' component of food production declined. This gradual transition did not follow a precise chronology and varied from place to place. The two competing systems must, however, have reached a significant point of balance between the seventh and eighth centuries when the combined recourse to wild and cultivated products probably achieved a maximum of complementarity.

The eventual outcome of this contest was already clear in the eleventh century, when Hildegard of Bingen wrote that only those plants domesticated and cultivated by man and, so to speak, made in his image were perfectly suited to human nutrition; those which grew naturally 'contrariae sunt homini ad comedendum' (are contrary to human consumption).[89]

It was clearly an ideological as well as an economic problem. The available sources are full of 'messages' of one sort or the other and suggest, for example, that there existed a distinction between the 'wild' preferences of the lay nobility and the 'domestic' ones of the ecclesiastic (and especially monastic) world.[90] Of the blessed Meneleus Queen Brunichildis asked angrily: 'Why do you knock down the woods in which I go hunting?'[91] We read also that Remigius dealt out large wooded plots to the freed slaves from a forest given to him by King Clovis in order for them to plough the land and learn to live by working the fields.[92] Throughout Europe, monks sponsored important deforestation projects and expanded cultivation as well as a lifestyle and diet very different from that of the hermit. According to the Life of John, abbot of Réome (written by Jonas about the mid-seventh century), the saint, having gone off one day to pray came upon a pauper who was seeking sustenance among the plants of the forest. John urged the poor man to place his hope in God and take up again his work as a peasant. The pauper followed John's advice, enjoyed abundant harvests and no longer had to search elsewhere for food.[93]

The diligent entrepreneurship of the monks – the monasteries rapidly became the wealthiest and most powerful households in Europe – ran into conflict not only with the hunting practices of the nobility but often with the interests of the peasants as well, who remained dependent on the use of uncultivated nature. Judicial documents from the ninth century, especially in Italy, recount numerous arguments between monks and peasants regarding the use of forest land. For the large monasteries, laying claim to these lands on the basis of real or alleged royal concessions meant not only increased resources and income, but also and above all the elimination of any possibility of independence for rural communities. For the latter, use of the forests formed the foundation of their economy and social solidarity. The fatal compromising of their interests – the cases were almost invariably settled in favour of the monasteries – made these communities easy prey for seigniorial power.[94]

Meanwhile population had begun to increase; after centuries of decline and then stagnation, the demographic curve turned up in the eighth and ninth centuries. This may have been due to a favourable nutritional cycle resulting from the combination of resources described above, or else perhaps for entirely different reasons, as demographic phenomena do not obey strict dependence on food production. In any case, while on the one hand this growth depended upon a hard-won productive system, on the other it threatened to trigger the destruction of that very system. In fact, given that particular society and economy, increased demand for food could be satisfied only by expanding cultivation and emphasizing the role of agriculture over that of other uses of the land.[95]

Projects of deforestation, tilling and colonization undertaken by churches, monasteries, the aristocracy, peasant communities and later cities throughout Europe, especially beginning in the ninth century, signalled a radical change in the manner of attacking the problem of food. It was the most straightforward – and for the moment efficient – response to progressively and at times sharply increasing demand. In some ways it was also the response to an increasing demand for *civilitas*: nature and the wild were henceforth relegated to the margins of productive values and of the dominant ideology. It was the beginning of a 'boom', or perhaps a crisis.

2

The Turning-Point

A Forced Choice

An inventory in 883 of the Bobbio monastery, one of the richest
and most powerful of northern Italy, includes reference to thirty-
two farming properties (rented out) which had not been mentioned in a previous inventory of 862. These were new plots,
reclaimed from a forested area that the monks had only recently
decided to cultivate. The tone of the document, which attempts
to *justify* the choice, is significant: 'we did it out of necessity',
following a reduction of the monastery's overall property holdings
imposed by the Emperor Ludwig II.[1] Only necessity (*proper necessi-
tatem*) drove them to fell trees and expand their cultivated area.
This expression of regret derived from a profound contradiction
inherent in the economic situation in Italy – and in Europe in
general – from the ninth century: on the one hand the desire to
preserve the uncultivated spaces so important to daily sustenance,
and on the other the inevitability of their sacrifice in the face of
increased demographic pressure. 'The choice between cereals and
meat depends on the number of people.'[2] Braudel's aphorism finds
undeniable confirmation in the observation that a hectare of forest
might nourish one or two pigs, and a hectare of pasture a few
goats; while a hectare of cultivated land, even given the paltry
yields of the day (until the fourteenth century a seed yield of three
to one was rarely exceeded), certainly produced more.[3] Moreover,
grains keep much better than meat – in ideal conditions of

temperature and humidity millet may last as long as twenty years – and are in some ways more versatile for food preparation. At a certain point the ploughing of virgin land becomes a 'forced choice';[4] it was regarded as such, particularly so long as attachment to the traditional productive models remained strong.

The agricultural and forest–pastoral productive systems were in fact not well co-ordinated: agriculture and the raising of livestock everywhere coexisted, but draught animals were few and their manure was scattered in the forest. The latter situation was the primary reason for the low productivity of the fields, and so for the need to sow large areas. Land dedicated to pasture was kept to a bare minimum, and consequently so was the quantity of stabled livestock that otherwise would have provided both greater animal power and more manure. It was a closed circle with no way out. So long as demographic pressure was contained, the system continued to function; but each increase in population endangered the unstable equilibrium upon which the system was based. The *extensive* character of production allowed no other outlet but the enlargement of ploughed fields at the expense of uncultivated lands.[5]

Initially, this process was undertaken cautiously. According to ninth-century agrarian contracts, the forests to be felled were only those deemed 'barren' (with reference of course to their usefulness for foraging); that is, forests lacking acorns or other animal fodder.[6] In the tenth century the rhythm of forest reclamation slowed, perhaps because some positive results had been achieved, only to pick up again in the mid-eleventh century and carry on to the end of the thirteenth. In general this conversion was slow, progressive, almost timid (one might even say respectful). Only in a few areas did the scale of reclamation become truly destructive. None the less, there was a turning-point: references to *novalia* or *runca* – lands newly employed for agricultural cultivation – become ever more frequent in post-1050 documents.

The gradual conversion of forests (or in some cases their

destruction) was not the only sign of a more agricultural economy. The forests themselves were domesticated and cultivated. This period saw the spread of fruit-bearing chestnut groves in southern central Europe reach a maximum; the trees were selected from among wild varieties and often planted in place of pre-existing oak groves. The reason for this choice was obvious: the chestnut produces flour, and so its nutritional role was similar to that of grains. It was not by coincidence that the chestnut was called the 'tree of bread'.[7]

The basic steps of agricultural expansion (a first wave in the ninth century and another more decisive one between the eleventh and the thirteenth) seem to have been closely correlated to what little we know of the productive and nutritional crises of the period. If we ignore local famines – and we should not underestimate their importance in a period when consumption was largely dependent on local production – existing texts record twenty-nine *general* European famines between 750 and 1100, on average one every twelve years. But as Bonnassie (on whose work these calculations are based) has noted, there were important chronological variations: the years of famine appear to have been especially frequent in the second half of the eighth century (six) and in the ninth (twelve); they were less frequent in the tenth century (only three, all in the first half of the century), only to recur more often again in the eleventh (eight).[8] We derive similar results from consideration of regional or national famines: in all cases the eleventh century appears to have been particularly hard hit by disaster. For France, a list penned in the eighteenth century (to be considered with caution, though the general picture presented cannot be too far off the mark) records twenty-six famines in the eleventh century, by far the largest number for any century in the country's history; only the eighteenth century comes close to so dramatic a level with sixteen.[9] It should come then as no surprise that one of the most terrifying descriptions of famine in European literature – that of the chronicler Radulfus Glaber – comes from exactly that period.

Between 1032 and 1033, according to Glaber:

famine began to spread throughout the world, threatening
nearly the whole of humanity with death. The weather
patterns were so confused that the right moment for planting never came, nor was there time enough for harvesting,
in particular because of flooding . . . The soil was so dren-
ched by incessant rain that for three years in a row one
could not plough a single adequate furrow for planting. At
harvest time, weeds and harmful darnel covered the fields
entirely. Where the harvest was best, a *modius* (peck) of seed
planted yielded a bushel at harvest [that is, less than the
amount planted] and from that bushel one could barely get
a handful of grain. This vengeful famine began in the east;
having laid waste to Greece, it travelled to Italy, then Gaul,
and finally all regions of England. The food shortage
struck all classes of the population. The wealthy and the
less wealthy became as wan with hunger as the poor, and in
the face of general indigence, the tyranny of the powerful
ceased. If there was any food to sell, the seller could raise
the price to whatever level he pleased and it would be paid
. . . Meanwhile, having consumed the quadrupeds and
birds, people began, in the grip of terrible hunger, to eat
any sort of meat, even that of dead animals, and other
disgusting things. Some tried to elude death by eating
forest roots and aquatic plants, but to no avail. There was
no escape from the wrath of God . . . In those times – ah,
misfortune – the madness of hunger drove men to eat
human flesh, as one had only rarely heard of in the past.
Travellers were seized by men stronger than they, cut into
quarters, cooked over a fire, and devoured. Many of those
who travelled from place to place in order to escape starvation were beaten to death in the night where they found
refuge, and so provided nourishment to their hosts. A great
many lured children with a piece of fruit or an egg to an
isolated spot where they were killed and eaten. In number-
less places, even the cadavers were dug up and used to slake
hunger. This insane fury became so widespread that untended

animals were less likely to be seized than people. Acting as though the cannibalism had become a standard practice, one man even brought cooked human flesh, like normal animal meat, for sale at the Tournus market. When arrested, he did not deny his crime and was tied and burned at the stake. The meat was buried, but another dug it up in the night and ate it. He too was burned.

This was only the first of a series of horrible tales which we should perhaps not attribute entirely to exaggeration, literary references and hearsay.[10]

Similar stories appear in many other texts.[11] According to Adam of Bremen, famine reigned in his city from 1066 to 1072 'and many poor people were found dead from starvation in the public squares'. In 1083, again in Germany, 'many children and old people died of hunger'. There was much death in 1094 as well when, according to the chronicler Cosmas of Prague, the German bishops, returning from a synod in Mainz, were unable to enter the parish church of Amberg because of the large number of corpses covering the floor. These are only a few examples of the many that could be cited: hunger, malnutrition, sickness and epidemics all figured prominently in the European chronicles of the period. As population growth forced ever greater dependence on grain, the importance of each harvest increased and so also the negative impact of bad weather. The period during which this new productive/nutritional system was established, the eleventh century, was in fact that most characterized by tension and breakdown. It became necessary to strike a new balance, to create a truly agricultural system of the sort that previous centuries had only partially achieved. This process led to difficulties, failures, successes, dramatic famines, and the spread of new diseases linked to excessive dependence on grain. Epidemics of ergotism (a skin disease caused by the consumption of fungus-infested rye) were frequent in Europe in the tenth and eleventh centuries, and especially virulent in 1042, 1076, 1089 and 1094. Successes followed: from the twelfth century, both the frequency and intensity of famines declined, while the food production system was made more robust (with the attendant risks we shall discuss below).

The beginning of agricultural expansion coincided (in the eleventh century, as previously and to a lesser extent already in the ninth, and then again in the sixteenth and eighteenth) with a period of increasing nutritional tension which could not be attenuated in the context of the pre-existing productive system. Can we conclude that expanded cultivation was a response to food shortages? Recall the Bobbio inventory: 'we did it out of necessity'.

Power and Privilege

From this point on the European economy became ever more markedly agricultural. In the short term, however, this development would not have brought about, in and of itself, a fundamental change in the dietary regime of most people; a decisive change in the social order was needed as well. Although the forests shrank, they none the less remained an important element of the landscape and in some areas would continue to be so for many centuries, even to the present day. The further development which took place was the progressive limitation of the right to their use. As demographic growth and the reduction of uncultivated spaces increased the competition for forest resources, social tensions grew sharper, and so also did the definition of the privileges associated with power. With varying degrees of rigidity and exclusivity, forest use was reserved for the more powerful social strata, to the detriment of the weak. In those countries where monarchy was strong, such as France or England, forest control and use were in the hands of the king and his aristocracy. Elsewhere local potentates held the advantage: lords, bishops, abbeys, and even cities in those cases where the economic and social fabric favoured their development.[12]

The first skirmishes over forest resources date back to the eighth and ninth centuries. We have already seen how some monasteries exerted their power over local populations by the appropriation of these resources from rural communities. During the tenth and eleventh centuries, lay masters in particular asserted themselves: it was the period in which the power of local lords reached an apogee as they brought men and land under their control and directed productive activities as well as public and judicial administrations. Relations with the peasantry became tenser. The seigniory demanded more than in the past, not only privately (as property owners) but also in terms of public levies. Church and monastery assets (people, land, animals, stock) were themselves targets of pillage, as the nobility was overrun by a frenzy of power, a sort of 'hunger' similar to that which afflicted the peasantry.[13] It was hunger born of the need to carve out a niche in the local wealth and power structure, for the nobility too felt the effects of demographic expansion.

Seigniorial appropriation of the right to use untilled land took place in this turbulent climate. Everywhere the number of 'reserves' increased, areas in which the rural classes were forbidden to hunt, and hunting itself entered into the hierarchy of privilege; poaching came to be punished with the severity reserved for the enemies of class. Pasturing was rigidly controlled as well: the use of grass for the pasturing of sheep and of acorns for pigs were subject to specific limitations, as was the right to gleaning; previously stubble had been freely used, following the harvest, for feeding livestock. In the thirteenth and fourteenth centuries, these rights 'had practically disappeared in much of the hills and plains of north-central Italy',[14] just as they had in the more agricultural regions of other parts of Europe. These rights did none the less long survive in marginal areas, but they no longer held the importance they once had. Even the cities, which in some regions, such as north-central Italy, successfully competed with the rural nobility for territorial rights, took part in this general appropriation, reserving large sections of forest for the exclusive use of the *cives*. An important semantic transition was made as the 'common forest' became the 'forest of the *comune*', that is of the city.[15]

The peasants understandably viewed this process of expropriation as a hardship and sought when possible to contest it, a fact born out by court proceedings from the ninth century on recording an interminable series of accusations, court battles and humiliation. Occasionally they succeeded in defending their rights, negotiating a degree of reciprocal respect with the lords; in the twelfth century, for example, several rural communities in northern Italy successfully secured (or regained) the right to hunt in public spaces. More often expropriation was brutal and definitive. In any case, the right to use untilled spaces would long remain at the heart of peasant concerns. The eleventh-century chronicler William of Jumièges confirmed as much in recounting the bloody peasant revolt of 966 in the duchy of Normandy: 'the only particular manifestation of peasant self-assertion mentioned by the chronicler is that they intended to exploit at their will the woods and the rivers'. The revolt was brutally suppressed by Raoul, Count of Evreux and uncle of Duke Richard II. Noble privilege was strictly defended in England, where the king reserved larger game (deer and other large animals) for himself, leaving smaller game to local lords. Keeping in mind this state of affairs, 'it might well be thought that the popularity of outlaw ballads (such as those later tales of Robin Hood) reflected not only an interest in the adventures of these rebellious men living outside settled society in the wilds, but also some Utopian vision of free communities of hunters eating their fill of a forbidden food'. Access to natural resources would continue to play a central role in peasant demands in the following centuries, in the English revolt of 1381 as well as in that of 1525 in Germany.[16]

The limitation or denial of the right to use untilled spaces constitutes not only an important chapter of social and economic history, but also a decisive event in the history of nutrition. A significant qualitative change followed as diet became ever more socially differentiated. Differences had of course always existed between rich and poor diets, but had been primarily quantitative; subsequently they took on a more markedly qualitative character. The food of the lower classes came to consist primarily of vegetable products (grains and greens), while meat consumption (of wild game and fresh meat especially) became a privilege and gradually emerged as a status symbol. In some sense the old distinction between animal and vegetable foods, which had characterized the nutritional regimes of different *civilizations*, re-emerged with particular *social* connotations. Such was the new language of food which, with increasing clarity and self-consciousness, Europeans spoke from the eleventh century on.

These changes did not, of course, occur all of a sudden, though there were periods (the eleventh century, for example) when the process was speeded up. In some cases they took place rapidly and definitively, while in others they represented only an incipient trend. None the less, it was still generally the case that the dietary regime of the European peasantry in the twelfth and thirteenth centuries – the period most strongly characterized by the process of agricultural transformation, both economically and culturally – was relatively rich in meat. Around 1130, Peter Abelard wrote a letter to Héloïse and her Paraclete nuns full of advice regarding the material and spiritual organization of their lives; in it he did not fail to point out that the required abstinence from meat, strongly advocated by traditional monasticism, could itself become a temptation to gluttony. Meat in fact was relatively abundant, and all could enjoy it without difficulty. It was a 'common' food, much more so than fish which the monastics often substituted for meat: fish, on the other hand, 'is much more expensive than meat for the poor and harder to obtain; what is more it is less filling'. It was in effect an indulgence for sophisticated palates and those who could afford it. According to Abelard, a more humble solution, in substance if not in form, was to cease vaunting the renunciation of meat and choose instead a truly modest and simple diet which might even include eating meat 'three times a week'. In this way one might nourish oneself with ordinary foods which are less tempting than fish or birds, though 'Benedict does not forbid eating these either'.[17]

The nutritional importance of meat, considered (as it would not be later) an indispensable component of a poor diet, is mentioned in many other texts of the period. In the thirteenth century, the first *Battle of Lent and Carnival* – a story frequently retold in the European literature of the following centuries – could still conclude with the victory of a meat diet over that without, a victory which found justification in that the poor needed meat. Lent was certainly cruel in that he afflicted only the poor, while the wealthy could seek out other delicacies. This message was similar to that of Abelard.[18]

The twelfth- and thirteenth-century peasant was ever more confined to his plot of land. Forest access had become more difficult, and hunting and animal breeding no longer played the decisive role they had several centuries before. Meat procurement declined: less wild game, less pork. Domestic poultry raising continued, though chicken always appears in the literature of the period as a luxury reserved for feast days. The world of the peasant was itself diversifying. The rebirth of trade and a money economy in the context of continually increasing agricultural production brought about changes which were at first barely perceptible. Next to the wealthy peasant, who recognized the opportunity to carve out a niche in the market economy, many others continued to live in a traditional regime of autarky in consumption. Meanwhile, the category of salaried workers grew, an agricultural proletariat particularly vulnerable in times of nutritional crisis.

Give Us This Day Our Daily Bread . . .

From the eleventh century, bread came to play a central role in the diet of the poorer classes. Other foods were of secondary importance and generally perceived as 'accompaniments' to bread. The best proof of this development was the spread of the term *companaticum* (literally, with bread) in the Romance language areas (those most strongly marked by a bread culture). Bread's role had changed radically, indeed had been inverted, from that of the seventh century when Isidore of Seville wrote that bread's name (*panis*) derived from the fact that it is served (*adponatur*) with other foods: 'panis dictus, quod cum omni cibo adpona-tur.'[19] Subsequently it was all the rest that was added.

Reference to bread in the documents of the period verges on the obsessive. In agrarian contracts, arable plots were referred to as 'bread lands'. Agricultural production became by antonom-asia the 'bread harvest'. Both rent and land tithes were reckoned in terms of bread. Above all, bread (or grain, or flour) con-stituted the stores of peasant families (as recorded in property inventories). The kneading chest in which bread was kept and on top of which dough was kneaded was a domestic item of utmost importance. The household, which ate and slept under the same roof, was described as those who lived off the same bread (*ad unum panem*) and also off the same wine. A shortage of bread meant famine. Substitutes might be found to assure sur-vival, but the lack of bread signalled a state of emergency and was borne with ever greater difficulty. The attachment to bread – the well-rooted habit of preparing and consuming that particu-lar food – was such that it was procured at all costs, using, in times of crisis, any possible ingredient.[20]

This behaviour was not new; we have already seen its like in the sixth century (recall Gregory of Tours) and it would not be difficult to find other examples: 'famine bread' – mixed even with earth, as for example by French peasants in 843[21] – is a frequent and ubiquitous player in the history of want. Radulfus Glaber relates that during the famine of 1032–3, 'an experiment was tried which appears never have been tried anywhere else. In an attempt to combat hunger, many gathered a clay-like white sand which they then mixed with whatever quantity of flour and bran was available in order to fashion loaves.' Unfortunately 'their efforts were in vain: their faces all became pale and hollow;

many suffered from bodily swelling and taut skin; their voices became so faint as to resemble the cries of half-dead birds'.[22] In spite of these unfortunate consequences, such remained the most 'rational' response to famine, before panic or madness forced resort in the most extreme cases to different behaviour: eating grass 'like animals' and all sorts of unclean food. To make bread from earth was an act of controlled desperation. It represented the employment of survival techniques which had been developed and passed down orally by generations of famine sufferers: a chronicle describing the Swedish famine of 1099 relates that 'it was customary for peasants to mix some grain in with the flour'.[23] Scientific texts of the period also considered this problem: there are many references to 'famine bread' in the agronomic texts of Moorish Spain. Heirs to the Graeco-Roman agronomic, pharmacological and dietetic tradition, these texts 'brought important knowledge to bear on the problems of daily nourishment at the moment of European agricultural expansion'. They included a series of progressively unusual techniques for the use of grains, legumes, forage, domestic fruit and vegetables, wild herbs, nuts and medicinal plants: 'the pharmacopoeia became more and more important as the plant used to make bread became less and less adapted to domestic use'. Ibn al-Awwam wrote, for example, that 'if the fruit is inedible, its basic taste must be identified and if possible eliminated according to the appropriate procedures; when this is accomplished, dry the fruit and grind it and then proceed to make bread'.[24] Ignorance of certain rules, haste, choice of the wrong herbs or their improper treatment could be fatal: the chronicle of the German famine of 1099 reports that 'among the wild herbs gathered there was a poisonous one called *collo*, and many died'.

It is clear in any case that with the passing centuries, the possibility of resolving a nutritional crisis by recourse to grain alternatives (or their unlikely surrogates) became ever more distant. According to the Life of Benedict of Aniane, a multitude of starving poor flocked to the monastery gate in 779 and were fed 'mutton, beef and goat's milk' until the next harvest;[25] a few centuries later this solution would have been inconceivable. Gradually the idea that 'it is difficult to survive without agriculture' forced its acceptance – this citation is taken from a hagiographic text describing the famine of 1095 in an area of what is now Belgium[26] – and only then did the lack of bread (the *penuria panis*, *exiguitas panis*, *inopia panis* of the chronicles) become intolerable.

In truth, it was not just 'bread'. As we have already mentioned, this name comprised other foods as well, and symbolically it represented all food obtained by working the fields. Between the eleventh and thirteenth centuries, European agriculture witnessed considerable wheat expansion, as its cultivation gained ground from lesser grains. As a result, bread consumption – in particular, white bread consumption – increased.[27] This development, however, benefited almost exclusively two select categories of consumers (which occasionally overlapped): landowners, who collected rent from peasants in the form of wheat (partly for consumption, partly for sale) and scorned other grains, and city-dwellers, who, if not landowners themselves, could purchase wheat at the market. The peasants, on the other hand, who only marginally took part in the market, and primarily for the sake of selling excess production, generally contented themselves with what they produced, that is what remained after the rent was paid. As a result, their diet was based primarily on lesser grains and legumes, and occasionally, as we have seen, on chestnuts: mostly black bread, polentas and soups. Bonvesin de la Riva, a Milanese writer of the thirteenth century, confirmed that 'an abundance of chestnuts, Italian millet and beans often nourished many people in place of bread' (*panis locis*).[28] Only in certain regions (and not before the thirteenth century) did wheat and white bread make their way into the peasant diet: in the Tuscan countryside, for example, between Florence and Siena where the urban imprint on the rural economy was such that the peasants imitated city consumption patterns;[29] or in southern Italy, where a Roman productive model persisted, one based on wheat and barley. Even there, however, wheat was intended primarily for the market, for the rich cities of the north and for overseas kingdoms; while barley (in soups, flat-breads, and other miserable 'breads') and greens played a large role in local peasant diets.[30]

With a few possible exceptions, white bread made from wheat remained a delicacy available only to a few. A twelfth-century poem by William of Aquitaine placed bread on a plane with pepper (an extremely dear food) and fine wine: 'the bread was white, the wine good, and the pepper plentiful'.[31] In a sermon to the lay Cistercian brothers, Humbert of Romans recounted – or invented, which for our purposes is the same – a significant episode:

> Brothers often come to us from poverty, attracted by the hope of a better life. It happened once upon a time that a man, from a family which only ate black bread, wanted to become a brother in order to eat white bread. On the day of his admission, prostate before the bishop, he was asked, 'what do you desire?' He answered: 'White bread, and often!'[32]

As for the image which the city-dwellers had of these rustics, we shall limit ourselves to citing a novella by Giovanni Sercambi in which a Florentine gentlewoman exclaims: 'and what do they know, these peasants, of good and bad flour who think millet bread the equal of wheat?'[33] During the twelfth and thirteenth centuries, a new nutritional dichotomy arose which would long characterize European culture: that between town and country.

The Throat of the City[34]

'You who control the transportation of food supplies are in charge, so to speak, of the city's lifeline, of its very throat.'[35] Cassiodorus, in addressing this circular to the urban food prefects,

touched upon a vital aspect of the organization of the Roman
state (a state which was itself controlled in the sixth century by
a 'barbarian' like Theodoric who none the less generally respected the traditional political models). The city played a
central role of administrative co-ordination; it was the hub
around which rotated the entire economic as well as political life
of the state. It was the centre into which flowed every sort of
agricultural product and food, directed in particular to the
urban market, but also to the storehouses of the major landowners. Victualling policy (the management and control of
urban food supplies) was a basic public function, carried out by
specific officers.[36] When the social fabric of the empire – in the
West at least – unravelled, the European countryside came to
recognize other reference points: village communities, courts,
abbeys and rural churches. Indeed, it may have been in part due
to this process – the decline of a dominant and demanding
urban state apparatus – that peasant society succeeded in reorgan-
izing itself on new bases and developing different production
patterns focused primarily on domestic consumption. The agricultural growth of the ninth to eleventh centuries coincided
with the rebirth of the markets, in particular on a local level:
villages, castles and monasteries became the centres of renewed
commerce. Local lords did not hesitate to secure the new sur-
pluses for their own purposes; in certain regions, Italy and
Flanders for example, the process took on a markedly urban
character as these 'lords' became the cities themselves, around
which the rural economy began again to organize. A new urban
imperialism developed, and the resources of the 'colonized'
territories were evaluated in terms of their role in the market
and in urban consumption. A meticulous (if at times impro-
vised) victualling policy served to focus all energies on the
single objective of supplying the city, of satisfying – as Cassiodorus would have said – its throat.[37]

The legislation imposed by urban authorities (single ordinances and comprehensive statutes) covered all phases of the production process: the care of the agricultural terrain, including

directives intended to increase productivity; the control of the peasant's labour, minutely regulated with regard to both timing and activity; the control of food transformation processes, including in particular norms for mills and ovens; the control of the market, by means for example of varying tariffs, made higher or lower according to whether importation or exportation was to be encouraged. Agricultural contracts, privately negotiated by landowners with the surrounding peasants, resembled the laws passed by public urban authorities. It is no surprise that we find there the same interests, even the same wording; for these landowners were generally also the city leaders.[38] The defence of their private interests coincided with that of the urban market: to protect their own rights as well as urban consumption. The work to be done was as a result carefully spelled out: how often and when to plough the fields, how much fertilizer to use and which crops to sow (with particular insistence on wheat as the city-dwellers did not care for other grains). The peasant came to be viewed in a new way: no longer a simple object of domination (as he had been viewed by the traditional nobility), he became instead a tool of power, used for increased production and greater profits. The profit motive was a new aspect of European culture which asserted itself from the eleventh and twelfth centuries among 'bourgeois' groups – a complex social grouping which included not only the bourgeoisie in its narrow sense but also sections of the lower and middle urban nobility.

Agronomic treatises, which began to reappear in the West after centuries of absence (with the exception mentioned above of Arabic literature in Spain), were generally an expression of this urban reality and clearly reflected its interests. It is worthy of note, for example, that Paganino Bonafede, a Bolognese landowner and agronomer of the fourteenth century, considered only the cultivation of wheat, passing over other grains like millet, Italian millet or sorghum, given that 'all men know more or less the season when they should be sown'.[39] Everyone knew how to cultivate the *biade* (as lesser grains were called in

Italy); the methods for wheat instead needed to be taught. Similarly, English treatises of the thirteenth and fourteenth centuries (that of Walter of Henley is well known) devote particular attention to wheat;[40] the point of view is less markedly urban but still clearly focused on a money economy and the market. It is in this context that we must evaluate the 'reconversion' to wheat which characterized the European agricultural economy (to varying degrees according to area) during the twelfth and thirteenth centuries. Wheat became the most important grain for city-dwellers and also for the rural lords; while the peasants continued to content themselves with *biade*.

In fact, the lesser grains (as well as legumes and chestnuts) continued to account for some of the bread consumed in the cities. The Bologna statutes of 1288, one example among many, consider three principal types of flour: that made from pure wheat (for which one paid a milling tax of four *denari* per *corba*), that from *mistura* (two *denari*) and that from fava beans and wheat (apparently a higher quality *mistura* given that the tax was three *denari* per *corba*).[41] Compromises of this sort, however, were made only by the lower urban classes, and not all the time: the giving up of wheat and white bread, a sort of status symbol of the urban diet and lifestyle, was conceded only under duress.[42]

For the urban classes, scarcity meant *carum tempus* (times of high prices). In normal times, urban dependence on the market meant higher levels of consumption and greater variety than were enjoyed in the countryside; this same dependence, however, in difficult periods put city-dwellers at greater risk than the peasantry who, though left to their own devices, were in direct contact with the means of production. There were occasions when the problem of dealing with the poor in periods of scarcity led to the assertion of privilege, and even of to the closing of the city gates from which not only the local rural population, but also the poor of the city itself were barred.

'It was a period of great scarcity in Genoa and the wretched there were more numerous than in any other land.' The authorities had ships fitted out and announced in the streets that 'all the poor should go to the shore and there they would receive bread from the city'. A crowd formed on the quays of the port, not only of the city's poor, but of 'wretches' come from elsewhere as well. City officials pretended to want to distinguish the two groups, instructing citizens to board one ship and foreigners another. All boarded, and then suddenly the oars were lowered and the poor (real as well as impostors) were taken to Sardinia. 'And there in the midst of plenty they were left, while in Genoa the famine ended.' This story comes from the *Novellino*, a book of stories, fables and apologues written in the late thirteenth century.[43] Even if we take this story to be an invention, it was none the less the product of that period's imagination. Nor would there be any lack in the following centuries, as documented in chronicles and legislation, of analogous examples of 'bourgeois ferocity',[44] as Fernand Braudel has chosen to call it.

To Eat Much and Well

Amid tension, contradiction and contrasts, European society seems to have reached the first half of the thirteenth century in a state of widespread if not generalized well-being. Taking into account the inevitable costs in terms of marginalization and inequality, economic growth none the less exercised a positive effect on city and country alike. The balance between population and resources remained fragile, as the succession of deforestations and agricultural colonizations – certain signs of a growing and unmet demand for food – attested. But this process also produced wealth and made possible higher levels of consumption and even a degree of luxury for a larger segment of the population than in previous centuries. Europe probably reached the height of this cycle of prosperity, begun about a century prior, around 1250; it was a partial prosperity that respected social distinctions, but no less real for this characteristic. What is more, it seems that even the lower classes managed to partake of the feast; as both the number and the frequency of famines declined in the twelfth and thirteenth centuries. For indeed it was the improved productivity of the peasants (which cannot be entirely put down to improved climatic conditions) which underlay the greater wealth of city-dwellers and the seigniory. In 1255, Bonaventure wrote in a treatise that famine was a problem of the past and took heart in the level of food consumption enjoyed by his generation.[45] Clearly this opinion was not a general one – just three years later Matthew Paris wrote that famine had killed 15,000 in England[46] – but it none the less marks a significant social and cultural climate.

As we have already noted, this development applied in particular to the city. Towards the end of the thirteenth century, Riccobaldo da Ferrara referred to the era of Emperor Frederick II (a half-century before) as a time in which 'the habits of the Italians were unrefined . . . food was scarce and the common people ate fresh meat only three times a week. At midday, they ate greens cooked with meat, and in the evening that same meat served cold.'[47] Consider the quantitative aspect of this observation: for a city-dweller of the thirteenth century, eating *fresh* meat only three times a week was a sign of poverty and coarseness (and to that 'small' amount of meat we must add at least salt pork). It was certainly not a small amount, though to Riccobaldo (and the city-dwellers of his time) it seemed so. Qualitatively it is also striking: once upon a time people ate poorly, forced to consume simply prepared greens and cold meat. Moreover, given that nostalgia for the good old days seems to be an inevitable characteristic of the human spirit, the reversal of values represented here must be the sign of a strong and self-assured society.

Even the peasants – those who succeeded in taking advantage of an especially dynamic economic phase to increase their holdings of land and money – aspired to eat better and emulate the lifestyles of lords and city-dwellers. In thirteenth-century Germany, the old peasant Helmbrecht (protagonist of the tale in verse of the same name by Wernher der Gartenaere) recommended his own starchy diet to his son, maintaining that meat and fish were reserved for lords:

> You must live off that which I do, off that which your mother gives you. Drink water, my son, rather than buy wine with the profits of theft . . . Week after week your mother cooks for you a good porridge of millet; you should eat this and fill yourself up rather than trade a stolen palfrey for a goose . . . Son, mix rye with oats rather than eat fish paid for with shame.

The son, however, refused these councils: 'Father, drink water if you will, but I want to drink wine; eat polenta, but I want to eat what they call roast chicken.'[48]

As always happens in such cases, the rich shifted the threshold of class distinction upwards. In a world where abundance was fairly widespread (though not general), to eat much, as was the custom among the European ruling classes, was no longer sufficient, though it did of course remain a distinctive feature of the nobility: the heroes of chivalrous tales were also big eaters. The hero of the *Chanson de Guillaume*, having withdrawn from battle, comforted himself with a shoulder of boar, a roast peacock, a large loaf of bread and two large sweets. Witnessing this meal, his wife Guiborc scolded him, claiming that one who could eat in such a manner could not at the same time be capable of dishonouring his own lineage by laying down arms. On another occasion, Guiborc had served a similar meal to Guillaume's nephew Girart; just like his uncle, Girart had devoured it all without so much as raising his eyes from the table. At the sight of such a prodigious appetite, Guiborc commented to herself that certainly he must be a brave warrior; turning to her husband she added: 'You can see that he comes from your stock.'[49]

Alongside the depiction of cultural models and traditional lifestyles according to which noble valour was linked to an occasionally brutish image of force, there were also cases in which the courtly hero — or at least the author who described him – displayed a moderate attitude, almost one of detachment, with regard to food. It would be too simple to interpret this temperance as adherence to the religious morality of the 'Christian' warrior, a figure whose image coalesces in just these centuries. In the twelfth- and thirteenth-century romances, the nutritional aspects of aristocratic life are often only lightly touched upon: 'all that mattered was to eliminate any suggestion of shortage or stinginess by ensuring that everyone had enough to eat'.[50] Describing a meal at the court of Arthur, Chrétien de Troyes, in *Erec et Enide*, is brief: 'As to the quality of the meal, I shall not tarry over it.' We know only that there was fowl, game, fruit and fine wines. Even the description of the final banquet which brought to a sumptuous close the coronation of Erec is something of a disappointment for one who hopes to reconstruct the menu: 'One thousand knights served the bread, a thousand more the wine and still a thousand more the courses.' And again: 'I could certainly give a description of the various foods served, but I shall concentrate instead on other topics.' Hartmann von Aue, the German translator of Chrétien, was still more explicit: 'I prefer to pass over what they ate, because they paid more attention to noble behaviour than to eating much.'[51]

This was not then a case of simple Christian temperance. The apparent lack of interest in food shown by these individuals and the avoidance by the authors of over-accurate descriptions hide the careful attention paid to 'noble behaviour' and all those elements considered necessary accompaniments to food: the beauty of the table, of the tablecloth and of the crockery; good company and pleasant conversation; music, theatre and comportment. This attention signalled the birth of 'good manners',[52] of a ritual conviviality founded upon elegance rather than force, on form more than on substance (from a dietary point of view). In fact, in the twelfth and thirteenth centuries these 'manners' began to function as a sign of a social differentiation based no longer only on quantity but also on the quality and mode of consumption.

It was not, however, only the convivial dimension of dining that commanded the new aristocratic culture's attention. The foods themselves were expected to display more refined and elaborate flavours, smells and colours. Appetite alone, though it remained a fundamental attribute of nobility, did not suffice as a sign of initiation to courtly life; the ability to choose and to distinguish good from poor foods was also required. When the hermit count of *Tirant lo Blanc* (the famous romance of Joanot Martorell) finally abandons austerity and agrees to don the costume of a gentleman, it is just this sort of test to which he is subjected: 'many types of food were placed upon the table before him, but he, being both expert and wise, ate only the good foods, avoiding the others'. He reacted similarly when the sweets were later presented on a large golden platter, among which stood out the fruit preparations.[53]

We should not then be surprised to find in the European literature of the thirteenth century the first cookery books, a genre not seen since the late Roman handbook of Apicius. This development is the clearest and most tangible sign of renewed interest in the pleasures of food.

Gastronomy and Famine

Pope Innocent III's early thirteenth-century censure of worldly vanity (*De contemptu mundi*) did not spare the sin of gluttony and the new indulgences dreamed up by the insane passions of man. Wine, beer and cider were no longer enough – 'new emulsions and syrups are concocted'; nor were the good things which came from the trees, the land, the sea and the sky – 'spices are needed, and essences'; and each dish required the art of cooks.[54]

The need for spices was not entirely new. Spices had been widely used for some time in European cuisine (of the wealthy, that is), and there is evidence of a significant inflow of spices to the markets of Italy and France already by the ninth and tenth centuries. Documents reveal as well a growing interest in products such as ginger, cinnamon, galingale and cloves, products almost wholly absent from Roman cuisine (in which, judging from Apicius's handbook, the only spice used was pepper). Other spices first appeared in dietetic treatises and in a specifically medicinal context: Anthimus's sixth-century epistle *De observatione ciborum*, for example, prescribes the use of ginger, unknown to Apicius. Gradually spices made their way from the medicinal to the gastronomic sphere (a frequent and widespread process for many different products). When, at the end of the eleventh century, the expeditions and settlements of the Crusades brought westerners into closer contact with the East, the influx of spices increased and found fertile terrain among Europeans already familiar with those aromas and flavors. It was in this way that the Venetian merchants, who long dominated the spice trade, made their fortunes.[55]

The cookery books of the thirteenth and fourteenth centuries represent the first written codification of this gastronomic choice (and many others as well). To what can we attribute it? First of all, we should correct a false and widely held opinion which discerning scholars have shown to be entirely mistaken. This is the view that the ample use of spices (some even arrogantly suggest their *abuse*) served to cover, hide or 'camouflage' the flavour of poorly preserved or even spoiled foods (especially meats, with which spices are particularly used). Alternatively it is claimed that spices served to preserve meats. Both views are clearly unfounded. In the first place, the rich ate the freshest meats (and it was only the wealthy who could afford exotic and expensive products such as spices): game caught that very day if possible (recall Charlmagne who had prepared daily a spit of roasted game), or else meat bought at the market, which was also fresh as normally butchered daily and to order; the animals were brought *live* to the shops. The same held for fish, either caught directly or else bought at the market; some types (eels, for example, or lampreys – among the most sought-after) were even brought live to the fish vendor's. What is more, the cookery books are fairly explicit in calling for the addition of spices *after* cooking: 'as late as possible' we read in the four-teenth-century *Ménagier de Paris*. The 'preservative' argument falls as well; there were other methods for extending the life of meats and fish. These included above all salting, but also drying and smoking. In any case, spices were not involved, and the consumption of preserved meats was generally characteristic of 'poor' cuisine, that is of a social sphere in which spices were practically unknown. The rich did of course also consume some preserved meats, but in general the social class of the spice-eaters was more or less the same as that of the consumers of fresh (and the best-quality) meats.[56]

An alternative explanation involves the dietetic notions of the period. Physicians agreed that the 'heat' of spices aided in the digestion of foods; that is, in their 'cooking' in the stomach: hence their use, not only on foods, but also as a sort of confection to be taken at the end of a meal, or else in one's own room before going to bed. 'Bedroom spices' were sure to be found in the king's private chamber; the fourteenth-century *Ordinaciones* of Peter III the Great of Aragon numbered them among the few truly indispensable items (along with water and wine to drink, candles and torches for light).[57] Indeed, many gastronomic inventions, beginning with confectionery, are due to scientific and pharmaceutical practices.[58] We know, moreover, that health considerations have always exercised a strong influence on human dietary choices. The reverse, however, is also true: in the past, as today, the desire for novelty (new consumer products, new tastes) has always sought scientific confirmation, a rational justification for the folly of desire.

Braudel's characterization hits the mark with his phrase 'the folly of spices', and Rebora cites a relevant example when he writes: 'I challenge anyone to consume his or her share of a broth or sauce "for twelve persons", in which (according to the recipe of a thirteenth-century Italian cookery book) are stewed 26 grams of cloves, three nutmegs, pepper, ginger, cinnamon and saffron. An ounce of cloves suffices for the preparation of an efficient anaesthetic, and too much nutmeg can be poisonous.'[59]

These levels of consumption are hard to conceive of, and belong instead to the realm of desire and imagination, of the need for luxury and ostentation: the price of spices alone (beyond the means of most) sufficed to make them objects of desire. Indeed, why does one desire caviare or smoked salmon? It is not a coincidence that spices are called for even more abundantly in handbooks intended for an urban bourgeois public (for example, those produced in Tuscany in the thirteenth and fourteenth centuries) than in those intended for a courtly one (like those from the Angevin court of Naples or earlier French examples).[60] The bourgeois, more than the aristocrat, needs to emphasize his own wealth and social importance. Indeed, were it not primarily a question of luxury, it would be difficult to understand the many moral indictments, such as that of Pope Innocent, delivered in the twelfth and thirteenth centuries. Bernard of Clairvaux reproached the Cluniac monks for their use of spiced wine (*pigmentorum respersa pulveribus*), and Peter the Venerable prohibited the same in his *Statutes*. This did not prevent the continued use of spices for pharmaceutical purposes: the infirmary at Cluny – according to the *Consuetudines* of Ulrich – should never be without pepper, cinnamon, ginger and other 'healthy roots'.[61] We cannot, then, underestimate the pharmaco-dietetic convictions of the period, though it is certainly not in this area that we shall find the explanation for the spice boom in thirteenth-century European gastronomy. Gradually familiarity with these flavors became firmly established in the 'structures of taste' (as Flandrin likes to call them). Highly spiced foods came to be considered *good* to eat. Personal preferences, however, differed: European cookery books (which appeared in Catalonia, England and Germany after Italy and France) are generally unanimous in their enthusiasm for spices, though there were significant differences in those selected. Moreover, one often encounters the simple instruction to add 'good spices' to the food prepared. Rather than a lack of specificity, these indications reveal a degree of freedom left to the cook to choose as he likes, or else to use a mixture of spices, as seems to have been the norm. An

Italian book provides an example: 'take an ounce of pepper, an ounce of cinnamon, an ounce of ginger, half a quarter of cloves and a quarter of saffron'. This combination will go well with 'all foods'.

Nor did the image of spices end here. Signs of social distinction and of ostentation, spices also assumed dreamlike qualities, those same qualities that characterized the distant and mysterious Orient: an 'oneiric horizon' onto which westerners projected their desires and utopias.[62] According to the maps of the period, the Orient lay next to the earthly paradise, and so should be profoundly influenced by this nearness. These were the worlds of abundance and of happiness, and above all of immortality, inhabited by multiple-centenarians, evergreen trees and the ineffable phoenix; and it is there that spices grow. Indeed the latter come directly from paradise: Joinville describes the fishermen of the Nile who drag their nets, 'filled with the goods which this world produces, with ginger, rhubarb, sandalwood and cinnamon; and it is said that these come from the earthly paradise'. For shaken loose by the wind, these goods are presumed to have fallen into the river from the trees of Eden. 'It is said', but we cannot know to what extent our author or his readers actually believed this legend. 'Whatever the case, for the contemporaries of Taillevent spices undoubtedly had a flavour, and a smell, of eternity'.[63]

We have already referred to the dual context (bourgeois/aristocratic, urban/courtly) in which cookery books began to be produced at the end of the thirteenth century. In both cases, the public considered is explicitly identified: in the courtly recipe books, such as the Angevin example mentioned above, one reads 'give to the lord' or 'take to the lord', while the Tuscan examples envisage a company of 'rich' diners (an adjective not appropriate for the traditional nobility): 'twenty rich gentlemen', 'twelve rich epicures' etc. Neither group, however, is the *direct* audience for whom these books were intended. They were instead clearly written for professionals: cooks in the service of a lord or a 'rich man', or perhaps a tavern keeper. The advice included is for them:

for the eel pie, 'allow it to cool a bit or the wealthy will burn
their mouths'; for ravioli, 'make them with a fine crust or else
the wealthy will not like them'. It is the cooks, for example, who
are advised not to overcook the lamprey stew 'so much that the
pieces begin to fall apart', and not to oversalt it, given the
lamprey's already salty flavour, and it is to them that a good deal
of freedom is allowed with regard to the alteration of the flavours and ingredients used according to market and other restrictions.

According to a fourteenth century Italian text, 'as regards the
things here said, the good cook will in all cases be guided by the
specifics of his situation, and can vary or embellish the foods
accordingly as he sees fit.' And a German text: 'use these instructions to devise other dishes as well'. A lack of quantitative
detail is characteristic of many of the European recipe books and
seems to be linked to this same professional identity; the cooks
knew that theirs was an eminently creative and experimental art
and that proportions were for dilettanti and beginners. It seems
not to be a coincidence that the few handbooks which do
contain information of this sort, in Italy at any rate, belong to
the bourgeois tradition. Perhaps this was because the 'rich
epicures' were more attentive to their purse and wanted to keep
closer control over expenses, or perhaps because the city-dwell-
ing public interested in cookery books was more varied and
potentially wider. In a novella of Giovanni Sercambi, we read
that the professionals 'practise the art of cooking with books and
skill and devise such delicious foods that their shops are both
crowded and profitable'.[64] To these, however, we must add the
occasional amateur or gourmand, such as Meoccio, the priest
and main character of a novella by Gentile Sermini, who disguised his favourite cookery book as a breviary: 'full of cooking
recipes, including all possible foods and rarities, how they
should be cooked, with what seasoning, and at what time of
year; this it included and nothing else'.[65]

The cuisine described in these books was certainly not that of
every day, and above all not of everybody: the quality of the

ingredients (beginning with the spices) and the complexity of the preparations attest to an elite gastronomy. Among the elite, however, this cuisine was not simply described or written, but indeed prepared. Describing a visit by King Louis IX to the convent of Friars Minor in Sens, Salimbene da Parma wrote: 'On that day we had first of all cherries and the whitest bread . . . then fresh fava beans cooked in milk, fish and crayfish, eel pie, rice made with almond milk and powdered cinnamon, lightly roasted eel with an excellent sauce, cakes with curds and whey, and the usual fruit served in a refined and abundant way.'[66]

It was a strictly lean lunch and not particularly sumptuous, but the dishes served were more or less the same that we find in the recipe books, beginning with the famous 'blancmange', probably of Arab origin and made up entirely of white ingredients (rice, almond milk etc.); European cookery books include numerous variations on this dish including both fatty (made with chicken breast) and lean (made with fish or, as in this case, simply vegetables). Although the ingredients change from recipe to recipe – Flandrin, comparing thirty-seven recipes for 'blancmange' occurring in English, French, Italian and Catalan cookbooks, was unable to find a single common ingredient[67] – it is none the less the case that this dish, and others as well, was an international one, an expression of the gastronomic *koine* which European culture developed in the thirteenth and fourteenth centuries. Internationalism and regionalism were both characteristic: on the one hand, common traits, recurring foods and flavours, and trading and borrowing between different regions; on the other, local, regional or national peculiarities which suggest an early differentiation of European cuisines. 'Variety in tastes and practices – frequently cited, beginning in the sixteenth century, in works discussing food and in travel journals – did not await the Renaissance and Reformation.'[68] Nor was this fact lost on contemporaries, as attested to by the attachment of the names of countries to various foods (perhaps accidental or invented, but none the less significant), such as 'English broth', 'German broth' or 'Catalan blancmange'.

Among the distinctive characteristics of the 'new' European cuisine were cakes. Widely prepared in all countries, they bore little resemblance to ancient foods. Stuffed cakes seem to have enjoyed a particular success. These were extremely varied and known by a variety of names (*pastello*, *pastero*, *enpanada*, *crosta*, *altocreas* etc.); they might be filled with meat, fish, cheese, egg, greens, almost anything, either in layers or pieces, or else blended together and, in the style of a pie, covered with a crust. This was a gastronomic development dependent upon, or at least favoured by, the presence of an oven, and so one that transcended the domestic environment. It was characteristic of the cities' where the ovens of professional bakers were constantly in use – so the documents (statutes, novellas) tell us – for the preparation of food.[69] There were even rotisseries and 'cook's shops' where one could buy cakes and other ready-made foods: in a novella of Giuseppe Sercambi, a Pisan artisan states: 'I do not prepare food myself, and if someone comes to dine with me, I send out to the cook for a roast chicken.'[70] The cooks then provided a link to the cuisine of the common people, for foods intended for the nobility or the wealthy bourgeoisie often passed through the 'filter' of domestic cooks, or else public rotisserie operators and bakers, certainly not representatives of the higher social orders. A daily exchange of experiences and knowledge must have gone on, perhaps mediated by the cookery books we have discussed. 'Cuisine was not so much an invention of the upper classes, but rather a need of those same classes satisfied by popular art.' Nor is it a surprise that 'some of the preparations intended for the nobility came into general use, perhaps by means of certain economies', for example by reducing the quantity of spices used, or else substituting aromatic herbs – true 'poor man's spices' – in which the gardens abounded.[71]

Whether it was the general spread of an elite practice to the common classes, or else a popular custom which made its way into elite cuisine, cakes had become by the mid-thirteenth century a constant feature of European cuisine, or at least of urban European cuisine. Not even during the famine of 1246 were the citizens of Parma willing to give up their cakes, though agreeing to prepare them almost without a filling, stacking one upon another layers of a poor dough with a few herbs and roots: 'et fiebant turtae in duabas crustis, quatuor, et quinque' (and they made cakes with two, four or five crusts).[72]

3

To Each His Own

The Return of Hunger

From about 1270, the growth of the European economy came to a dramatic halt as agricultural expansion slowed and the cultivated area shrank. This development was not, however, due to the achievement of nutritional equilibrium. On the contrary, the situation became ever more serious as population growth did not respond adequately. The progressive spread of cultivation had reached an impassable limit, and to till new fields would have been wasted effort. The use of marginal fields, inappropriate for wheat, had already lowered productivity, and the precarious equilibrium between demographic growth and increasing production was being lost. Jacques Le Goff has described this development as 'the return of hunger',[1] which is not to say that the spectre of famine had ever ceased to torment urban and rural populations alike. None the less, as we have seen, during the twelfth and thirteenth centuries hunger became less oppressive amidst general well-being. Subsequently, it took on once again its leading role.

The last decades of the thirteenth century witnessed a decline in agricultural production. In the early fourteenth century a series of bitter famines began, which it would be impossible here to enumerate as their vicissitudes and timing varied – as always – from region to region. In 1302 famine struck the Iberian peninsula, and according to the *Cronaca* of Ferdinand IV of Castile 'death was so pervasive that a quarter of the population perished; never, in any epoch, had humanity known so great a scourge'. Between 1315 and 1317 a terrible famine afflicted much of Europe, in particular the Atlantic regions. The effects of climatic perturbations were aggravated by commercial speculation, and for two years the populations of France, England, the Low Countries and Germany were on the brink of nutritional disaster. Italy suffered especially in 1328–30 and 1347; these were, however, only the most memorable dates, as there were many other years of want. Price fluctuations in Florence indicate grain shortages in 1303, 1306, 1311, 1323 and 1340 as well. In 1333 and 1334, it was again Spain and Portugal's turn; between 1340 and 1347 that of southern France. In all, it was a half-century of famine. For the region of Forez alone, thirty-four years of famine have been calculated during the period 1277–1343, or one in two.[2]

Thus we encounter already familiar stories and expedients. A Florentine chronicler, for example, noted bitterly in 1329 that many went without wheat 'and ate cabbages, plums, lettuce, roots, melons and watercress, both cooked and raw, and different sorts of meat – horse, donkey, buffalo – but all without bread'. Another chronicle recounts that during the Roman famine of 1338, people ate cabbage 'without bread'; some even had meat, but always 'without bread'; and shouts of 'Bread, bread!' were heard in the streets. Pathetic attempts were made to mould even turnips 'in the shape of bread'. People were so accustomed to bread, the preparation and consumption of that particular food was so firmly established, that it had at all costs to be made, and with any ingredient.

In difficult periods the tension between city and country increased. City-dwellers, privileged in normal times, were also better protected during crises, especially if their city was wealthy and politically powerful. For example, during the 1328–30 famine, the *comune* of Florence undertook an expensive victualling policy, spending – according to the chronicler Giovanni Villani – 'more than 60,000 gold florins to support the people'; wheat and flour were sold at fixed prices in order to contain 'the anger of the people and the poor, and guarantee that everyone had at least enough to insure survival'. As a result, the peasants poured into the city streets in times of famine in the hope, often vain, of finding food. Describing the famine of 1347, the Bologna chronicles report: 'The peasants came to the city'. In Tuscany as well, during the crises of 1323, 1329 and 1347, there was a great influx of the indigent 'from the country to the city and from the smaller cities to the larger'.[3]

It also happened, and not rarely, that supplies were lacking or insufficient. In such cases the city-dwellers themselves went in search of food outside the city walls. An anonymous Roman chronicler describing the 1338 famine reported that 'all the poor of Rome, women, men and bachelors, left for the Castelli [translator's note: hills around Rome]'. They fled into the fields and the rural villages where perhaps they might find something to eat. This chronicler recalled as well an instance of rewarded generosity: a peasant voluntarily fed the starving with fava beans from his land until the famine ended; 'the poor returned to Rome', and his goodness was rewarded with an abundant harvest. One can easily imagine that the country might have more to offer than the city, especially for the poorest classes who, while they might find something to pick or gather in the fields or woods, were unable to turn to the urban market, either because it had no goods to offer or else because those remaining were unaffordable, in spite of fixed prices.[4]

The repeated incidents of nutritional stress suffered by the European population in the first half of the fourteenth century engendered a state of widespread malnutrition and physiological weakness which prepared the way for the plague epidemic that devastated the continent between 1347 and 1351. Clearly there is not a *direct* causal link between the two phenomena: each has its own life and history, and we know that the plague bacillus finds its carrier in the rat. It is equally clear, however, that the standard of living of a population – hygiene, quality of housing, type of nutrition – plays an important role in favouring or blocking individual defences to infection.[5] A 'pandemic' of the sort that attacked Europe at the mid-point of the fourteenth century 'cannot have been a simple coincidence; its onset was prepared by hard years which rendered precarious the existence of a population in excess'.[6] And perhaps it was for this reason that in the Low Countries, for example, the epidemic struck with considerably less force along the coast, where animal-raising and fishing guaranteed the inhabitants a higher level of protein and fat consumption than that of the peasants of the interior.[7] In all, the plague seems to have wiped out about one-quarter (and in some areas one-third) of the European population.[8]

A Carnivorous Europe?

After the tragedy of the plague, 'there was thought to be, due to the reduced number of people, an abundance of all the products of the earth'.[9] The Malthusian prediction contained in this passage did not, however, come to pass. Its author, the Florentine chronicler Matteo Villani, ascribed the hunger and famine that followed to the wickedness of the survivors who, rather than give thanks to God and beg forgiveness for their sins, instead gave vent to a sort of mad joy. None the less, the general situation did improve; nor could it have been otherwise after such a tragedy. According to Giovanni de Mussis, writing in 1388, the city of Piacenza was turned into a land of plenty:

> Marvellous foods were served by all, especially at the wedding banquets which generally fit the following model: red and white wines to begin with, but first of all confections of sugar. As a first course, one or two capons are served and a large piece of meat for every table setting [i.e. two persons]; it is cooked in a pan with almonds and sugar and other good spics. Next comes a great amount of roasted meat: capon, chicken, pheasant, partridge, hare, boar, deer or others depending upon the season; then cakes and curds

and whey with sugar confections on top; then fruit. Finally, after hand-washing and before rising from the table, drink is served and a sugar confection and then more to drink. In place of their cakes and curds and whey, some serve at the beginning of the meal a cake made of eggs, cheese and milk, topped with a good quantity of sugar. In the winter, gelatined wild game is served for dinner – capon, hen or veal – or else gelatined fish; then roast capon and veal; then fruit. After hand-washing but before removing the tables, drink is served, then sugar confections, then more drink. In the summer, dinner consists of gelatined hen, capon, veal, kid and pork, or else gelatined fish; then roast chicken, kid and veal, or else gosling, duck or other meats according to availability; and finally fruit. After hand-washing, the usual procedure ensues. On the second day after the wedding, lasagne with cheese, saffron, raisins and spices are served; then roast veal and fruit. All return to their own homes for dinner and the celebration is over. During Lent, drink and sugar confections are served first, followed by figs and peeled almonds, then large fish with a pepper sauce, then a rice soup with almond milk, sugar and spices [the blancmange already mentioned], and cured eel. After all this, pike roasted in a vinegar or mustard sauce is brought, together with mulled wine and spices. Then walnuts and other fruits are served. And after hand-washing but before the tables are removed, the last drink is served with the usual sugar confection.[10]

This abundance of food (*ciborum lauticia* in our text) seems not to have been limited to wedding feasts. While we know that it was above all on such occasions that wealth and generosity were put on display, the account of our chronicler betrays a more general outbreak of consumerism. Nor was this outbreak traceable only to a desire for social display – it was not by coincidence that city governments began in just this period to prohibit excessive displays of wealth, considered a threat to social equilibrium – but also perhaps to a rediscovered desire to enjoy life and festivity. We should note in any case the absolute priority given to meat (or else fish; the two seem to have belonged to distinct semantic categories and to have been mutually exclusive) in the menus proposed. The other items are not even mentioned. We learn nothing of bread, legumes or greens (common foods and so not worthy of mention), should they even appear on the tables of the wealthy bourgeois or urban aristocracy. From other sources we know that vegetable consumption – with the exception of white bread made from wheat – was of little importance.

Meat consumption had for some time – as we have seen – been a sign of social privilege, a status symbol. Aristocrats and bourgeois had made it the primary (if not the only) distinguishing feature of their nutritional regime. It appears probable none the less that meat consumption increased generally in the latter half of the fourteenth century, even for the lower classes. The gradual withdrawal of grain cultivation, which, as mentioned above, dates from the last decades of the thirteenth century, continued at a more rapid pace after the demographic collapse of the mid-fourteenth century. Pasture and natural meadows took over in many areas, while in others – from northern France to Lombardy – farms were for the first time used for the growing of fodder. There were even enterprises that specialized in the raising of livestock, especially in regions of medium-to-high mountains, from Sweden to Bavaria, the Tyrol, Carinthia, Switzerland and Alsace. This situation led to a notable increase in the meat trade, both over short and long distances (even the eastern regions – Poland, Hungary, the Balkans – began to ship livestock to the West). Urban markets were easily and plentifully supplied, which caused prices to fall, while the demographic crisis led to increased wages. As a result, meat became accessible to a larger group of consumers. It was the period of 'carnivorous Europe', as Braudel's coinage has accustomed us to call it: 'a favourable period as far as individual living standards were concerned' (within limits which we shall explore below) which lasted until the first half of the sixteenth century.[11]

According to Abel, referring primarily to Germany, meat
consumption in the fifteenth century averaged 100 kg per year
per capita. This is a huge figure, 'truly a physiological maximum', and translates – taking into account the days of abstinence imposed by ecclesiastical norms – into about 450–500
g of meat per day for 200–220 days of the year.[12] Limiting
ourselves to the northern countries, where meat consumption
was generally greater, there are indeed indications suggesting
the possibility, if not the plausibility, of similar figures for the
middle and upper classes, or at least the urban classes. The
German levels appear to have been matched in Poland, Sweden,
England and the Low Countries, where in the fifteenth century
'meat was so commonly used that a period of want only slightly
reduced demand' (van der Wee). A foreign observer in fifteenth-
century Paris noted that 'all the artisans and shopkeepers – no
less than the wealthy – want to eat deer and partridge on meat
days'.

In the Mediterranean regions, the nutritional role of meat was
less decisive; there too, however, fourteenth- to sixteenth-century documents reveal notable levels of meat consumption.
Stouff's studies of Provence suggest a figure of 66–67 kg of meat
for the family members of the Bishop of Arles in the period
1430–42. The average annual per capita consumption for the
population of Carpentras instead, for the years 1472–3, was only
26 kg; social class seems to have been decisive in determining
the level of consumption. Similar figures emerge for several
Sicilian cities from the studies of Giuffrida, Aymard and Bresc:
around the mid-fifteenth century, annual consumption seems to
have been about 20 kg, far below the 100 hypothesized by Abel
for Germany but none the less considerable if compared with
the present day. In Tours as well, annual per capita meat consumption fluctuated between 20 and 40 kg at the end of the
fifteenth century. It should be added that these calculations are
based upon market figures and do not take into account domestic production and consumption (pork, goat, poultry).

It is, however, not at all clear to what degree these high levels of meat consumption (as conditioned by geography and social class) were the product of a *new* situation established following the economic and demographic crisis of the fourteenth century, or instead the simple continuation, albeit intensified, of a previous trend. European cities seem to have been great meat consumers already in the thirteenth century, and data from the early fourteenth century give similar indications. In Sicily in 1308, a salaried butcher received, in addition to his monthly stipend, a ration of three loaves of bread a day and 2.4 kg of meat a week; while this quantity represents payment and not consumption, it is none the less indicative of an unsuspected abundance of meat. For the 1320s and 1330s, Fiumi has calculated per capita levels of meat consumption for several Tuscan cities which approach those of the fifteenth-century Sicilian cities: about 20 kg for Prato and 38 kg (certainly an overestimate but significant none the less) for Florence.

As soon as we go outside the city walls the situation changes; though not radically, as meat was not a rarity in the peasant diet of the fourteenth and fifteenth centuries (just as it had not been in the preceding centuries). However, one gains the impression – supported by minimal and still more conjectural data than the figures for the cities – that procurement was more difficult. According to Stouff, the Provençal peasants of the fifteenth century ate meat twice a week. Le Roy Ladurie's estimate for the agricultural labourers of the Languedoc is decidedly higher: 40 kg per year per capita. Salaried vineyard workers in Sicily also enjoyed relative abundance: in the fifteenth century they received a ration of at least 800 g of meat a week (but for some even double this figure), while non-specialized workers ate meat three times a week. Still better off were the Alsatian peasants: 'in exchange for their toil they received two pieces of beef, two pieces of roast meat, a measure of wine and two *Pfennige*-worth of bread'. These nutritional levels are, in any case, well above those that would be suffered by the European peasantry beginning in the eighteenth century.

The contrast between city and country would long remain a

fundamental feature of the social distribution of food. Cattle which, through the expansion of pasture and the development of livestock concerns, could be produced in greater quantity than previously were destined primarily for the urban market. The butchering of a cow was almost never a family undertaking, if for no other reason than its weight. It was an operation that only the presence of a large number of consumers – as were found in the cities – made profitable. There arose as a result the opposing images of pork, symbol of a quasi-autonomous family economy, and beef, symbol of a new and dynamic commercialism, which reflected the dichotomy between the old forest economy and the new livestock industry, between country and city. Cured pork had been the primary meat for city-dwellers and peasants alike in the twelfth and thirteenth centuries; it seems even to have played a role in the Origny fire described in *Raoul de Cambrai*: 'the hams burned, melting the lard, and the fat then fed the great fire'. Subsequently city-dwellers came to distinguish themselves as consumers of beef and veal, the most expensive and exclusive meats in the market-place. Those who could not afford such luxuries contented themselves with mutton and wether, a food 'type' which enjoyed its period of maximum expansion in the fourteenth and fifteenth centuries. This growth finds a double explanation. On the one hand, the transformation of the landscape had eliminated many previously cultivated areas without of course re-establishing the destroyed forests; in their place large natural pastures had grown up, more suited to sheep than swine. On the other hand, the rapidly growing wool industry needed sheep. This pair of circumstances created a situation in which sheep became a 'fashionable' animal in the urban society of the fourteenth and fifteenth centuries. Even though their meat was not greatly esteemed (suitable only, we read, for those with unrefined palates), sheep were none the less a sign of distinction, of emancipation from the rural diet and way of life of which cured pork had become the true symbol. The European urban lower classes consciously 'adopted' mutton as an alternative to pork, which became ever less frequent in the urban markets after the fourteenth century; it was a symbolic choice based on a need for self-identity as well as on the desire to eat fresh meat. This transition took place in Italy, just as it did in France and England, with more or less the same timing and in more or less the same way. Even in those areas where cured pork continued to be the day-to-day meat of the majority, its occasional substitution with the 'new' meats had clearly liberating connotations. In the Forez countryside during the fifteenth century 'a plate of beef or mutton substituted for the usual pieces of pork' on festive occasions; while in a novella of Gentile Sermini, a poor peasant states 'my family never eats fresh meat, except a little wether a few times a month'.[13]

During the fourteenth and fifteenth centuries, rights to forest use, in particular for the hunting of game or the grazing of animals, were pretty well established. Most uncultivated areas, except for certain mountainous zones, were closed to common use. Free pasturing (except of sheep) had given way to stabling, and by the fifteenth century the 'domestication' of swine on peasant farms was under way. Meanwhile, certain medical treatises counselled against the meat of 'penned animals, like cows or pigs raised in stalls'. They recommended instead free animals caught in the mountains, an option open to few.[14] Hunting rights, where they existed, generally took the form of *concessions* rather than actual rights, concessions granted (with ever less frequency) by those who held exclusivity, usually the public authority. They might also be cancelled for any reason and at a moment's notice, as in 1465 when the Republic of Venice prohibited hunting in the area around Brescia in order to put it fully at the disposal of the distinguished guest, the Marquis of Ferrara, Borso d'Este. Alternatively the temporary opening of reserves became in the fifteenth and sixteenth centuries a quick and efficient way for the princes to win over the good will of the lower classes. Among those who resorted to this expedient was Ludovico il Moro, who in 1494 needed to ensure popular support in a politically delicate moment: the king of France, Charles VIII, was entering Italy.[15] Beneficence of this sort was clearly demagogic (we might call it 'meat and circuses') and was revoked as soon as the circumstances that had created it were overcome and privilege could be reasserted.

A Meatless Diet

Ecclesiastical rules obliged this 'carnivorous' society (understood with all the necessary qualifications) to abstain from meat for between 140 and 160 days per year. This renunciation which, as we have already seen, indirectly confirmed the centrality of meat to the diet of the period, had become widespread in Christian culture over the preceding centuries. At first, hermits and monks in particular adopted the practice as a personal choice or else in observance of a rule; the 'model' then spread, reinforced by the ordinances of the religious authorities, to the whole of society and applied to certain days of the week (in particular Wednesday and Friday, then only the latter) and certain days or periods of the year (the eve of certain holidays and major and minor Lents – in addition to that leading up to Easter, there were three 'minor' Lents of varying lengths according to local customs).

The reasons behind this choice are complex and not entirely clear. Together with purely penitential reasons (renunciation of a significant daily pleasure), there must have been others as well: a 'pagan' image of meat consumption (animal sacrifice and ritual consumption were essential traits of pagan religions); the conviction, supported by scientific treatises, that meat encouraged an excess of sexuality (great enemy of the perfect Christian); and also the tradition of vegetarian 'pacificism' inherited from ancient Greek philosophy. Abstinence from meat, in fact, figured as a central theme of moral treatises and penitential rules from the first centuries of Christianity.[16] The resulting need for alternative foods led to the great (economic and cultural) success of 'substitutes' such as legumes, cheese, eggs and especially fish. The role of this latter as the meat substitute *par excellence*, and truly the symbol of meatless days and periods, was not achieved without deviations and opposition. During the first centuries of Christianity there seems to have been a strong tendency to eliminate fish as well as meat from the Lenten diet; subsequently, an attitude of tacit tolerance made headway which neither forbade nor prescribed fish consumption; only from the ninth and tenth centuries – by which time the practice must have been common in much of Christian Europe – was fish generally accepted as an appropriate food for the days of fasting. Only the so-called 'fatty' fishes were excluded from the Lenten diet; these were the large sea animals (whales, dolphins etc.) which in their 'meatiness' were too much like land animals, perhaps because they were so bloody. With a few exceptions, fish (and everything that was born and lived in water) took on with ever greater specificity the cultural definition of the meatless diet. It became the symbol of the monastic and Lenten diet (from which dairy products and eggs were meanwhile excluded) and its *opposition* to meat, initially muted if not in fact denied, became ever more clearly defined.[17] Menus came to be oriented drastically in one sense or the other in order to avoid contamination. The separation of roles was clear-cut and the borders unbreachable: the battle between meat and fish, between 'Carnival' and 'Lent', was a rhetorical device (spread from the thirteenth century) which masked the deep-set cultural integration of meat and fish consumption, opposed and complementary at the same time, and 'courteously' alternated during the course of the year.[18] It was not by chance that in certain European cities (Florence, for example) the management and sale of meat and fish was considered an 'art' in and of itself.[19]

The diffusion of Christianity played a significant, and perhaps decisive, role in creating a tradition of fish consumption alongside that of meat. Bede remarked that the Anglo-Saxon pagans did not fish even though 'their sea and streams abounded in fish'; and among the first tasks of Bishop Winfrid, who came to Christianize the region, was to teach the inhabitants 'how to procure food by fishing'. Moreover, as Zug Tucci has observed, in the eleventh century the *Domesday Book* counted a trivial number of fishermen and an exorbitant number of swineherds: seventeen as opposed to 1168 in Devonshire. Also in the eleventh century, according to the testimony of Thietmar of Merseberg, 'the Polish princes punished those who violated the ecclesiastical laws on meat abstention by using persuasive methods like the pulling out of teeth'; a lesser penalty, however, than that called for by Charlemagne in the capitulary *De partibus Saxoniae*, which was no less than death.

Several centuries, however, would have to pass before conservation methods advanced to the point that fish could truly become a 'common' food. It still possessed connotations of luxury in twelfth-century France, when Peter Abelard, taking up again an old theme of Christian pamphlets, counselled, as we have seen, against the renunciation of meat as requiring recourse to the rarer and more expensive fish delicacies.[20] The greatest problem was transportation, as fish spoils easily. Hence the great success of the eel which, according to Thomas de Cantimpré, 'can live for six days without water'; 'especially – following the advice of Albertus Magnus – if they are laid on a bit of grass in a cool and shady place and allowed to move about freely'. Fish that was transported and consumed was usually freshwater fish, which was more readily available and easier to transport. 'To find in Campania the herring that Thomas Aquinas had come to enjoy in France required a miracle': a basket of fresh sardines was marvellously transformed into one of herring, equally fresh. Fresh salt-water fish was in fact a rarity, and that which reached the urban markets was generally preserved. The practice of salting (and of drying, smoking or preserving in oil) was fairly old, but it was only in the twelfth century that the perfection of these methods, encouraged by increased demand, made preserved fish fairly common, as opposed to fresh fish, which was always identified as a luxury item.

It was in fact in the twelfth century that Baltic salted herring came to be commercialized on a large scale; in the following century, the already cited Thomas de Cantimpré confirmed that, preserved in this way, herring lasted 'longer than any other fish'. Towards the mid-fourteenth century, a Dutchman, Wilelm Beukelszoon, devised a system for quickly cleaning, salting and barrelling herring on the same vessel from which it was fished.[21] It was on this process that the fortune of the Hanseatic League was founded, and then of the Dutch and Zeelander fishermen. During the fourteenth and fifteenth centuries, however, the herring left the Baltic; and from then on the Dutch and Zeelander boats followed it to the waters off the English and Scottish coasts.[22]

Freshwater fish underwent similar treatment. Documentation from the thirteenth century mentions large fisheries on the Danube, where salted and dried carp was prepared (a fish apparently introduced to the region a few centuries earlier, together with Christianity, by monks from southern Germany). In time, it became one of the area's major resources: in the sixteenth century, the Venetian ambassador Giovanni Michiel observed that Bohemia 'has such teeming fisheries as to constitute a large part of that kingdom's wealth'. In the mountains, carp-raising gave way to that of trout and pike; while elsewhere salmon, lamprey and sturgeon were fished. Sturgeon was particularly prized, in part because of its great size, especially fish from the Po, Rhône and Gironde rivers, as well as the Black and Caspian Seas. Dried and salted, sturgeon were traded principally by Venetian and Genoese merchants.[23]

From the late fifteenth century, still another species came to dominate fish trade and consumption, gradually ousting the sturgeon and other competitors: this was cod, fished for centuries in the ocean, but discovered only at this point – and in seemingly unlimited quantities – off the shoals of Newfoundland. Exploitation of these waters precipitated a true war – involving Basques, French, Dutch and English – in which disputes were decided by force of cannon, with the result that only the most powerful navies, the French and the English, maintained access to the fishing grounds. Dried and salted cod, stockfish by weight or *baccalà* by the piece, became a frequent item of common diets, especially in the cities.

Fish consumption none the less continued to carry with it a series of cultural connotations which prevented it from becoming a truly 'popular' food. Preserved fish suggested poverty and social subordination, while fresh fish called up images of wealth, but not of an enviable wealth as fish *did not fill one up*: it was a 'light' food, intended for Lent, and one that could be fully appreciated only by those who did not have to deal with daily hunger. For both of these reasons, fish generally failed to achieve a positive nutritional image; one ate it, and even often and in large quantities, but it still remained a surrogate for meat.

A Question of Quality

Between the fourteenth and sixteenth centuries, a period of great social mobility even for sectors of the peasantry, the dominant classes were particularly sensitive to the problem of defining the *lifestyles* of the various social groupings: habits of diet, especially, but also dress and domesticity were all carefully catalogued. The intent, however, was generally proscriptive rather than descriptive, and a good example is provided by the so-called 'sumptuary laws'. These were intended to control 'private' behaviour and consumption – though the degree to which a banquet can be described as private is debatable – and so prevent waste and ostentation, excesses of the sort that occurred on the occasion of a wedding feast, in which the public image and personal power of a particular family or guild was in play. These laws found a basis not so much in moral considerations, but rather in problems of social and political control. They were intended to guarantee and maintain the institutional order and prevent the too rapid rise in prestige of certain social or professional groups which might otherwise threaten the existing equilibrium. It was not by accident that calls for temperance were particularly frequent and insistent in those political settings where ideas of equality and democracy were espoused, at least from an ideological and programmatic point of view. Such was the case in the Venetian Republic, where the control of banquet behaviour was entrusted to the appropriate officials, the *Provveditori alle Pompe*. A 1562 decree, for example, suggested that 'at each meal not more than one course of roast meat and one of boiled may be served, nor may these courses contain more than three types of meat or fowl'; wild animals 'both airborne and terrestrial' were prohibited. For meat-based meals one could offer 'two types of roast, two boiled meats and two fried along with the various appetizers, salads, dairy products, and the other ordinary things, a plate of common cake, marzipan and the usual confections'. Trout and sturgeon were instead prohibited along with lake fish, pies or *pastelli*, and confections and sweets made with sugar; only 'ordinary' pastries were allowed, those made by bakers. It was understood as well that 'meat and fish should not be served together in the same meal'. The decree also conferred upon the public authorities the right to control the work of individual cooks by inspecting kitchens and dining rooms.[24]

Rules of this sort revealed a desire for the normalization of dietary practices for the purpose of establishing order within the ruling classes during a period of intense social transformation, a period in which the bourgeois classes emerged alongside (or in opposition to) the traditional nobility. Manners and the 'style' of life provided a suitable starting-point for this effort. It was, however, the distinction between the ruling classes and other social groups (the urban *petite bourgeoisie*, the lower classes, the peasants) that commanded greatest interest. To a degree, all the literature of these centuries (private and public documents, narrative, polemics, agronomic and scientific treatises, medical–dietary manuals etc.) was marked by a basic characteristic: when the topic of food and dietary habits was discussed, it was done in the context of specific social categories and groups.

The preliminary assumption was that one's diet should be determined 'according to personal qualities'; a proposition not easily disputed if we take 'qualities' to indicate the sum of individual physiological and behavioural characteristics. This idea constituted a central aspect of Graeco-Roman thought, indeed that upon which European medical science was based: individual food consumption should be determined taking into consideration age, sex, 'humoral disposition', state of health and occupation, as well as climate, season and all environmental factors which might have an impact on the individual according to his 'qualities'. The result was an ambitious and clearly elitist dietary regime, elitist in that it required attention, time and study. Hippocrates was perfectly aware of this aspect when he directed his careful instructions to a wealthy and educated minority, reserving for 'the mass of people' a few general prescriptions. None the less the proving-ground for this science was clearly not any particular category of individual, but the 'free' person, which for Hippocrates meant people in general.[25] Subsequently, with the progressively more social connotations of 'personal quality', this idea began to change, and quality came to correspond more and more with social class, rank, wealth, and above all power. This 'quality' took on – at least according to the dominant classes – an immutable and innate character, a rigid and unassailable personal definition, like that of the social order in general.

This concept was well developed by Carolingian times, when the royal capitularies instructed that the *missi* travelling throughout the empire should be provisioned 'according to personal quality' (*iuxta suam qualitatem*). For his part, Alcuin, in his description of gluttony, included the condemnation of those who prepared foods which were overly refined in relation to the 'quality' of those persons ('exquisitiores cibos . . . quam . . . suae qualitas personae exigat'). This hierarchical conception of diet came even to involve the symbolic image of the 'spiritual repast', of the 'internal satiety' provided by faith: in the Life of the monk Appianus, written in the twelfth century, we read that 'with the word of God, he fed the poor, filled up the better off, and satisfied the spiritual banquets of the rich and powerful'. The paradoxical crescendo of the terms used for the three categories (*recreavit, pleniter refecit, spiritualis epulis saturavit*) reflects the mentality of a culture accustomed to identifying food consumption according to social rank.[26] In the thirteenth century, Salimbene da Parma wrote that 'being made to a higher status, the nobility are entitled to better food and clothing than are the common people', though he did not agree with the patriarch of Aquileia who, 'for the honour and glory of the patriarchate', interpreted the spirit of Lent in an unusual fashion: on the first day he ordered forty different dishes served, and then one less each day until Holy Saturday.[27] King Peter III the Great of Aragon, instead, required that differences of rank be indicated with mathematical precision at table: in the *Ordinaciones* of 1344, we read that 'since it is appropriate that some persons are honoured more than others according to their status, we desire that our plate should include food enough for eight persons'. The royal princes, the archbishops and the bishops should instead receive enough for six, while the other prelates and knights at the king's table were assigned a portion for four.[28]

The relationship between nutritional regime and social status had initially been mostly a question of quantity (though not entirely, as revealed by the excerpt from Alcuin cited above). We have already seen how in the 'barbaric' age a hearty appetite and the possibility of satisfying it constituted an essential trait of the powerful. With time, the qualitative aspect took on ever greater significance; this too we have noted in the birth during the twelfth and thirteenth centuries of a 'courtly' ideology of food. Given these cultural assumptions, it is clear that the consumption of certain foods (and of foods prepared in a particular way) was not simply a function of habit or choice, but rather a sign of social identity and so to be correctly observed in the interest of maintaining the proper social equilibria and hierarchies. Considerations of health reinforced these convictions, and to eat according to 'one's own qualities' was considered a physiological necessity; physicians from Hippocrates on had said as much. All hinged on the at once clear and ambiguous idea of *quality*. In fourteenth- to sixteenth-century Europe, the cultural image of the dominant classes was unequivocal on this point: quality equalled power; and this equation represented an enormous simplification, as social status and diet confirmed one another in a straightforward way. Expensive, elaborate and refined foods (those which only wealth and power could procure on a daily basis) were intended for noble stomachs, while coarse and common foods went into the stomachs of peasants. The poor – the growing mass of the poorest and socially outcast – had to content themselves with the leftovers. The *Ordinaciones* of Peter III the Great of Aragon stipulate that sour wine, stale bread, rotten fruit, acidified cheese and similar foods be put aside for the ritual alms given to the poor.[29]

Those who failed to respect these rules did so at their peril. Attacks on class privilege – which, in literature, at least, might be premeditated and intentional – were fiercely punished. Zuco Padella, a peasant from the countryside around Bologna, went each night to steal peaches (like all fresh fruit, a decidedly upper-class food) from the garden of Messer Lippo, his master. Discovered and captured in an animal trap, Zuco was 'washed' with boiling water and berated: 'In future leave my fruit alone and eat your own foods which are turnips, garlic, leeks, onions and shallots with sorghum bread.' There were foods for peasants and foods for the aristocracy, and anyone who did not observe these differences violated the social order: in the fourteenth-century novella of Sabadino degli Arienti from which this episode is taken, the recurring behaviour of the peasant is clearly intended to be transgressive, confrontational and challenging.[30] A similar situation might arise as a result of error, but this too led to dramatic results: in Giulio Cesare Croce's *Bertoldo*, the court physicians sought to cure a sick rustic by giving him rare and delicate foods, completely unsuited to his peasant stomach; in vain he begged that 'they bring him a plate of beans with onion and turnips cooked under the ashes'. Only by eating according to his own 'nature' might he have been saved. His pleas, how-ever, went unheeded and Bertoldo died 'in great pain'.[31]

We might simply be amused by Croce's text (published in the early seventeenth century), were it not a parody of authoritative scientific theories appearing in the medical, botanical and agronomic treatises of the preceding centuries. In the early fourteenth century, Piero de' Crescenzi, a well-known agronomer from Bologna, observed that wheat was unquestionably the best grain for making bread; none the less he recommended bread made with other grains (sorghum, for example, well suited to peasants as well as swine, cattle and horses) for those who engaged in heavy labour.[32] Giacomo Albini, physician to the princes of Savoy, predicted aches and illness for those who ate foods not appropriate to their social rank: the rich should not partake of heavy soups, like those made from legumes or entrails, which were not very nutritious and difficult to digest; the poor instead were to avoid excessively select or refined foods which their coarse stomachs could not easily manage.[33] The scientific theory of nutritional privilege was a recurrent theme among intellectuals of the period and reinforced – as was often the case – the interests of the powerful. In the mid-fifteenth century, for example, Michele Savonarola authored a well-received dietary treatise which was careful to distinguish between courtly and peasant meals: with regard to kid he wrote that 'its meat is delicate and not suitable to peasants', while parsnips 'are a meal for poor men and peasants'.[34] Between 1542 and 1546, the physician Jacques Dubois, called Sylvius, published in Paris four booklets on the diet of the poor in which he was careful to suggest 'appropriate' foods and recipes: 'the poor have their own particular diet which is heavy and hard to digest, but perfectly suited to their constitutions'.[35] Garlic, onions, leeks, legumes, cheese, beer, beef, cured pork, soups – all of these were part of the 'peasant' or 'popular' world of food explored by the French physician (and many of his colleagues). The relation between 'quality of person' and 'quality of food' was not a simple fact tied to the chances of wealth or need, but rather a basic and ontological postulate: to eat well or poorly was an intrinsic individual characteristic (and hopefully unalterable), just as was social class. French and Spanish treatises on nobility frequently refer to the relationship between diet and social rank and emphasize its reciprocity: membership in a social class implied a certain type of consumption, but was itself also a product of that consumption.[36] Great importance was attributed to infant nourishment as well which had to be adapted to the baby's 'nature' (or rather social rank). Even its prenatal nutrition was regulated.[37] A late seventeenth-century booklet by Girolamo Cirelli reports that the peasants, except on feast days, ate 'like pigs', an observation delivered without surprise or really even regret. The title of the work ('The Peasant Unmasked') resolves any doubts regarding the cultural vision within which reflections of this sort were considered: one's manner of eating (and general lifestyle) reveal or unmask one's social status while at the same time confirming it. The bad manners ('like a pig') and inferior food of the peasant were natural and just; so long as this distinction remained, the social order was intact.[38]

It is no coincidence that these nutritional ideologies, which had already appeared in previous centuries, took on a new and unprecedented systematic rigour between the fourteenth and sixteenth centuries. As we have seen, this was a period of social and economic elasticity, of mobility, demands and revolt: the popular classes of city and country alike had never been so restless. The result was a reassertion of privilege and barring of the too easy and numerous avenues leading to the acquisition of power. The ruling classes progressively closed ranks and pursued a profound aristocratization of society and culture. The exclusion of the 'people' from enjoyment of the more refined pleasures of the table – a highly symbolic exclusion, more ideological than actually enforced – allowed the powerful both to celebrate and to represent themselves at the moment of greatest, or at least most concrete, social discrimination.

The parallelism between food and society, between the hierarchies of foods and of men, was firmly rooted in the culture and image of power, and, as we have seen, both medical and literary opinions reinforced this idea. Further reinforcement came from certain scientific theories dating from several centuries earlier according to which a strict parallelism existed between human and, let us call it, 'natural' society. Of the various interpretations and classifications of the natural order of the world, that which described living things – plants and animals – as links in a vertical chain or rungs on a ladder had enjoyed considerable success (even if it was not perhaps at the height of its popularity in the fifteenth and sixteenth centuries). In both cases the value of each plant and animal was determined by its place on the chain or ladder, and increased or decreased as one moved either up or down (in keeping with the usual symbolic understanding of high and low). In the vegetable world, intermediate between the mineral and animal, bulbs and roots were considered the lowest by virtue of their close contact with the element earth in which the edible part was buried. Then came herbs and grasses, bushes, and finally trees, the fruit, branches and leaves of which wave in the sky. The nobler character of the fruit of trees as compared to roots and bulbs was explained not only metaphorically – in terms of their relative distances from the heavens and divine perfection – but also scientifically: it was claimed that the 'digestion' of the food by the plant, that is the assimilation of its nutritional characteristics, was more complete the more the plant strove upward, perfecting the process. Piero de' Crescenzi, for example, wrote that 'the nutritional humour of the plant is more insipid in the roots, and according as it distances itself from these, the flavour improves'. Another agronomist and naturalist, Corniolo della Cornia, affirmed that 'many fruits are flavourful when they come from the tops of trees, but near to the ground become insipid through the dominance of the watery substance'. Similarly, the top of the animal kingdom was occupied by animals that fly.[39]

This 'image of taste' must have influenced the preferences of those who had the means to satisfy them. The high position occupied by birds, for example, in the animal chain suggested that they were a particularly appropriate food for the higher classes of human society. It may also have been a question of taste, but then taste underwent a considerable transformation after Charlemagne (and all those like him) who enjoyed above

all large game roasted on a spit. During the fifteenth and
sixteenth centuries, few doubted that pheasant and partridge
represented the height of culinary refinement, at once the no-
blest of foods and a reference point below which other types of
meat might be ranked. Deer and boar, to be sure, were less
frequent in Europe than they had been because of the massive
destruction of forests during the eleventh to thirteenth centuries, but this fact is not sufficient to explain their reduced
frequency in the aristocratic diet; indeed, rarity might have
made them more rather than less desirable. Lifestyle, instead,
had changed: warrior nobility had given way to that of the
court; refinement of custom had oriented preferences more towards 'white' and 'light' meats, so that an Italian physician of
the sixteenth century did not hesitate to describe them as 'well
adapted to those who are dedicated more to the exercise of the
spirit than of the body'.[40] Nor was it a coincidence that monastic
culture devoted special attention to these meats, likening them
occasionally to fish and so excluding them from the list of
prohibited foods. According to Andreolli, 'the change was naturally not immediate, and the fifteenth century can be considered
from this point of view a period of transition, frequently characterized by mixed gastronomic practices in which two opposed
and not well co-ordinated nutritional models coexisted'.[41] The
theories of the natural order of the world also aided the change,
adding scientific conviction regarding the foods best suited to
the aristocratic table. The greater prestige of birds in relation to
quadrupeds quickly became a commonplace. In a novella by
Matteo Bandello, a woman complains that her husband 'went
off to eat fine capons and partridges while I am left with a few
bits of beef and lamb'.[42] The pheasant in particular seems to
have especially enjoyed universal admiration; Ortensio Lando,
in his 'Commentary on the Most Notable and Monstruous
Things, in Italy and Elsewhere', recalls having eaten exquisite
fruit in Piacenza, and having been 'satisfied as if I had eaten a
perfect pheasant'.[43] Lazarillo de Tormes instead sought to de-
ceive himself, claiming that the beef on his plate 'is the most

delicious morsel in the world, and there is no pheasant that pleases me so much'.[44]

Among the vegetables, bulbs and roots (leeks, onions, turnips) were left to the peasants, as were the 'lower' and more common greens. Fruit from trees instead was suited to the aristocrat, except for those unusual varieties whose abundance, culinary uses and potential for storage ensured popular consumption; such was the case for the chestnut which never constituted part of the ideological universe of the nobility. Chestnuts aside, we can now better understand the symbolic import of Sabadino degli Arienti's novella cited above: beyond questions of taste and even of the defence of property and power, the angry words of Messer Lippo, invoking the privilege to eat peaches and enjoining Zuco Padella to stick to his onions and garlic, hide an unexpected philosophical and scientific dimension. Excessive love of fruit, moreover, is frequently portrayed as one of the characteristics of aristocratic gluttony.[45] Many examples might be cited, from the *chansons de geste*, novellas, cookery books and dietary treatises. The reasons for this preference seem in any case to have been more tied up in prestige and ostentation than in taste: fruit made an impression, both because (and in so far as) it was expensive and difficult to come by, and also because according to the scientific co-ordinates of that culture it occupied a 'high' position in the hierarchy of the vegetable world. Culture, power, image and reality all intertwine inextricably.

A Table to Admire

In the social rituals of the upper classes, the elementary opposition between ruler and ruled was the one most frequently represented (and shown in a favourable light). Both the consumption of food and the social context in which that activity took place were, above all, tools for the expression and manifestation of power.

The concept of power in fourteenth- to sixteenth-century Europe,

however, was not what it had been 500 years before: the attributes of a leader were no longer principally physical strength
and skill in combat, but rather administrative and diplomatic
ability. Similarly, the expression of power through food had also
changed. The nobleman no longer distinguished himself by his
individual ability to consume, but instead by his organization of
a well-orchestrated kitchen and table, by surrounding himself
with the right people who – before eating – might properly
admire the quantity of elaborately prepared food which his
wealth and the imagination of the cooks and master of cere-
monies presented. The wealthy table came increasingly to be
characterized by *ostentation*; not that this quality had ever been
lacking, but it became the principal underlying motivation, a
sign of profound social, political and cultural modification. It
represented the progressive introspection and closure of the
dominant classes, the separation of the leader from his 'people',
as well as a new image of power that asserted itself and its
prerogatives from afar. The table was no longer a place of social
cohesion centred on the leader, but rather one of separation and
exclusion: a few were invited to participate; the rest were left to
watch. Describing the great banquet arranged by Giovanni II
Bentivoglio in Bologna in 1487 to celebrate the wedding of his
son Annibale to Lucrezia d'Este, the chronicler Cherubino Ghirardacci wrote: 'Before being served, [the dishes] were paraded
with great ceremony around the piazza of the castle . . . to show
them to the people that they might admire such magnificence.'
The feast, similar to many others described in chronicles and in
culinary treatises, lasted seven hours, from eight in the evening
till three in the morning, during which were served: small
appetizers and wafers with several types of sweet wine; roasted
pigeons, bits of pork liver, thrushes, partridges 'with sugared
olives and grapes', and bread; and a castle of sugar 'with artfully
constructed merlons and towers' and filled with live birds which
as soon as the platter was brought into the hall flew out 'to the
great pleasure and delight of the diners'. There followed deer
and ostrich surrounded by various *pastelli*, veal's head, boiled

capons, veal breast and loin, goat, sausage and partridge, all served with various sauces; then peacocks 'dressed up in their own feathers as if spreading their tails', one for each guest; then mortadella, hares, and stewed deer dressed in its own skin so perfectly 'as to appear alive'; followed by turtle-doves and pheasants 'from whose beaks issued flames' accompanied by citrus and sauces. Next came sugar and almond cakes, 'junket' (a preparation of fresh cheese) and biscuits; and again goat's head, turtle-doves, roast partridge, and 'a castle full of rabbits' who ran out to the delight of the guests; then rabbit *pastelli* and 'dressed capons'. There followed an 'artful castle' – banquet architecture, it should be noted, took as its primary model this symbol of power – containing a 'large pig' which, trapped inside, grunted and snorted among the merlons. Meanwhile, the servers brought 'whole golden-brown roasted suckling pigs', various other roasts, wild duck 'and the like'; and finally sweets made from milk, jellies, pears, pastries, candies, marzipans 'and other similar favours'. Before leaving, the guests (who would in any case return the next day for breakfast) were given spiced confections and 'precious wines'. This entire feast, before arriving at the table, was paraded through the piazza so that the people 'might admire such magnificence'.[46] The guests too must have limited themselves to admiring many of these dishes, for not even a Pantagruelian appetite would have enabled one to try them all. Nor was it presumed otherwise: dishes were not presented one after another, but rather *displayed* in large groups. Each diner chose according to his or her preferences, but was expected above all to admire (just like the 'people') the abundance and quality of food, to marvel at the presentation and scenic invention, as if in the theatre. It was as much a *show* as a meal.

The image of splendour that the ruling classes of the fifteenth and sixteenth centuries left behind owes much to efforts of this sort, and a great part of their energy was devoted to image, appearance and theatricality. Pressing formal and aesthetic requirements seem to have imposed themselves on the gastronomic art in these centuries, engendering an explosion of fantasy and creativity. The visual aspect has (rightly) always played a role in this art, but for a time it became predominant. The search for forms became the rule: gastronomic forms (the composition of the dishes, their appearance and colour), environmental forms (banquet 'stage-direction', the presentation of food, the rituals of service), and behavioural forms ('good manners', the correct use of utensils, the rules of chewing). All of these forms served to define a separate dining space: protected, different, distinct and isolated. The area of social privilege and political power was ever more glaringly opposed to the world of hunger and fear.

The Abundance of the Poor

The best cure for the fear of hunger lay in dreams: dreams of tranquillity and a full stomach, of abundance and overindulgence; a dream of the land of Cuccagna where the supply of food was inexhaustible and readily available, where huge pans of macaroni were dumped over mounds of grated cheese, where the vines were tied up with sausages and the grain fields surrounded by fences of roast meats. The image of Cuccagna, a sort of popular version of the more 'refined' mythology of Eden, took shape between the twelfth and fourteenth centuries. In a well-known French *fabliau*, the first to provide a detailed description, the *païs de Coquaigne* was one in which

> the walls of all the houses are made of bass, salmon and herring, the trusses of sturgeon, the roofs of ham, and the beams of sausage . . . the fields of grain are all fenced with roasted meats and pork shoulders; along the roads fat geese are browned on spits which rotate on their own and are basted with a garlic sauce; and I tell you that wherever you go, along the roads and lanes, you shall find tables laid with white tablecloths where anyone may eat and drink freely, either fish or meat, as there are no rules or restrictions, and may even carry away a cartload if he wishes . . .

And it is the sacred truth that in this blessed land there
flows a river of wine . . . half of it red, of the best that can
be found in Beaune or overseas; and the other half white, of
the strongest and most excellent that can be found in
Auxerre, La Rochelle or Tonnerre.'[47]

From the fourteenth century, lands of this sort – which our
unfortunate author had left and never again been able to find –
appear in the literature of many parts of Europe: England,
Germany, France, Spain, Italy . . . . In a novella of Boccaccio, it
is called Bengodi, and Maso sings its praises to the ingenuous
Calandrino: 'there stood in Bengodi a mountain of grated par-
miggiano on top of which were people who did nothing else but
make macaroni and ravioli, cook them in a capon broth, and
then toss them down the hill to whoever wanted to take them'.[48]
These utopian descriptions also included the suggestion of a free
and happy sexuality as well as a dream of eternal youth, more
directly connected to the ancient age of Saturn or the mythical
Eden. The urban and 'bourgeois' reference to easily acquired
wealth and an always full purse was there too, but while the
desire for fine clothes and expensive shoes plays its role,
the theme of food, initially one of several (only fifty out of
the Fabliau de Coquaigne's 186 verses refer to the pleasures of the
palate), gradually expands to become the dominant and almost
unique characteristic of Utopia; by the seventeenth century the
connotations are ever more concentrated on the belly. The 1691
etching by Giuseppe Mitelli, the *Gioco della Cuccagna*, is little
more than a review of gastronomic specialities. 'The reduction
of Cuccagna to pure and simple gastronomy, the progressive
assimilation of Cuccagna to carnival' were also signs of a deter-
iorating food situation, of the increasing difficulty after the
sixteenth century of satisfying one's appetite; hence the repres-
entation of a clearly 'popular' desire, even if the texts by which
it was transmitted were not themselves exactly popular.

Without entering into the merits of arguments made by
cultural historians regarding the much debated question of

whether and to what degree 'educated' culture might transmit, directly or indirectly, explicitly 'popular' traits, there is none the less a greater degree of correspondence between the two spheres than one might imagine: the culture of ostentation and waste, for example, is incomprehensible if divorced from that of hunger. In particular, the 'two' cultures refer to one another dialectically and are each expressions of the other. In addition, they coexist, intertwined, as both contrasting expressions of different social and cultural categories, and also within those same categories. Real hunger was unknown to the privileged classes, but not the fear of it, the concern to maintain a daily supply of food in keeping with their (high) dietary expectations. On the other hand, the world of hunger was under certain circumstances also a world of ostentation and abundance; peasant society too knew moments of squander: on important holidays and to celebrate the principal rites of passage. This was, to be sure, ritual waste and of primarily propitiatory value, but no less real for its rituality; on these occasions the dietary behavior of the 'poor' came to resemble that of the 'rich'. Everyone had to see and to know: in eighteenth-century Naples, a band of town criers passed through the streets of the city listing the animals butchered and describing the amount of food consumed during the Christmas holidays, a practice whose significance resembles that of the show of food put on in the noble palaces (and outside them in the streets and squares) on the occasion of great feasts and great waste. This was, however, a relative similarity as in both cases nothing was really wasted.[49]

It would appear that *Homo sapiens* has historically displayed an extraordinary degree of physiological adaptation with regard to the assimilation of food, adjusting his needs from time to time as the situation warranted: abundant consumption in one period (for example during the hunting season) and meagre in another. This adaptation explains the ability both to eat large amounts (to the point of excess) and also to survive on little (within limits). It has been a biological characteristic of the species since its activities were primarily predatory and has conditioned certain cultural attitudes: the antithesis of abundance and scarcity has become a mental characteristic as well as a physiological one and was historically transmitted by the adaptation to concrete social situations. Only the fantasy, or self-interest, of the privileged few was able to conjure up images of happy poverty or else contented frugality (and indeed frugality was the necessary behaviour of the majority). While it may be that to eat lightly is healthy, only those who eat abundantly (or at least are able to) succeed in thinking so; only the long experience of a full stomach allows one to derive pleasure from controlling one's appetite. Those who are truly hungry have always wanted only to fill themselves to bursting, a desire satisfied from time to time in practice and often in dreams.

4

Europe and the World

A Wonderful Land Beyond the Sea

The excitement over discoveries and new knowledge which characterized the era of transoceanic voyages seems to have captured the popular imagination as well. The utopia of Cuccagna and dreams of abundance were projected on to the lands across the sea, thought to be overflowing with food and all the bounty of God. These lands were celebrated in verse, as in the poem of an anonymous Modenese of the first half of the sixteenth century, who sang of a 'wonderful land . . . which is called Good Life', discovered by 'sailors who set out upon the ocean'. In this new place, 'which has not been seen or heard of since', exotic foods and unusual drinks are not found, but instead 'there is in the middle of a plain a lone mountain of grated cheese on top of which has been placed a cauldron'; this cauldron measures a mile across and 'is always boiling and cooking macaroni, which it then tosses out when ready' so that they tumble down the mountainside covering themselves in cheese; 'and the fountains are full of wine'. There were in addition good vegetables, rivers of milk with which flavourful ricotta was made, grapes, figs, melons, partridges and capons, cakes and white bread; 'the donkeys are tied up with sausages'; and when it rains, 'it rains ravioli'. This poem represents a broad inventory of the best fifteenth- and sixteenth-century cuisine; in it the Italian culture of the period was projected on to the wonderful lands beyond the sea.[1] Thus there are limits even to fantasy, ones imposed by the culture out of which they are born. Each aspect of this culture has its place, its particular role as defined in relation to all the other aspects: cuisine and dietary regime are not a casually assembled number of ingredients, but rather a coherent and global system. Difficulty in accepting, or even understanding, what is different derives from this fact; and so we must 'filter' the unusual through our own value system, often denaturing it, or at least adapting it to familiar measures.

In the face of new realities, of unknown plants and animals and unusual foods, European explorers and conquerors reacted with both diffidence and curiosity. Great efforts were made to contextualize or theoretically 'classify' these new experiences; European descriptions sought to 'translate' them into familiar language, to place them in a familiar cultural setting. Consider for example – one example among many – the anonymous 'Relation of Some Things from New Spain', perhaps written by a companion of Cortés and published for the first time in 1556. Maize becomes 'a grain similar to chick-peas', which grows ears 'like millet'; tortillas are described as a sort of bread (that is, in terms of the Mediterranean food tradition); chillis are presented as 'a sort of pepper'; and turkey as 'a large peacock-like chiken' The references to European culture are frequent and inevitable.[2]

The problem, however, was not simply one of terminology and – so to speak – technical understanding. From a practical point of view, acceptance of these new realities within the European cultural context long remained marginal. A long interval of time passed between the discovery of new foods by Europeans and their integration into the European dietary regime. It was a process of assimilation which required two or three centuries, a delay too great to be simply physiological, even taking into account the slower rhythms of earlier times. It suggests instead an extended period of indifference on the part of the nutritional culture of Europe to the new American products. There were of course exceptions and notable differences between regions and social classes, but overall the reaction was lack of interest, a state of affairs which can have only one explanation: the new products lay outside the structural balance of the European model of consumption as it had developed from the fourteenth century. We might say that in some sense they served no purpose; indeed they were finally adopted to that system at the moment (and to the degree) that the system began to fall apart. This process occurred in two distinct and separate phases, so that we can speak of a double introduction of new foods to Europe. The first took place in the sixteenth century, just after the voyages of conquest; its motivation, like that of the second, was hunger.

New Players

In the sixteenth century, the populations of many European countries increased. That of Castille doubled between 1530 and 1594, growing from 3 to 6 million. As a result, the country, which had been a grain exporter in the previous century, was forced to buy foreign grain from English and Dutch traders. Elsewhere growth was more modest, but the overall population of Europe is estimated to have grown from 84 million in 1500 to 111 million a century later. Production structures felt this change generally; nutritional resources became scarcer; and a familiar mechanism came again into play (the same which had spurred the agricultural colonization of the eleventh and twelfth centuries).[3]

The years of underproduction were more frequent than in the fifteenth century; the previously cited seventeenth century statistics list thirteen years of famine for France in the sixteenth century, as opposed to seven in the fifteenth.[4] Agricultural technology had improved in the interim, both in terms of the tools used and of irrigation systems. Fertilization, however, was imperfect, and grain yields remained low in spite of the fact that certain fifteenth-century agronomists understood the crux of the problem perfectly well, namely the need to include periods of fallow in crop rotation, alternating growing and pasturing. With only sporadic exceptions, a harvest-to-seed yield of five to one was rarely exceeded. The traditional solutions were sought: expansion of cultivation, land reclamation, the clearing of new plots. This period saw the establishment of polder in the Low Countries and the first capitalist initiatives in agriculture. The single-crop system of rice farming in Lombardy, for example, had already developed by the fifteenth century. Pasture land correspondingly shrank, and some governments were forced to apply controls to prevent the peasant cultivation of pastures; similar restrictions appeared in agricultural contracts.

The many agronomic treatises published throughout Europe in the sixteenth century reflected this renewed attention to working the fields. At the same time, essays specifically dedicated to nutrition, or rather famine, appeared: their purpose was to instruct the poor how to survive by the use of every possible resource, including unusual plants and foods never before eaten. Clearly the appearance of these treatises during a period of economic and production difficulty was not a coincidence. The booklets of Jacques Dubois, the Sylvius already mentioned – *Regime de sante pour les pauvres, facile a tenir* ('A Simple Scheme of Health for the Poor') and advice for combating famine (*Conseil tresutile contre la famine, et remedes d'icelle*) – were written between 1544 and 1546;[5] the *Discorso sopra la carestia, e fame* ('Discourse on Shortage and Hunger') of Giambattista Segni dates from 1591.[6] We now know that both the central decades of the century (culminating in the general crisis of 1556–7) and also the last (the famine of 1590–3) were particularly hard hit by famine, with of course regional variations. We are then faced with a 'militant' literature, dictated by pressing problems and needs. The degree to which it was useful to the poor is of course another matter.

The growing need for food suggested the possible recourse to new products. Such was the case for rice in certain regions; we have already referred to its early spread in Lombardy, explained by financial and commercial interests as well as strictly nutritional motivation. It is not clear whether rice (previously an exotic import sold in spice shops and used sparingly, primarily in sauces) came to northern Italy by way of the Sicialian Arabs or else from Spain. Spain had in fact, through the influence of Arabic cuisine, been the only European region in which rice had early enjoyed a significant degree of diffusion. From Spain rice spread to the Low Countries, and this example suggests – keeping in mind the links between the two countries in the sixteenth century – the way in which the history of food is linked to that of power and politics.

Another new 'discovery' was buckwheat. This grain had in fact been known and cultivated in the West for at least 200 years, but it was only in the sixteenth century that it enjoyed general diffusion, first perhaps in the Low Countries, then in Germany, France and northern Italy. In addition to the traditional yellow polenta made from millet, a new grey-coloured one was now added.[7]

In retrospect, the impact of maize was greater still. Discovered by Columbus on his first transatlantic voyage, it came to Europe in 1493. For reasons of both curiosity and need, it was soon planted in the Iberian peninsula. By the early sixteenth century maize had appeared in Castille, Andalusia and Catalonia; around 1520 it was grown in Portugal. In the following years, it spread to south-western France (the first citation is for Bayonne in 1523) and northern Italy (especially the western Veneto where its cultivation took hold in the 1530s). From there it spread to Pannonia (Slovenia and Croatia) and the Balkan peninsula. Maize only occasionally replaced other grains; sometimes it was used as fodder and planted in fallow fields, or it was planted experimentally in vegetable gardens. In both cases its presence is not easily discerned from the existing documentation which represents the agricultural terrain primarily in terms of the landowners' interests and so rarely reveals the 'minor' aspects of production not affecting property revenue. Vegetable gardens in particular were free from rent, and the peasants could plant whatever they pleased there. In fact maize seems to have often been introduced in this way: quietly, almost furtively, and protected from landowners' demands for tithes and agricultural taxes. Even from a terminological point of view of maize tended to be disguised: in France it was *millet*; in Italy *melega* (sorghum); in Hungary *tengeribúza* or maritime millet; in the Balkans it was fava, millet, sorghum, grain and coarse grain. Then there were the exotic names – Rhodian, Indian, Turkish, Arabic or Egyptian grain – all of which were intended to describe the foreign and distant origin of this new arrival.[8] Peasants must have been quick to recognize the nutritional potential of maize, together with its extraordinarily high yield. None the less the spread of maize in Europe was initially contained; in fact, it came to a halt after the successes of the sixteenth century. This may have been because many remained doubtful about it or thought it to be a food fit only for animals; or else because it made no inroads in the dominant culture (there is no mention of maize in books on *haute cuisine*, almost to the present day); or again because the general nutritional situation had, after the great famines of the mid- and late century, regained that minium degree of necessary elasticity. Indeed, even demographic growth seems to have stopped towards the end of the sixteenth century.

The similar successes enjoyed by these several new products in the space of a century (from the late fifteenth to the late sixteenth century) are significant. Rice, buckwheat and maize all tentatively approached the traditional European nutritional culture; they enjoyed almost immediate success, but failed to find a firm niche and retreated into relative disuse in the seventeenth century, only to re-emerge strongly in the mid-eighteenth. The chronology of the potato's appearance in Europe is shifted forward a little, but the pattern is the same. The Spaniards came across it in Peru in 1539, and it spread across Spain with little fanfare. It received greater attention in Italy – according to Braudel because of that country's particular situation of over-population – and there it acquired one of its first nicknames: *tartuffolo* or white truffle. The first mention of its use as food comes from Spain: in 1573, the potato appears among the purchases of the Sangre de Sevilla hospital. A German reference appears late in the century, while England acquired the potato in 1588 directly from America thanks to Sir Walter Raleigh. Even in the case of the potato, however, one has to wait until the eighteenth century for a definitive success and a significant impact on the European dietary regime.[9]

Bread and Meat

Fernand Braudel has suggested that we accept at face value the lament of a gentleman from Gouberville who wrote in 1560: 'In my father's time we ate meat every day; our plates were full; and wine was drunk like water. Now all has changed and everything is expensive; the diet of the wealthiest peasant today is worse than that of a servant of old.' A literary commonplace? Perhaps, as identical sentiments are expressed in a German text of 1550, but commonplaces can be revealing of the social and cultural climate. Why, for example, did the writers of two centuries before use just the opposite example?[10]

All manner of documentation and study confirms that European meat consumption began to decline (for the poorer classes, of course) from about the middle of the sixteenth century. According to Abel, consumption declined from a maximum of 100 kg per capita per annum estimated for Germany in the fourteenth and fifteenth centuries to a minimum of 14 kg between the eighteenth and nineteenth.[11] There are many possible causes for this: population increase, agricultural land reclamation and the reduction of pasture and forest, a reduction in real wages, increased building density and the associated prohibition of keeping animals in the city, and a reduction of importation from the East after the Turkish conquest of Hungary. We have already listed the estimates of Abel, and a similar pattern seems to emerge more or less everywhere. Careful studies such as that of A. M. Piuz for the region around Geneva confirm as much: in the seventeenth century the availability of meat was generally reduced, except in certain mountain areas dedicated primarily to pasturing.[12] A statistic reported by Braudel tells us that in Montpézat, a city of lower Quercy, 'the number of butchers was in continual decline: 18 in 1550, 10 in 1556, 6 in 1641, 2 in 1660, 1 in 1763. Even if the population declined in this period, it certainly did not do so in a ratio of 18 to 1.'[13]

The result of this process was an ever greater dependence on bread for daily sustenance. The urban market continued to offer city-dwellers a wider range of products than available to peasants, but the daily ration of bread was still at the centre of their attention. This ration varied in both quantity and quality according to regional nutritional customs, purchasing power, the success of the harvest and the time of year (in the spring supplies dwindled). There were, however, standard levels of consumption which seem not to have varied greatly between the fourteenth and seventeenth centuries. Fourteenth-century documents allow calculation of daily bread (or wheat) consumption in the cities of central and northern Italy, which varied between 550 and 700 g per capita; public authorities considered 'normal' consumption to be a bushel a month or about 650 g a day. Sicilian consumption in the fifteenth century appears to have been decidedly higher: over 1 kg a day. In the sixteenth century, average individual consumption seems not to have fallen below 500 g, though tending upwards (as high as 800 g). The usual values for the area around Siena in the seventeenth century ranged between 700 and 900 g, with a peak at 1,200.[14] By using these and other data, it has been possible to establish a general schema: from the fourteenth to the seventeenth century, the daily bread ration amounted to 500–600 g and in some cases 700–1,000 g; it was in any case not below 400–500 g (except of course in times of famine). Perhaps, however, the picture is not entirely static, as one can also read a general increase over the centuries from the available data, however fragmentary and varied.[15] Nor should this increase come as a surprise in the context of decreasing meat consumption. In seventeenth-century Geneva, 2 lb of bread (1,100 g) were considered sufficient, while 1 lb (a little less than the quantity considered 'normal' in the fourteenth century) was 'the minimum necessary to escape starvation'.[16] Again in the seventeenth century, representatives of the charity institutes of Beauvais in north-eastern France estimated 3 lb a day of bread as a bare minimum (almost 1,300 g) or else 2 lb (850 g) and soup.[17] In the eighteenth century, the poor population of Paris ate as much as $1\frac{1}{2}$ kg of bread a day,[18] and well into the nineteenth century the workers of Nivernais ate from 2 to 4 lb.[19] It would seem then that those levels, which were only occasionally reached in the fourteenth and fifteenth centuries, gradually became the norm; nor do I believe that this increase was an indication of improved diet, but instead signalled its qualitative deterioration, as daily fare became ever more monotonous and ever more limited to breads and grains.

In some cases the quality of bread deteriorated as well. From at least the thirteenth century, European city-dwellers had been accustomed to eat bread made from wheat; subsequently other grains also came to the fore. In the sixteenth and seventeenth centuries wheat lost its monopoly of the urban market of Geneva and was progessively complemented by spelt; at the end of the seventeenth century both spelt and *méteil* (a mixture of rye and wheat, or of other grains) were widely use in bread-making. 'Not without resistance, however: in 1679 the population rejected *méteil* and preferred instead to purchase wheat for 25 per cent more, claiming that *méteil* was a poor substitute.'[20] The situation resembled that of the food shortages of the fourteenth century. Again the 'hierarchy of bread' reproduced that of society: there was white bread for the wealthiest, less white for the middle classes, and a dark bread for the least well off. As for barley, oat or legume bread, the Genevan physician Jacob Girard des Bergeries (author of the 1672 *Governement de la santé*) considered it unhealthy and difficult to digest, and recommended that it be left for the poor 'who are unable to afford better and, moreover, are very hearty, work a lot and have always been used to this sort of bread'.[21] We have already encountered similar opinions. In 1585 Naples, the population refused the chestnut and legume flour proposed by the merchant Vincenzo Storaci. His insolent response was 'Eat stones!', for which he was subsequently murdered and quartered.[22]

Lesser grains had instead never ceased to figure in the bread of peasants; breads which in the city were signs of famine or poverty were the norm in the countryside. Even the wealthiest peasants, those who grew a surplus for sale in the market-place, often sold their best produce (all the wheat and often the rye as well), keeping lesser grains, legumes and chestnuts for their own use. To cite another example from the area around Geneva, in 1696 the granary of the wealthy Jacob Lombard contained only barley, millet, rye *méteil*, peas and lentils.[23] We can already guess at the significance: soups, polentas etc. continued to occupy a more important place than bread in peasant diets. As Marc Bloch has perceptively noted, this diet at least allowed the peasants to escape the double monopoly of the landowners, namely of both the mills and the ovens, and indeed the enduring rustic attachment to these sorts of foods may be in part explained by similar motivations.[24]

In any case, grains supplied the better part of lower-class energy needs, all the more so the lower the social position of the consumer. Grains never accounted for less than 50 per cent of this group's caloric intake and even reached 70–75 per cent. Hence the seriousness of the famines, and even simple grain shortages, which afflicted Europe with considerable intensity in the seventeenth century. Their timing varied, as always, from region to region. The years around 1630 were particularly difficult, as famine seems to have broken out everywhere, as were those around 1648, a critical year for all of Europe (though the crisis continued until 1652–4 with frequent recurrences in the 1660s). Another difficult period was between 1680 and 1685, while 1693–5 witnessed a general collapse of the European productive system (and 1697–9 a sudden recovery).

Bourgeois Ferocity

As the food situation worsened and the threat of famine increased, expressions of rage and intolerance became ever more desperate and violent. The lootings of bakeries were not literary inventions; hundreds took place over a wide area in the sixteenth and seventeenth centuries. It was the era of food riots; these were not merely the result of productive shortages, but also of the development of capitalism and the consequent process of proletarianization. The period of great food conflicts centred on the two centuries running from the beginning of the seventeenth century to the first decades of the nineteenth, though the chronology varied from country to country (earlier in England than in France, for example). The public authorities, and above all the king, were increasingly seen as the guarantors of the nutritional equilibrium of their subjects; when this equilibrium collapsed, revolt followed. The mythical king-who-feeds-his-people took on new cultural significance. Kaplan has called this figure the 'baker king', a description which recalls Louis XVI, called 'the baker' by the crowd that brought him from Versailles to Paris in October 1789.[25]

In moments of crisis, crowds of peasants and paupers thronged to the gates of the cities, which enjoyed relatively greater political protection. This practice had gone on for centuries, and for centuries city-dwellers had defended themselves from invasions of this sort. The mass of paupers had grown enormously, however, and the nutritional privilege of the cities was in danger. Defence of this privilege became ever more dramatic, and social marginalization (certainly nothing new) became a more frequent occurrence as extra mouths – obviously the weakest – were forced out.[26]

In 1573 crowds of famished paupers coming from the surrounding countryside and still farther afield filled the city of Troyes.

The city administrators gathered together with the wealthy

citizens in an assembly in order to find a solution to the problem . . . They ordered a large amount of bread baked for distribution to the paupers at one of the city gates. Each of these would be given a loaf of bread and a silver coin as he passed through the gate; and this gate would then be closed behind the last of these, and from the wall above they would be told to go with God and find food elsewhere   This was done and the poor were driven out of Troyes.[27]

Episodes of this sort tend to make us forget the measures often taken on behalf of the poor by these same cities, though even in charitable moments it was preferred that the peasants stay outside the gates. During the 1590 famine, the city of Bologna, 'wishing to provide for the poor, ordered that the peasants, large numbers of whom had come to beg in the city, be expelled'. Out of charity, but also to keep them under control, each was provided with a small daily ration of food, 'four ounces of rice so they can fend off hunger until spring'.[28]

This 'bourgeois ferocity' – in the well-known expression of Braudel – hardened towards the end of the sixteenth century and still more in the seventeenth. The poor came to be imprisoned together with lunatics and criminals, and their marginalization was pursued in a more 'rational' and systematic fashion.[29] In England the Poor Laws were introduced – 'Poor Laws, which were in fact laws *against* the poor' – and in 1656 the authorities of Dijon 'went so far as to forbid the town's citizens to take in the poor or to exercise private charity'.[30] In 1693, the municipality of Geneva counted 3,300 religious refugees, half of whom enjoyed public assistance; because of a catastrophic harvest, however, the refugees were invited to leave and, in anticipation of their departure, a little bread was given to the poorest. Many of these were old, women and children and truly had nowhere to go. None the less, the city council decided to stop all assistance in order to force them out before the winter.[31]

The Two Europes

'Tomorrow I have to lecture on the drunkenness of Noah, so I should drink enough this evening to be able to talk about that wickedness as one who knows by experience.' To this line of reasoning Dr Cordatus replied: 'By no means, you ought to do the opposite'; and Luther said in turn: 'One must make the best of the vices peculiar to each land. The Bohemians gorge themselves, the Wends steal, the Germans swill without stopping. How would you outdo a German, dear Cordatus, except by making him drunk – especially a German who doesn't love music and women.'[32]

The convivial conversation repeated above, recorded by Martin Luther's disciples in the last months of 1536, provides significant testimony that the image of the drunken German – a frequently recurring theme in European literature – was shared by the Germans themselves. It was an ancient image and derived directly from the consumption behaviour which the Germanic peoples introduced to European society from the third century AD. Some considered heavy eating and drinking evil behaviour, and also harmful; others instead took it to be a sign of individual dignity. It was in any case generally agreed to be characteristic of certain peoples (the Franks, the Saxons), and whether praised, condemned or ridiculed the *national* character of such behaviour was unquestioned.

In spite of the fact that European food culture has undergone a degree of normalization and that both the quantity and quality of food consumed are generally *socially* determined, these national distinctions endure. We encounter them in the literature and popular imagination of recent centuries, and they show no signs of disappearing. The peoples of the south – moderate, frugal, fond of the products of the earth and vegetable foods – are contrasted with those of the north, voracious and carnivorous. These are of course stereotypical characterizations, and make little sense if divorced from social variables. 'North' and 'south', for example,

constitute an abstract geographical antithesis; they do not cap-
ture local varieties and cut horizontally across national distinctions, as both the Italian and French examples show.

We ought to advance further, into 'regional' stereotypes and
images. This is, however, a path that, once taken, has no end,
and so we shall restrict ourselves to the persistence of the 'major'
stereotypes, which, it should be noted, have significant links to
concrete realities. It was only relatively recently, for instance,
that the habit of drinking wine, an old Mediterranean practice,
came to characterize the northern regions, where the habit of
heavy drinking was compatible with the lower alcohol content of
beer. The impact of wine on northern customs must have been
comparable to the 'discovery' of alcohol by the Indians of North
America, where the white population used it as a real instru-
ment of destruction. A passage from Tacitus comes to mind in
which referring to the Germans, he writes: 'If you humour their
drunkenness by supplying as much as they crave, they will be
vanquished through their vices as easily as on the battlefield.'[33]
The vanquishing was only relative, however, as a few centuries
later the Germans conquered the Roman Empire; moreover, wine is not whisky. None the less, this 'vice' – on which
both the Germanic and Celtic peoples prided themselves –
continued to characterize both their habits and their cultural
identity.

Nor were Italians and Spaniards slow to deride northern drinking habits, and their romances, novellas, letters, chronicles,
plays and poetry abound with these images. When one of Teofilo
Folengo's characters comes upon a Utopian fountain of muscatel
and malmsey and drinks copiously from it, he begins to utter
'trinch trinch! and other German ravings'. Cervantes's *morisco*
Ricote 'is turned into a German' in order to drink. As for the
French, 'they go after food and wine like fish after bait' according
to Ludovico Ariosto.[34] Francesco Redi attributed this intemperance
to climate and to a true ethnic predisposition: 'It is not
gluttony, but their natural behaviour, and not a naturalness of
recent date but very ancient.' And he cites Sulpicius Severus

when affirming that voracity is 'gluttony among the Greeks, but natural to the French'.[35]

In addition, the Germans and French ate more meat. Although, as noted earlier, this behaviour was probably limited to the middle and upper classes, there is little doubt that the food culture of the 'north' was more markedly carnivorous (as was of course northern food production). Travelling through Italy in 1580–1, Michel de Montaigne observed that 'the provisions are neither half so plentiful as in Germany, nor so well dressed. They serve up without larding in both places [in contrast to French practice], but in Germany they are far better seasoned, and varied by sauces and soups.' Again with reference to Italy, he writes: 'These people do not, as a rule, eat as much meat as we do . . . a banquet in Italy is no more than a very light meal in France – several pieces of veal and a couple or two of fowls, that is all.'[36]

These are not off-hand observations, and the diversity of European regional dietary regimes, in particular between central European and Mediterranean regions, is well established and finds documentary confirmation. This basic distinction characterized army rations as well, generally meatier than the ordinary diet. During the sixteenth and seventeenth centuries, Dutch soldiers seem to have consumed excessive quantities of meat while their Spanish, Provençal and Italian counterparts received a smaller amount and, in compensation, more bread.[37] Nor was the importance of meat in the Dutch diet limited to soldiers. In a 1672 travel guide, P. Boussingault wrote: 'Around November, the Dutch buy a cow or else half a one depending on family size. They salt or smoke it . . . and every Sunday cut off a good piece which they then cook and eat over several meals: all week it returns cold to the table with a few pieces of boiled meat and some greens.'[38] We can make similar observations regarding England, which in spite of the general reductions of the sixteenth and seventeenth centuries none the less enjoyed a relatively rich and diverse diet. Some scholars attribute England's lesser dependence on harvest fluctuations (as compared to France for example) to this situation; and the English demographic curve seems to have been generally less sensitive to the changing price of wheat.[39]

The Modenese Giacomo Castelvetro, exiled from Italy because of his Protestant ideas, went to England, where in 1614 he wrote a *Brief Account of all the Roots, Greens and Fruits that are Eaten in Italy either Raw or Cooked*. It is a sort of list of Italian gastronomy and captures one of its most original and distinctive aspects, namely the emphasis on these roots, greens and fruits which Castelvetro most missed during his stay in carnivorous England (or such anyway was the high London society in which he circulated). Castelvetro also considered the reasons for which 'the Italians eat more greens and fruit than meat':

First of all, Italy is not so rich in meat as either France or this island [Britain]; and so we must find other foods to feed such a large number of people confined to so small an area. The other reason, no less important, is the great heat which we endure nine months out of the year and which causes us to lose interest in meat, especially beef which we cannot even look at let alone eat.

Reasons of poverty, then, and also climate abound, though it is with a deep sense of nostalgia that Castelvetro describes at length the vegetables of his native land (and all cultures do love themselves above all others).[40] Others before Castelvetro had written on gastronomic botany in systematic manuals that fall somewhere between natural science treatises and cookery books. These include the long letter of Costanzo Felici, 'On the Salads and Plants that are in any way Used as Food for Man' (1569), and the treatise of Salvatore Massonio, 'Archidipno, or on Salad and its Use' (1627). In the first of these, Felici observes that for 'this food salad . . . Italians are truly greedy (or so say those from beyond the Alps), and they have snatched away sustenance from the animals who eat raw greens'.[41] Dietary satire apparently did not travel in one direction only.

The divide between food cultures deepened in the sixteenth

century when the Protestant Reformation rejected, along with much else, the dietary norms of the Roman Church. 'Just as the father says to his family: "Obey my will, and for the rest, eat, drink and dress as you please", so God does not care how we eat or dress.'[42] These words of Luther are clearly and forcefully polemical: recalling the evangelical and Pauline texts, he denies the legitimacy of ecclesiastical dispositions in dietary matters and assigns the choice entirely to the conscience of the individual. Hence away with Lent, with abstinence, and above all with the war on meat.

European food culture was thrown into confusion. Centuries of Lenten precepts had accustomed people to alternate meat and fish, animal fat and vegetable oils, and these precepts had played a role, as we have seen above, in uniting European dietary practices, not standardizing them, but at least integrating them within the same cultural context. 'Liberation' from Roman Catholic norms reignited conflicts which had never been entirely placated: carnivorous Europe – in so far as means permitted – promoted its preferred food almost as a symbol of newly won independence. During the sixteenth and seventeenth centuries, treatises on the unrestricted consumption of meat abounded in Protestant Europe – to cite a single example, Arnoldus Montanus' *Diatriba de esu carnium et quadragesima pontificiorum* ('Treatise on Meat-Eating and the Popish Lent') published in Amsterdam in 1662 – and provided an interesting counterweight to the spate of Lenten dietary treatises which appeared in Catholic areas. The casuistry of prohibited and permitted foods was specified ever more minutely and bureaucratically, as for example in 'Lenten Food'.[43] In reaction then, the post-Tridentine Catholic Church manifested a strong resolve to conrol private behaviour. It seems that in seventeenth-century Florence an inquisitor patrolled the streets on the appropriate days in order to determine, by smell, whether anyone was eating meat.[44]

It is of course difficult to measure the *real* imact of this break, as opposed to the obvious cultural impact. Although 'it is normally assumed, particularly by English writers, that the

Reformation struck a particular blow at the fishing industries of Europe', this judgment merits further scrutiny in order to distinguish between artificially created demand for fish (for days of fasting and Lent) and that demand which constituted a basic dietary element (as for example in Holland, Scotland and Norway). In England, the number of fishing boats certainly declined; though 'elsewhere it seems to have had a relatively minor impact, probably hitting freshwater fishing (where the yield was lower) hardest'.[45] There was in any case a noticeable impact.

There is no evidence that this process also affected wine, which enjoyed too prestigious an image to suffer seriously. It was, however, considered to be ever more a luxury product in the Protestant north, where beer production and consumption increased considerably in the seventeenth century; thanks to Dutch hegemony beer conquered territory in the south as well.[46]

The two Europes disagreed over the choice of fats as well. While previously, 'in all of western Europe, oil was used on meatless days and lard or other animal fats on meat days', this aspect of culinary uniformity 'did not survive the Reformation'.[47] In the Catholic countries numerous dispensations permitted the re-establishment of regional differences. It seems that Charlemagne hoped to obtain permission from the pope to use *oleum lardinum* in the monasteries of the north, 'because, unlike those beyond the Alps, they had no laurel oil';[48] butter was in fact included among the meatless foods from at least 1365 (the Council of Angers) and from that date spread as an alternative to oil (and in opposition to that fattiest of fats, namely lard). It continued to be banned during Lent, but there were even concessions and dispensations in this latter case. The story of the so-called 'tower of butter' built by the citizens of Rouen who had obtained permission to eat butter during Lent may be legend; but there is documentation confirming that this privilege was obtained *in perpetuum* by Anne of Brittany and her family in 1491 and later extended to all their subjects. So in spite of cultural integration, not even ecclesiastical rules were able to ignore the realities of production and differences of taste and dietary tradition.[49] The case of the cardinal of Aragon who travelled through the Low Countries in 1516 accompanied by his personal cook and a good supply of olive oil reminds us that the 'structures of taste' are a tenacious historical reality.[50]

A final observation: although the Reformation represented a decisive rift in western Christianity, it also, paradoxically, precipitated opposed processes of cultural integration and exchange. Dedicating his *Brief Account* on the nutritional virtues of vegetables to his London hosts, Giacomo Castelvetro observed that 'over the past fifty years' – recall that he was writing in 1614 – the 'noble nation' of England had learned new gastronomic habits thanks to 'the influx to this secure asylum of many refugees seeking to escape the angry claws of the cruel and impious Roman Inquisition'. He too sought to make a small contribution by teaching the appreciation of foods 'that many today, whether out of neglect or ignorance', are not in the habit of using. When people circulate, so do ideas, and this is perhaps the one positive aspect of forced migrations. Who can say whether or not Castelvetro's work did not play a role in encouraging John Evelyn to publish in 1699 the first English treatise on salads: *Acetaria, a Discourse of Sallets.*

Changing Tastes

Along with many of his contemporaries, Evelyn held that salad must be dressed with oil and vinegar, and the oil had to be olive oil. We know that the oil merchants delivered a decidedly inferior product to northern Europe. The English expression 'as brown as oil', noted as early as the fifteenth century, would, for example, have been incomprehensible in Provence or Italy. It was for this reason, according to Flandrin,[51] that northern Europeans dreamed of a colourless, odourless and tasteless oil; the oil they received was instead cloudy, acrid and acidic. They used it none the less. They had learned to do so over a period of many centuries, not for reasons of taste – again according to Flandrin – but out of necessity as ecclesiastical rules forbade the use of animal fats on at least one day in three during the course of the year. There were dispensations, but these were exceptions, issued to single individuals or communities, and difficult to obtain. As a result, the use of oil spread throughout northern Europe, both as a condiment and for cooking (especially of 'meatless' foods). It continued to be used raw on salads for a long time, at least in France and England; Evelyn's work is from the end of the seventeenth century. As a basic ingredient for cooking or as a hot condiment, oil was instead gradually replaced by butter.

This change began during the fourteenth and fifteenth centuries and clearly bore a relation (though the direction of causality is debatable) to the increasing availability of butter made possible by the spread of cattle farming. It was a fashion that conquered Europe in general, and not just the northern countries, but Italy and Spain as well to some degree. As early as the fifteenth century, the recipe book of Maestro Martino signals butter's entry into Italian cooking, and later we encounter it also in Spain. Flandrin describes it as a 'second invasion' of northern food habits, following that of a millennium before which had broadly spread the 'barbarian' use of lard through southern Europe. As for France and England, while the cookery books of the fourteenth and fifteenth centuries propose oil as a substitute for lard, by the sixteenth and seventeenth centuries it had been almost entirely replaced by butter. On the one hand, this replacement was the outcome of a process begun long before, but it was the Reformation – in those countries where it triumphed – which dealt oil the fatal blow. Oil continued to be called for only on salads, and there not for long. Even in the seventeenth century, Dutch salads were dressed with melted butter, and a French traveller recounts being ridiculed in Ireland for requesting oil. Finally, the English and French also converted to creamy dressings.

The butter-based sauces which took hold in European *haute*

cuisine in the seventeenth century, as well as those using oil
which came to be modelled after them, represented a true
'transformation of taste' as compared with those sauces used a
couple of centuries before. In the fourteenth-century cookery books, which codified practices widely used in preceeding
centuries, most sauces contained no fat of any kind, neither
oil, butter nor any other. The sauces which normally accompanied meat and fish were lean and acidic; they contained above all
wine, vinegar, verjuice (the juice of unripe grapes), citrus juice,
or the juice of wild fruits, to which were added various
herbs and spices. In order to thicken or 'bind' a sauce, the soft
part of bread, almonds, walnuts, egg yolks, liver or blood were
used. Occasionally they were sweetened with sugar or lightened
with meat (or fish) broth. But they were all lean sauces, and
none of them – except perhaps for mustard – has survived to the
present day, or only after transformations which have radically
changed their character: the addition of oil and butter (as, for
example, in green sauce or garlic sauce) has revolutionized their
nature and taste.[52] This 'transformation of taste' took place during the sixteenth and seventeenth centuries, and Flandrin – to
whom we owe the most careful studies of the question – does not
hesitate to assert its independence from external factors and
necessary causes, with the exception of those circumstances (above
all the Reformation) which served to 'liberate' new desires. He
writes: 'I fail to see how demographic, economic or technological
transformations can explain this culinary revolution; it did not
take place on the plain of material restrictions, but on that of
desire.' It was in fact the upper classes, social groups which were
certainly not concerned to use a product (butter) because of its
availabilty and economy, that 'launched' the new cuisine. Indeed,
we know that it is just the opposite phenomenon, namely a
product's scarcity, which heightens its distinction and therefore
its desirability. We might then reverse the direction of causality:
new tastes and preferences – which rapidly spread among the
upper to the middle bourgeoisie – must have played a part in
European agricultural transformation, for example the tendency,

already evident in the seventeenth century and marked by the eighteenth, to favour the raising of milk-producing live-stock.

An apparently paradoxical phenomenon which accompanied these changes clearly demonstrates that elite demand is driven by the rarity, expense and exclusive character of the goods consumed. Spices, which for a millennium had distinguished the cuisine of the rich and been desired perhaps above all other things, slowly began to disappear from culinary use, at just that moment when their abundance would have allowed (as, in fact, for a period it did) more widespread use. The procurement of spices directly from their sources in order to supply this demand had been among the goals of the globe-circling voyages of exploration and conquest. But the inundation of aromas and flavours which assaulted sixteenth-ccentury Europe quickly brought fatigue. When saffron, cinnamon and 'fine spices' came within the reach of anyone, the wealthy looked elsewhere for signs of distinction. Preferences even turned to indigenous and (in some respects) 'peasant' products: in the seventeenth century the French elites gave up spices and replaced them with chives, shallots, mushrooms, capers, anchovies and the like, more delic-ate flavours and certainly better suited to the richer cuisine then coming into fashion. Another element was the satisfaction ex-perienced by those who from the lofty height of their wealth could allow themselves to enjoy even 'poor' foods, a sentiment which today is fortunately widespread.

The French example enjoyed general success among European elites and renewed in a profound way the gastronomic culture of the continent, or at least in the western regions such as Italy and Spain. The countries of the east and centre-north, such as Ger-many, Holland, Poland and Russia, persisted (and continue to persist) in their affection for spices, and contrasting or strong flavours; perhaps, as Braudel suggests, because spices had ar-rived there later and so remained a 'new' luxury. The cuisine of these latter countries was then conservative as compared to the abrupt change which took place in France; and it was from this point that France took the lead in European cuisine and became generally fashionable.[53]

The 'new cuisine' distinguished itself for other reasons as well. Bitter and sweet flavours, traditionally combined, came more and more to be carefully separated. Sweetness in particular came to the fore as evidenced by an increased use of sugar in many preparations.[54] Sugar had been used for centuries in Europe, but primarily for medicinal purposes, while honey was used to sweeten foods. Especially in Italy and Spain, this Arabic 'spice' – sold by the spice-sellers together with other oriental products – began to be used in confectionery, a practice which emerged in pharmacology long before it did in gastronomy. Confectionery lay somewhere between the two worlds, as suggested by the practice we have described above of consuming small spiced sweets before bed to aid digestion. Only in the fourteenth and fifteenth centuries did sugar find its way into culinary practice, a passage first noted, as one might expect, in Italian and Spanish texts, but also precociously in English ones. An Anglo-Norman treatise of the fourteenth century explains how sugar serves 'to combat the strength of spices'; that is, to lessen the acidity of foods and sauces. Also in the fourteenth century, German cuisine, though still tied to the traditional use of honey, seems to reveal a particular attention to sweetness: the *Buoch von guoter spise* ('Book of Good Foods') repeatedly suggests that foods should not be oversalted.[55] In the fifteenth century, sugar established itself in France as well, first in the 'new' recipes and then in the re-elaboration of traditional ones. From that point on, sweet preparations spread throughout Europe, though not always with the same intensity: Mediterranean cuisine (and to a degree that of England) was more strongly influenced. The humanist Bartolomeo Sacchi, known as Platina, suggested the addition of sugar to 'Catalonian blancmange' and then apologized for such an obvious recommendation, given that 'no food refuses, so to speak, sugar'.[56] By the following century, sugar had become an indispensable ingredient, and cookery books called for its almost universal use, just as Platina had suggested. Nor was this phenomenon limited to elite cuisine: in the mid-sixteenth century sugar appeared together with bread, wine, oil and cheese among the foods distributed to the poor at a monastery in the Emilian Apennines. This radical transformation which took place in the space of two centuries is perfectly captured by Abraham Ortelius who in 1572 wrote, 'Whereas before, sugar was only obtainable in the shops of apothecaries, who kept it exclusively for invalids, today people devour it out of gluttony . . . What used to be a medicine is nowadays eaten as food.'[57] In order to satisfy and increase this demand, Europeans established sugar cane plantations (worked by slaves) in the American continent from the sixteenth century; this was in itself a fundamental chapter of political, economic and social history significantly linked to habits of food consumption which emerged in Europe between the fourteenth and sixteenth centuries.[58]

Old and New Drugs

The consumption of alcoholic beverages – beer or wine according to region – has in the past reached extremely high levels. It is of course impossible to calculate an average which is valid across periods, regions, social classes, age and sex, but scholarly estimates rarely fall below a litre of wine a day per person and more often reach 2, 3 and even 4 litres a day. These figures have been verified for various places and social groups, both rural and urban, from the thirteenth and fourteenth centuries (though documents from before the year 1000 allow reasonable and similar calculations).[59] Beer consumption was greater still. In sixteenth-century Sweden, consumption was forty times greater than it is today; English families in the seventeenth century drank about 3 litres a day per person (a calculation which includes all age groups).[60]

Various factors explain this situation. The first is simply thirst, probably more acute than today – an English writer of the sixteenth century defined it as 'oceanic' – given the widespread practice of preserving food with salt (meat, fish, cheese, etc.). Moreover, beer and wine are nutritional foods and supply a daily caloric contribution that is easily and quickly assimilated and becomes ever more important the more monotonous the diet. Johann Brettschneider wrote in 1551 that 'some live more off drink than real food, and all have need of it whether men or women, old, healthy or ill'. Alcoholic beverages, and wine in particular, were also held to have important therapeutic powers: they served as the basis for many pharmaceutical preparations, and were themselves considered medicine, almost a universal remedy for all ailments. Research conducted regarding consumption at the Hôtel-Dieu hospital in Paris during the fifteenth and sixteenth centuries has confirmed 'the general belief in the invigorating and curative powers of wine as reflected in levels of consumption'. Wine was in fact given with every meal 'in abundance if not excess', and ever more generously according to the seriousness of the illness.[61] It was also common practice to 'correct' water with wine; indeed, water was almost never consumed unadulterated as it was not often fit for drinking (a serious problem until at least the nineteenth century), and the addition of alcohol served as a sort of antiseptic.[62] Nor should we overlook the festive aspects of wine and beer consumption, a form of escape and at the same time of sociability. While it is difficult to find examples of 'sacred' drunkenness in Christian Europe like those which characterized pagan religions (both in Graeco-Latin and Germano-Celtic traditions), as its religious dimension was reduced and culturally marginalized, the social and ritual character of drinking re-emerged on a secular level in the meetings of congregations and confraternities, in domestic toasts and in both rural and urban taverns. In this context it is impossible to determine the point at which wine and beer cease to be simple foods and take on the status of *drugs*. It is clear at any rate that drunkenness, tenaciously and uselessly combated by Christian preachers from the fourth century on, had an important collective dimension: it was more a social than an individual phenomenon and constituted a clearly *euphoric* use of alcoholic beverages. We may choose to call this practice 'secular', but it does not differ greatly from that which in other cultures represented an ecstatic voyage to mystical horizons. The appeals of moralists and preachers for moderate and *controlled* wine consumption is simply a milder version of the terrible penalties inflicted upon those who used toxic and stupefacient substances for purposes of 'demonry' or 'witchcraft'. We should also recall that this same Christian culture had carried out an intense propaganda campaign in favour of wine as both an alimentary symbol and a ritual tool of the new faith.[63]

From the seventeenth century, new beverages spread throughout Europe, as both complements and substitutes for wine and beer. The cultural dominance of these two standards, until then absolute, was challenged by new methods of distillation, by coffee, tea and chocolate, products at first restricted to the elite but later enjoying wider success, even with the working classes. Differing in both their geographical and social diffusion, these new drinks had in common the fact that they were not properly foods, but rather drugs the primary functions of which were euphoria and escape, combined with advantages of taste and sociability. These were functions (especially the first two) that Christian Europe could not easily accept. As always in such cases, justifications in terms of health were quickly invoked. Physicians and scientists explained that alcohol, coffee and tea were healthy, as was said of wine and beer. Hence a small intellectual alibi, perhaps sincerely proposed, served to open the doors of desire.

The distillation of alcohol was born of alchemy. Greeks and Romans were familiar with the alembic, reportedly an Egyptian invention. It was used, however, only to distil substances such as mercury or sulphur and at very high temperatures. The process was then perfected by the Arabs, and European alchemists achieved the distillation of wine by a new technique for chilling the serpentine. The earliest description of this method for preparing 'fiery water', which 'burns without consuming the material onto which it is poured', comes from a technical treatise of the twelfth century. Initially, the miraculous *aqua vitae* was used only for chemico-pharmacological purposes, as a solvent or antiseptic; such was the case also for *aqua ardens*, obtained by subjecting the alcohol to further distillation. According to Arnoldo di Villanova, a physician who lived between the thirteenth and fourteenth centuries, *aqua vitae* drove off unnecessary humours, reinvigorated the heart, healed colic, dropsy and fever, calmed toothaches and gave protection from the plague. In 1735, a chemical treatise affirmed that 'the spirit of wine, properly used, is a sort of panacea'. As early as the fifteenth century, however, *aqua vitae* had begun its journey from the phamacist's to homes and taverns. In the seventeenth century, it had become a beverage and for certain functions competed with wine. To it were soon added distillates of molasses (rum), of fruit (calvados, kirsch, maraschino), and of grains (vodka, whisky, gin), as well as those sweet liqueurs (rosolio, ratafia) which were so much in fashion in seventeenth-century Europe; yet another example of that 'triumph of sweetness' which constituted an aspect of the new gastronomic tastes of the period.[64]

Originally from Ethiopia and other parts of eastern Africa, coffee was imported to south-western Arabia in the thirteenth and fourteenth centuries; there its cultivation spread and the practice of preparing a beverage with the roasted seeds was established.[65] According to Arab tradition, this beverage dates from the fourteenth century and was discovered by a holy man from Yemen who first used it for the prolonging of mystic vigils. Coffee then arrived in Egypt and spread through the Turkish Empire and to the east as far as India. From the second half of the sixteenth century, it began to be imported to Europe, in particular by Venetian merchants. In spite of hostility and scepticism – Francesco Redi claimed that he 'would sooner drink a cup of poison than one full of bitter and evil coffee' – the new drink enjoyed great success and led to the creation of coffee plantations in European colonial possessions, first by the Dutch

(Java) and French (Antilles) and then in the Spanish and Por-
tuguese colonies of Central and South America. The success of
coffee in Europe was determined primarily in the Paris market,
where it is said to have arrived by 1643. Some opposed the new
product, including some physicians who advised against its
consumption or else recommended it only as a medicine. Others
proposed it as a cure for a variety of ailments, and judging from
the results, these latter opinions enjoyed greater success. Jacob
Spon, for example, celebrated the ability of coffee to dry out
cold humours, strengthen the liver, combat scabies and the
corruption of the blood, refresh the heart, relieve stomach aches,
protect (with its steam) against eye infections and colds, and
other similar fantasies. Alongside the colourful itinerant pedlars
dressed in Turkish costume, the first shops for the sale and
consumption of coffee opened in Paris in the 1670s; the famous
Procope was founded in 1686 by the Italian Procopio Coltelli,
who had previously worked in another shop run by an Armen-
ian. The fashion quickly spread to Germany, Italy, Spain,
Portugal and England. The first London coffee-house was opened in 1687–8 by Edward Lloyd in Tower Street, and a statistic
from the time, certainly exaggerated but none the less significant for its exaggeration, suggests that around 1700 the city's
600,000 inhabitants frequented some 3,000 establishments of
this sort. Although the English soon came to prefer tea, thanks
to the self-interested complicity of the British East India Company, coffee took on importance as a symbol of the rationalist
culture of the age, of its aspirations to clarity, acuteness and
freedom of thought. The brilliant conversation in the coffee-
house or in the drawing-rooms of the upper bourgeoisie provided
a privileged arena for Enlightenment culture. The bourgeois
work ethic and insistence on productivity – not a secondary aspect
of emergent capitalism – also found a valuable symbol and ally in
coffee. In 1660 James Howell noted that artisans and employees
who used to drink beer or wine in the morning, and so had heads
too heavy to permit serious work, had now adopted this middle-
class beverage, which kept them awake.[66] The 1671 *Traité nouveau*

et curieux du café, du thé et du chocolat by the Lyon merchant Sylvestre Dufour, which quickly became a sort of bible for the use and advertisement of the new drink, praised the ability of coffee to keep one sober and awake. Initially a drink of the elite, it had conquered the working classes by the end of the seventeenth century, at least in France and especially in Paris, where it seems to have replaced wine as the drug of the masses. While Le Grand d'Aussy wrote in 1782 that 'there is no bourgeois household where you are not offered coffee', Mercier added in his *Tableau de Paris* the observation that workers 'have found more economy, more sustenance, more flavour in this foodstuff than in any other. As a result, they drink it in prodigious quantities, saying that it generally sustains them until the evening.'[67]

As we have already mentioned, coffee's fortunes were challenged in England, and also in Holland, by the suppliers of tea, who won out in the end.[68] The first load of tea arrived in Amsterdam around 1610 and came from India, where Europeans had come to know this ancient Chinese drink. There are reports of tea in France from 1635, but only after 1650 (from the Dutch) of its arrival across the Channel. Tea had by then become the new drug of the Dutch and replaced all alcoholic beverages (including beer) as an inebriant. It would appear that in the last decades of the century, Amsterdamers drank as many as 100 cups of tea a day per person, a level of consumption which found the usual medical support. Cornelius Bontekoe, courtier to the Great Elector Frederick William and lecturer at the University of Frankfurt, recommended tea to 'all the peoples of the earth', and prescribed that 'all men and all women drink it every day and at all hours, beginning with ten cups a day and increasing the dose as much as the stomach can stand and the kidneys can expel'; to the ill he administered as many as fifty cups a day. From 1720–30, tea caught on in England as well: the agricultural workers of Middlesex and Surrey began to drink it in place of the more expensive beer. Between 1760 and 1795, annual English tea imports grew from 5 to 20 million lb, that is to about 2 lb (900 g) per person; contraband imports, estimated as about equal in volume to legitimate, should be added to this figure. Next it was the turn of the urban proletariat: by the 1820s the consumption of English industrial workers consisted above all (and in some cases only) of bread and tea.

The *functional* substitution of these new drinks for beer and wine is clear and confirms our claim that coffee and tea served not only as foods but also as drugs in the European system of consumption, at least until the seventeenth century. The transition is neatly linear in Holland and England. Elsewhere it is less consistent but equally clear, as in the public lecture delivered by Dr Colomb on the occasion of his joining the medical college of Marseille in 1679. Asking 'Is coffee use harmful or not to the inhabitants of Marseille?' he concludes that coffee is harmful for a series of medical and physiological reasons, but above all because of its 'despotic' and 'authoritarian' character: 'It is with real terror that we view this beverage which, due to attributes foolishly assigned to it, has almost completely taken the place of wine; in truth we must admit that neither the taste, smell, color nor substance of coffee merit comparison with even the dregs of wine.'[69] Colomb's is clearly a rhetorical statement, but the fact did not escape him that coffee threatened to occupy – to borrow an anthropological term – wine's 'ecological niche', just as it threatened elsewhere that of beer. In an autarkically inspired eighteenth-century ordinance issued by the bishop of Hildesheim we read: 'Germans, your fathers drank *aqua vitae* and were brought up on beer, just as was Frederick the Great; they were happy and good-hearted. You should send wood and wine to the wealthy half-brothers of our nation [the Dutch], but no more money for coffee.'[70]

Analogous in some ways, the use of chocolate, another new product, also took hold, especially in Spain and Italy. It did not, however, become a product of mass consumption, but was restricted to social and religious elites: The Jesuits attached special importance to the spread of chocolate as a drink for fast days, as it was both allowed (as were all liquids) and also particularly nourishing. The elitist image of chocolate was so strong that it came practically to be a symbol of aristocratic luxury and idleness, in apparent contrast to the activity and clear rationalism of the bourgeoisie.[71]

Apart from chocolate, which was socially and culturally less significant, it was doubtless the case that these new products brought about a change in the traditional nutritional balance: in particular, they altered the role of wine and beer in the popular diet. Their spread – extremely lucrative for mercantile companies – was, above all, a response to new needs and desires: the need or desire for new and stronger drugs, for energy and euphoria. Nor is it difficult to understand why this should be the case in eighteenth-century Europe, tormented by famine as perhaps never before.

5

The Century of Hunger

Does History Repeat Itself?

The nutritional history of eighteenth-century Europe follows a familiar pattern and seems to repeat that of the eleventh and twelfth centuries or of the sixteenth: demographic expansion coupled with insufficient production and agricultural development. This time around, however, the dimensions of the phenomenon had grown. The population of Europe peaked at perhaps 90 million before the great crisis of the mid-fourteenth century; subsequently it recovered gradually and reached 125 million by around 1700, after which it grew rapidly: 145 million by the mid-eighteenth century and 195 million at the century's end.[1] The productive system was severely tested, and the population regularly hit by times of shortage. Some of these (for example the infamous famine of 1709–10) affected all of Europe: Spain, Italy, France, England, Germany, Sweden and the countries to the east. Others were specific to certain regions: that of 1739–41 hit primarily France and Germany; that of 1741–3 England; the famine of 1764–7 was especially severe in the south (Spain and Italy); and that of 1771–4 in northern Europe. As for local famines, it seems that an economy based on trade was better able to cope than that of a few centuries before. Even so, we need to keep in mind the day-to-day difficulties created by a chronic shortage of grain. Grain had become the principal (or only) nutritional resource of the poorer classes, and its lack must have had a decisive influence on the quality of individual life. Added together, the 'difficult' years of the eighteenth century seem to have been more numerous than ever (except perhaps for the eleventh century). Not that people generally died from hunger. Had this been the case, the demographic expansion of the century would not have been possible. There existed instead widespread malaise, a state of permanent malnutrition which came to be physiologically and culturally 'assimilated' as a normal condition of life.

The initial response to increased demand for food was, as usual, the expansion of cultivation. In the thirty or so years before the French revolution, tilled land in France expanded from 19 to 24 million hectares. In the second half of the century, hundreds of thousands of hectares of untilled land and forest were enclosed and cultivated in England. In Ireland, Germany and Italy, swamps and marshes were drained.[2] New productive technologies were also introduced, as a climate of scientific fervour and agronomic experimentation succeeded for the first time in meeting the needs of farmers and property owners. We can properly speak of a true *agricultural revolution* in this period from a technological point of view: fallowing was abandoned and replaced by the regular planting of leguminous fodder in rotation with grains. On the one hand, this development allowed for the integration of animal raising and agriculture, traditionally separated. On the other, crop yields were notably increased thanks to the presence of legumes (which fix nitrogen in the soil) and the greater availability of animal fertilizer. The introduction of new technologies often accompanied enclosure movements and the elimination of common lands; together with social transformations of this sort, technological innovations signalled the beginnings of agrarian capitalism. In certain regions, especially England and France, they also represented the first step towards an industrial economy.

In addition to technological improvement and the expansion of tilled acreage, sturdier and higher-yielding crops were more widely planted. Those same crops which had spread in limited areas during the fifteenth and sixteenth centuries were now 'rediscovered' as a low-cost response to pressing nutritional needs. Rice, for example, after suffering a decline in the seventeenth century that was in part linked to questions of the advisability for health and environment of filling fields with stagnant water, came into vogue in the eighteenth as an alternative to traditional grains. In some areas it was introduced for the first time; in others it was in a sense reintroduced. In both cases it took on the connotations of poor man's fare intended primarily for the lower classes, quite a change from the exotic and precious image it had enjoyed previously.[3] Buckwheat, also rediscovered or else introduced for the first time in the eighteenth century, took on similar social significance.[4] Maize and potatoes, however, were the crops which took on the greatest importance and replaced many traditional competitors. During the eighteenth and nineteenth centuries, traditional varieties of lesser grains – the basis of popular diet for many centuries – progressively gave way before these new players. The explanation is simple if we consider the greater dependability (in terms of resistance to climatic adversity) and much higher yields of the new crops. Consider the case of Pannonia where in the eighteenth century maize gave a harvest to seed yield as high as 80 to 1, while rye gave less than six and wheat still less. The potato achieved similar 'miracles': for the same cultivated area, potatoes could feed double or treble (or even quadruple according to Arthur Young) the number of persons that traditional grains could.[5] And yet for over two centuries these crops had remained on the margins of the European productive and nutritional system, only to emerge at that moment when the problem of hunger took on proportions large enough to require new solutions. Nor did this development fail to engage cultural and scientific debate. As previously in the sixteenth century, there appeared a spate of treatises on famine foods: a 1762 volume published in Florence by Giovanni Targioni Tozzetti entitled 'Alimurgia, or the Way to Lessen the Seriousness of Famines for the Relief of the Poor' is among the many examples we might cite. Methods were even devised for making bread from acorns, a complicated procedure explained by Michele Rosa in his treatise 'On Acorns and Oak Trees and Other Useful Things for Food and Cultivation' (1801).[6] Scientific academies encouraged research and experimentation of this sort, offering prizes for the 'invention' of new foods that might appease people's hunger. A competition sponsored by the Academy of Besançon in 1772 was won by Augustin Parmentier for a treatise on potato cultivation.

A choice in favour of *quantity* underlay this eighteenth-century upheaval of European productive and nutritional structures (a process that continued into the nineteenth). It was, however, only a relative upheaval, as the grain option had for centuries been imposed on the lower classes as really the only dietary alternative; it was a necessary and in some ways forced choice, given population growth and, above all, the socially unequal distribution of meat. The eighteenth-century success of maize and potatoes (or in some areas of rice; and we shall encounter other variations on this theme) constituted a logical development (and end result) of this process. It was a process characterized by a sense of urgency and emergency; the first accounts of dietary conversion are everywhere linked to years of famine and want. This recurring and constant connection confers an important unity of meaning on experiences varying otherwise in time, place and form. Can we conclude then that these 'American' products changed the eating habits of Europeans? Personally, I have reservations about such an interpretation. First of all, it was only the *internal* evolution (or better, crisis) of the European nutritional system that succeeded in modifying the initial attitude of distrust and refusal with regard to those products, and so in bringing about their acceptance. Their success was therefore more the result than the cause of this transformation. Moreover, their acceptance was made possible only by a process of cultural confirmation which changed, sometimes radically, their utilization in such a way as to adapt them to specifically local traditions. Maize was 'interpreted' by the

European peasantry according to their own culture (as polenta) and used in way very different from that of the indigenous American populations. The potato too was received with the idea – in this case mistaken – that it might be adapted to the traditional canons of European culinary culture. Experts in fact held (and taught) that it could be used to make bread. The 'new arrivals' then did not really overturn the European nutritional system, but were instead called upon – as late as possible, with a thousand precautions and with the appropriate disguises – to restore it.

The Hard-Fought Rise of Maize

We have already discussed the early introduction of maize to the European countryside in the decades immediately following its 'discovery' on the American continent; and described its free adoption by peasants for use in gardens, as opposed to fields from which it long remained absent. We have also pointed out the advantage to the peasant of this situation, which excluded maize from any tax by the landowner; the garden plot had traditionally been a sort of 'free zone', not subject to fees and reserved for the personal use of the peasant family.[7] It was above all for this reason, and also for an understandable degree of caution with regard to the introduction of anything new, that the earliest uses of maize in Europe were restricted to the peasant garden and so in a way hidden (not to mention its presence in botanical gardens). But, as Kula has written, 'a new food means new production; and new production means new sorts of economic relationships and so a social struggle over those already existing'.[8] This is just the process which occurred in the agricultural regions of southern and central Europe (those where the new crop took hold) during the seventeenth and eighteenth centuries.

Following these first, almost unobserved, experiments, maize cultivation began to spread. In certain areas, north-eastern Italy for example, it was already an important economic reality at the end of the sixteenth century.[9] The possibility of planting maize in open fields caught the interest of landowners at different times and in different ways; it was a move which meant that maize would be included in agricultural contracts and placed on an equal footing – in terms of fee payments – with traditional grains. At this point the enthusiasm of the peasants diminished, and in some cases they even ceased to cultivate it. A struggle began, but with the roles reversed: the landowners sought to encourage maize planting and the peasants refused to do so. The owners had redefined the terms of the question in their own favour: the high productivity of corn opened the way to possible new and increased income, both in terms of the profit to be made off the new product as well as the possibility of obtaining a quantity of low-cost food for the peasants; at the same time they might increase the (more or less forced) exaction of prestige products. The divergence between wheat and lesser grains, gradually replaced by maize, became ever greater. Two separate and non-communicating levels of consumption emerged: the peasantry (directly in the case of tenant farmers; by means of the market in the case of day and salaried labourers) was encouraged and in fact forced to eat maize, while wheat found its way at high prices to the market. This mechanism, furthered by a series of contractual norms as well as oppressive systems of loans which exploited the unarmed poverty of the peasantry, was one of the methods by which landowners were able to increase their wealth during the eighteenth century. In this way the impoverishment of the peasant diet, which became still more monotonous than it had been in the past, contributed to the development of capitalist agriculture.[10] The European peasantry noted, with varying degrees of awareness, the seriousness of this transformation for their living standards; hence their resistance to planting fields with maize, in apparent contradiction with a centuries-long interest in the new crop. Clearly theirs was not a simple resistance to novelty. 'The rebellion against the cultivation of maize in the eighteenth century and later took aim at the regime of lords and other large landowners who sought to transform maize into a field crop and the cultivation of grains into a single-crop system.'[11]

The pressure of the property owners was seconded by that of hunger, and in fact the critical moment for this transformation came in the middle decades of the eighteenth century, a period marked as we have seen by severe famine. After the crisis of 1740–1, maize assumed a more visible presence in the Balkans alongside the traditional crops of barley and millet, which it came gradually to replace. 'Barley and millet biscuits and porridges were transformed into biscuits and porridges made from maize.'[12] It was a true metamorphosis, and polenta above all became an indispensable ingredient of the rural population's survival system.

This moment was decisive also in Italy. In 1778 Giovanni Battarra, an agronomist from Rimini, wrote: 'No more than forty years ago peasants planted a shoot or two of maize around their gardens . . . But as plantings became bigger and bigger, harvests grew abundant and filled nice large sacks.' Clearly outlining the socio-economic mechanism we have described, our author continues: 'The property owners, who had ignored those small harvests, came to want their half, and for the past twenty-five, or at most thirty years this new and much greater source of income has been introduced in our lands.' The landowners' interests combined with the necessity of hunger: 'Now, my children, had you been present in 1715, which the old folk have always called the year of famine, when this grain was not yet in use, you would have seen poor children dying of hunger'; until finally 'it pleased God to introduce this grain here and elsewhere so that even in years when wheat is scarce we can fall back on this food which is both good and nutritious'.[13]

Maize was good and nutritious according to the family head into whose mouth Battarra put the preceding passage, though we should add 'on condition that it is consumed together with other foods'. Maize polenta by itself is not sufficiently nourishing as it lacks niacin, an indispensable vitamin. Thus a diet based exclusively on polenta is harmful, while the addition of a tiny amount of meat or fresh greens supplies the daily requirement of niacin. Dependence on maize brought on a terrible disease, pellagra, which in its initial stage covers the body with purulent sores before leading to madness and death. Pellagra was first noted in Spain around 1730 (in the region of Asturias); it appeared shortly afterwards in France and northern Italy. In the second half of the century, together with increased maize consumption, it spread throughout the countryside of southern France, the Italian Po valley and the Balkans, where it continued its scourge well into the nineteenth century, and in some areas (in Italy, for example) into the twentieth.[14] It was evident to all that it was a food-related disease, but a heated debate followed between those who blamed spoiled maize or flour (and so ultimately those who chose to eat it) and those who held that it was the dietary regime itself – its monotony and so a state of chronic and excessive indigence – which brought on the illness. Only in the first decades of the twentieth century was this debate definitively resolved in favour of the latter opinion, nor can we help asking whether those who supported the former might have done so out of personal interest (whether direct or second-hand), that is whether they chose to close their eyes to the serious social implications of this situation. For their part, the peasants had perfectly understood the crux of the problem: an Italian physician complained in 1824 of the difficulty encountered in treating those afflicted with pellagra, many of whom 'do not consult a physician because they believe that every cure calls for drinking wine, and eating meat and wheat bread, which most of them simply do not have'.[15]

The spread of pellagra followed the fortunes of maize, its success from the 1730s and 1740s and its further strengthening following the famine of 1816–17. For a century or two the disease constituted an endemic scourge throughout much of the countryside of central and southern Europe, both sign and symbol of a nutritional poverty without precedent.

The Potato, Between Agronomy and Policy

The potato also spread as a famine food, encouraged by both hunger and landowners, much as did maize. The potato had the added benefit of being a crop that grew below soil level, and so was less exposed to the devastation of war, a sort of 'artificial famine' to which rural populations were periodically subjected: the potato 'is never exposed . . . to the ravages of war' an Alsatian document tells us.[16] The massive introduction of the 'white truffle' as a substitute for traditional grains characterized above all northern and central Europe, and its spread was almost a mirror image of that of maize. Together the two crops came to cover the entire continent, with areas of overlap in culturally and climatically intermediate zones such as southern France and northern Italy.[17]

By the first half of the eighteenth century, public authorities sought to encourage potato planting, while scientific writers launched an intense propaganda campaign praising the virtues and nutritional potential of the new crop. Measures to this end were taken by Frederick William I of Prussia (1713–40) and his son Frederick the Great. None the less, the major factors which led to the introduction of the potato in Germany were the nutritional crises linked to the Seven Years War (1756–63) and the Famine of 1770–2. Coincidentally it was during the Seven Years War that Augustin Parmentier, held prisoner in Prussia, presumably encountered the potato and so became its champion in France (we have already cited his prize-winning essay on the subject for the Academy of Besançon in 1772). Meanwhile the potato spread to Alsace-Lorraine, Flanders, England and above all Ireland, where it encountered great favour among the peasantry and became a staple of their diet. In Germany as elsewhere, however, it was the famine of 1770–2 which signalled a general leap forward in potato cultivation: in some areas (Auvergne, for example)[18] it appeared for the first time, while in others where it was already planted, production intensified and the potato was confirmed as a fundamental element of the dietary regime; in Lorraine the potato was criticized and opposed in 1760 and then in 1787 described as a 'usual and healthy' food of the peasants. By the century's end it had become established in Sweden, Norway, Poland and Russia, while the Austrian military sought (with some difficulty) to impose its cultivation on the Balkan peninsula: an 1802 edict issued by the border command threatened forty lashes with a stick to those Serbian and Croatian peasants who continued to refuse to plant potatoes in their fields.[19] Famines, however, had greater impact than edicts, and it was as a result of the former that the potato (like maize) enjoyed rapid 'promotion'. In Nivernais, for example, it was only after the crisis of 1812–13 that the potato became an important food.[20] In Friuli (as in much of north-eastern Italy) the famine of 1816–17 achieved 'what the impassioned appeals of the academics could not'.[21]

Production relationships were none the less decisive. As was the case with maize, a social divide opened between consumption patterns: the potato (a 'filling' food for the peasant masses and the urban proletariat) was contrasted to higher-quality foods sent to market. Foreseeing in 1817 the spread of the new crop in the territory of Venice, Pietro Zorzi noted that the interests of wheat merchants would not be harmed, as only 'that amount [of potatoes] which will feed for a short time those who in any case do not eat bread' would be cultivated, that is only that which sufficed for domestic consumption and perhaps as a substitute for maize. In any case 'this development, which may be useful to the needy classes, will not be disadvantageous at all for the better off'.[22] Resistance on the part of peasants, who saw behind these plans a possible further impoverishment of their diet, was also due to the low quality of the products proposed: poorly selected, the first tubers often had an acidic, watery and even toxic pulp. Moreover, potatoes were long proposed to the peasants as suitable for bread-making: Parmentier suggested this, as did many manuals and booklets of the late eighteenth and early nineteenth centuries. The error of these suggestions, namely the inappropriateness of potatoes for bread, must have dissuaded many from using potatoes. All possible means were employed to convince the reluctant. In Italy even priests were enlisted in the struggle, recognized by the public authorities as 'confidants of the peasants' and 'one of the most efficient tools for impressing upon and spreading among the people those useful truths and practices which are advantageous to society and the state'. So stated an 1816 circular of the Royal Delegate to the province of Friuli sent to all the parochial priests together with an *Instruction* on potato cultivation to be explained and spread among the faithful.[23] Legal coercion was used as well, for example the insertion into agrarian contracts of a clause requiring a new tenant to reserve a percentage of his fields for potatoes.

Refined gastronomic elaborations of the potato soon emerged. Cookery books of the early nineteenth century provide evidence of 'high' culture's interest in the potato. Perhaps this development was inevitable, given the energy which intellectuals and scientists had devoted to exploring its marvellous qualities. Early on then, the potato came to occupy a socially heterogeneous cultural space, something which did not happen to maize which was confined to poor diets.[24] We should not, however, forget the spirit with which the potato was accepted (when it was) by the European peasantry of two centuries ago: a food for animals it would seem, but also (though perhaps we should say and *therefore* also) for peasants. In his 'Agrarian Practices', Giovanni Battarra wrote: 'The potato is an excellent food for both men and beasts'.[25]

Describing the German countryside, another Italian advocate of the potato wrote in 1767: 'The poor peasants of those lands survive for at least six months out of the year on potatoes alone, and they are handsome, robust and healthy'.[26] Perhaps they were not entirely 'healthy', although it is true that a diet of potatoes does not present the same risks as one of maize. Still, dependence upon a single food always represents a threat to individual survival, not only because a varied diet is the only guarantee to healthy growth, but also because daily nutritional security is a function of the diversification of the resources available. The single-crop farming of the eighteenth and nineteenth centuries and the associated single-food diets were the extreme manifestation of a centuries-long trend toward the 'simplification' of the popular diet; and the most striking outcome of this trend was the Irish tragedy of 1845–6. The rotting of two potato harvests was sufficient to destroy a peasant society which had unluckily based its survival system on that food alone. This dependence, thanks to the high yield of the potato, had allowed the tenant-farming families to support themselves on ever smaller plots, while English landowners shipped the better products (wheat, pork, poultry and butter) across the sea. Thus the combination of two years without potatoes and a policy of criminal neglect on the part of the British government was enough to wipe out by means of famine, infectious disease and forced emigration one-third (and in some areas more) of the population. Subsequently, the depopulation of the island (which in 1841 counted 8 million inhabitants and sixty years later fewer than 5 million) proved to be a good occasion to eliminate many of the small property holdings and transform them into great pastoral estates the better to supply the British meat and wool markets.[27]

In the face of this tragedy, the exclamation of the Italian peasant reported by Giovanni Battarra strikes one as ironic: 'We should be happy if we could introduce large plantings [of potatoes] and so suffer no more from famine.'[28]

Macaroni Eaters

The history of pasta is still to be written.[29] It is another 'filling' food on which popular attention focused during the eighteenth and nineteenth centuries. In a geographically and culturally more limited region – essentially central and southern Italy – pasta came to fill the same function as maize and potatoes did elsewhere. A distinction, however, must first be made between fresh pasta (a simple dough of flour and water or egg made for immediate domestic consumption) and dry pasta (which is dried immediately for the purpose of long-term conservation). The first of these is a food of ancient date, widespread among Mediterranean populations and also in other parts of the world, for instance China. Dry pasta is a more recent invention and has been attributed to Arabic origin, the technique of drying being developed in order to supply provisions suitable for desert travel. A more careful examination of the available texts, however, suggests a degree of caution with regard to this attribution. Rosenberger has noted that the very notion of 'pasta' seems to be absent from Arabic gastronomy. We can only say for certain that the first European reference to pasta comes from Sicily, an area profoundly influenced by Arabic culture. In the twelfth century the geographer Idrisi refers to the existence of a true dry pasta industry – *itrija* – at Trabia, about 30 km from Palermo. In that zone, he writes, 'a great quantity of pasta is made and exported all over, to Calabria and to other Muslim and Christian lands; and many shiploads are sent'. It is also worth noting that the term *tria*, borrowed from Arabic to designate the elongated form of pasta, appears in the *Tacuina sanitatis* and other Italian culinary treatises of the fourteenth century.

Moreover, there are many reasons to look to Liguria as well as Sicily. By the twelfth century Genoese merchants were the principal agents for the spread of Sicilian pasta in the north. From the thirteenth century Liguria and nearby parts of northern Tuscany appear as areas for the production as well as sale of vermicelli and other sorts of pasta. Nor can it be accidental that the *tria* recipes found in fourteenth-century cookery books are regularly described as 'Genoese'. During the fifteenth century, new centres of production developed, especially in Apulia, alongside those in Sicily and Liguria. Dried pasta seems instead not to have caught on in those areas of central north Italy (Emilia and Lombardy for example) where fresh pasta has traditionally been made at home.[30] Pasta then appeared in the gastronomy of other countries as well: in particular, in Provence (perhaps the route for its spread to northern Europe) and England (the only European country besides Italy where pasta recipes appeared in fourteenth-century cookery books). Varieties included both long (vermicelli) and short (macaroni) pastas; filled pastas (ravioli, tortelli, lasagne) enjoyed considerable success as well.[31]

The role and image of pasta in the food culture of the period is difficult to define. In cookery books it was awkwardly described as a category on its own, combining (at least until the fifteenth century) pastas both boiled and fried, sweet and savoury, simple and filled; in fact, even meat or vegetable balls dredged in flour and fried were described as 'pasta'. Its social role too was problematic. On the one hand, it seemed to be a 'popular' food for fishermen and others who needed stores that would keep for long periods. On the other, it appeared to be a luxury food, restricted to a limited group of consumers: dreams of macaroni or dumplings that roll down mountains of cheese – as in the Utopia of Bengodi already referred to – suggest that those foods represented unrealized desires. Perhaps we need to differentiate – just as for bread – two socially (and to a degree regionally) distinct levels of pasta consumption. Dry pasta may already in the twelfth and thirteenth centuries have been a true 'popular' food in those areas where it was produced; its conservability certainly qualified it for admittance to the cultural universe of famine. Fresh pasta on the other hand, like any perishable product, bore connotations of luxury and gluttony, with the exception of that made not from wheat but from other lesser grains; the 'strozzapetti' or 'gnocchi' described by the seventeenth-century agronomist Vincenzo Tanara, made from bits of leftover millet bread crumbled and made into a dough with water, certainly did not resemble aristocratic fare.[32] The image instead of macaroni and lasagne dishes included in 'upper-class' cookery books, richly prepared with butter and cheese and liberally sprinkled with sugar and sweet spices, was entirely another affair. As with bread then, it is pointless to attempt to define the 'social status' of pasta.

The nutritional importance of pasta long remained limited. The phrase 'macaroni eaters' was still applied to the Sicilians in the sixteenth century and suggests that the practice was unusual. In most of southern Italy, pasta was still considered something special, a delicacy, which one could (indeed had to) forgo in difficult times. In Naples (where it appears that pasta began to be imported from Sicily only at the end of the fifteenth century) a proclamation of 1509 prohibited the production of 'taralli, susamelli, ceppule, maccarune, trii vermicelli' and any other sort of pasta in periods when the price of wheat 'rises as a result of war, famine or inclement weather'. Clearly pasta was not the primary food of the Neapolitan population which in that period ate, in addition to bread, a great deal of meat and vegetables (especially cabbage). Even in Sicily pasta was fairly expensive: only in 1501 was it included among those necessities subject to price controls, and at mid-century the price of macaroni or lasagne was still about three times that of bread.[33]

Only in the seventeenth century did pasta begin to assume a central dietary role. This development took place, for a change, in the face of necessity. In the 1630s, overpopulation in Naples created a difficult food situation made worse by the political and economic crisis of the city, once the rich capital of the kingdom. Resources for the urban population declined, and the Spanish governors did not guarantee adequate supplies. As a result, meat consumption declined, and grains took its place. At the same time, a small technological revolution occurred: the spread of the kneading machine and the invention of the mechanical press made possible the more economical production of macaroni and other sorts of pasta. Suddenly pasta took on a central role in the diet of the urban poor, and in the eighteenth century the Neapolitans took the title of 'macaroni eaters' away from the Sicilians. Pasta and cheese (the normal condiment for pasta from the thirteenth to the nineteenth century) replaced the traditional pair of meat and cabbage. This was in a way an ingenious dietary solution as it guaranteed both adequate protein and a desirable quantity of food. Southern Italy would not witness the dramatic instances of malnutrition associated with dependence on maize or potatoes alone. Thanks to the gluten of durum wheat – a coarser but more nutritious variety that grows only in the south – the peasants and poorer city-dwellers of southern Italy were better protected than their neighbours to the north. Moreover, durum wheat flour keeps well, and this longevity was the key to pasta's success in that part of Europe, the reason for its becoming – only there – an important element of popular nutrition. Elsewhere, whether more or less widespread and valued, it remained something extra.[34]

The 'second' introduction of pasta to Italian food culture began in Naples, though its success was not everywhere so rapid. In certain parts of southern Italy, pasta still played a marginal role at the end of the nineteenth century and was eaten only by wealthy families.[35] None the less the stereotype of the Italian spaghetti or macaroni eater was by then well established and corresponded to a wide if not uniformly spread phenomenon. Pasta could be bought at kiosks along the street (as prints and paintings of the period depict); it was eaten with the hands and without any condiment, or only with a little grated cheese. Only from the 1830s was it dressed with a sauce made from tomatoes, another 'American' product destined to enjoy great fortune in Italian and European gastronomy.

Population and Nutrition

During the eighteenth and nineteenth centuries the growth of European agricultural production (through both technological advances and the introduction of new crops) somehow managed to meet the nutritional demands of a rapidly growing population. And so a disaster of the sort precipitated by the conditions, in some ways analogous, which characterized the late thirteenth and early fourteenth centuries was avoided. Demographic growth was not only not dramatically interrupted, as it had been in the mid-fourteenth century, but continued with increased intensity: the 195 million Europeans estimated at the end of the eighteenth century became 288 million half a century later. Can we then conclude that increased food availability was the basis of demographic expansion? That population grew in reponse to improved nutritional conditions?

This view, whose most authoritative and well-known advocate is probably McKeown, has been given much credit. The story, however, is not so simple.[36] If by 'improvement' we mean that famines were less disastrous than in the past, that they caused fewer deaths, then the hypothesis is tenable. If, however, we mean to say that the nutritional regime was richer and more substantial, then just the opposite was the case. The progressive 'simplification' of the popular diet, ever more concentrated on one food or a few, effected a true impoverishment as compared to the past. We have seen both the endemic undernourishment and dramatic disease caused in many countries by dependence on maize alone; we have also seen the tragedy caused in Ireland by a similar dependence on potatoes. Even if we ignore these extremes, the overall nutritional regime of the poorer classes became monotonous and impoverished. Maize and potatoes served to fill up the peasants, while wheat became more than ever a luxury product, almost entirely sent to the urban markets. The same was true of meat, which could now be produced in greater quantities thanks to new agrarian systems and zootechnical progress, though for a considerable period of time those who profited were few in number. Statistics suggest that after 1750 the declining purchasing power of large sectors of consumers caused a rapid drop in meat consumption even in the urban centres. One example should suffice: in 1770 in Naples 21,800 cattle were butchered for a population of about 400,000; two centuries before, 30,000 were butchered for about 200,000 inhabitants. Nutritional impoverishment affected the middle and working classes generally and characterized all regions: Italy, Spain, Sweden, England and so on.[37] Statistics on the height of population (closely correlated to the quality of life and nutrition) also confirm these observations: during the eighteenth century the average height of soldiers recruited by the Habsburg monarchy seems to have declined noticeably, and a similar shortening characterized Swedish recruits towards the end of the century. Also at the end of the eighteenth century and beginning of the nineteenth, the average height of poor London adolescents declined, while the height of Germans at the beginning of the nineteenth century seems to have been decidedly below the average of the fourteenth and fifteenth centuries.[38]

It seems fair to say that in the eighteenth century (and well into the nineteenth) the population of Europe ate poorly, or in any case considerably worse than in previous periods. 'Caloric' calculations made for earlier periods and based on uncertain and incomplete data are always risky and not to be heeded in any detail. None the less it would appear that the decades around 1800 represented a historic minimum with regard to food available per capita. In comparison with the data for other periods, the lowest nutritional levels, those closest to the barest necessity, are regularly those from the end of the eighteenth century and the beginning of the nineteenth. It was a time of rapid population growth, and one might suggest (turning McKeown's hypothesis on its head) that it was just this growth that, through insufficient production and the related nutritional 'choices', created a general dietary impoverishment. This situation may appear paradoxical, but we have none the less to observe that it occurs repeatedly throughout history. The periods characterized by a more richly varied and abundant popular diet seem to have been, until the nineteenth century, those marked by demographic stagnation or regression, when reduced demand allowed more elastic and diversified production. Are demographic and nutritional curves then inversions of one another? It would appear that they are, so that it is difficult to explain demographic growth in terms of an improved dietary regime.

This is not, however, to say that dietary regime and demographic regime are independent of one another, though the position of Livi Bacci, according to whom the relationship between food and population tends to manifest itself only in short-run phenomena (that is, mortality crises), seems the most convincing. These crises, provoked in times of famine either directly by hunger or else more frequently (in precarious hygienic, environmental and cultural conditions) by epidemic or individual infectious diseases, strongly influence demographic growth, especially if repeated over a short period. In the medium and long term, however, the nutritional factor (as also the demographic) seems to acquire its own autonomy. Under 'normal' conditions – if we can speak of such for a population continually threatened by hunger – the degree of adaptation is high and allows for the 'normal' operation of survival and growth mechanisms. Three years after the famine of 1812, the French *préfet* Fiévée wrote, 'During the famine which struck France, we offered a loan from the amortization fund to the district of Morvan so that inexpensive soups might be distributed. They answered that they were not wealthy enough to nourish themselves in such a luxurious way and that, as poverty was their habitual state, they had not suffered more than usual that year.'[39]

We must then seek elsewhere for the causes of demographic growth (a problem beyond our scope), nor should we detect any contradiction in describing the dynamic European society of the eighteenth century as one characterized by a low and even miserable level of nutrition in spite (or perhaps because) of that growth.

Another paradox which repeats itself in history, at least in the long period we call pre-industrial, is that the poorer classes enjoy greater security (which is not to say that they live better, but simply with more stability and less subject to crises) in the marginal, less cultivated, less urbanized and less commercially developed areas, as opposed to the more intensely urbanized or agriculturally developed ones. The case of Auvergne studied by Poitrineau for the eighteenth century is instructive in this regard: in the more 'developed' plains and hills, where grain and grape were intensively cultivated, the peasant nutritional regime was limited and monotonous, lacking in vitamins and animal protein, while in the mountainous areas, pasturing and chestnut gathering contributed to a more balanced and abundant diet with the result, it seems, that average life was longer and resistance to disease greater.[40] Equally significant are the observations of Kula, who has compared the general situations of France and Poland, again for the eighteenth century. Poland, less populated, less urbanized and characterized by less intensive agriculture, did not suffer famines comparable to those of France in either their frequency or their devastation.[41]

The Evils of Meat

Having called for the introduction of the potato as a means to combat peasant hunger, Giovanni Battarra also explained in his 'Agrarian Practices' (1778) how to make bread from that odd tuber: mixed with a little wheat flour, a delicate and pleasantly scented bread was obtained, in all respects a product fit even for the gentry. But 'can one make a flour out of potatoes and use that for bread without adding wheat flour?' asks Mingone, son of the peasant in whose mouth Battarra puts his teachings. 'Yes', he answers, 'but the bread is said to be very hard to digest'. Surprisingly, Mingone is not put off by this observation but instead filled with joy: because, he explains, 'indigestion does not bother peasants; indeed it makes them feel more filled up'. Here then is the true desire of the peasant: a nice bout of indigestion in order to stave off as long as possible the frustrating desire to eat.[42]

This point of view was of course that of the landowner. No peasant of the eighteenth century (or before for that matter) has left a *first-hand* account of his or her gastronomic preferences; and as taste and habit are not the same thing (goaded by hunger, one might well eat unpleasant foods), it is hard to escape the conclusion that the nutritional model attributed to the peasantry in various treatises and other writings was more the product of forced habit than conscious choice.[43] Hence the intrinsic ambiguity of so many descriptions of popular 'taste'. Not going beyond the codification of visible behaviour, they risk overlooking (or else overlook intentionally) the possibility of different desires. Nor is it always easy to identify the point at which social concern and philanthropy give way to class interests and an ideology not far removed from that which in previous centuries described the bad and indigestible food of the peasants as an inevitable and necessary attribute of their social 'quality': we have already noted the comments of Girolamo Cirelli, according to whom peasants, 'except at wedding feasts', ate 'like pigs'; and this behaviour served to 'unmask' their fundamentally bestial and uncivil nature.[44]

By the eighteenth century, a spirit of philanthropy and 'enlightened' paternalism towards the poor had come to characterize much of the ruling class, in contrast to the attitudes of two or three centuries before when the defence of privilege and the enforcement of an ideology of social difference based in part – as we have seen – on models of life and nutrition held sway. It had become more difficult openly to advocate exclusion of the 'poor' from the enjoyment of good-quality foods, and the malicious cynicism of the powerful (and of many intellectuals) had to be softened. There is, however, still something sinister, or at least grotesque, in the 'Warnings to peasants with regard to their health' included by Marco Lastri (author of many agronomic treatises and handbooks at the end of the eighteenth century) as an appendix to his 'Rules for Landowners'. Here we read that peasants eat poorly, or rather do not know how to eat properly! In an effort to economize (a guilty economy he adds), they are willing to eat spoiled food, and prefer (recall the words of Battarra) heavy and indigestible foods in order to save on quantity and stave off hunger. If the peasants eat poorly then, it is because they *want* to do so.[45] This condemnation of bad habits resembles the attitude of those who a century later attributed pellagra epidemics to the inability of the peasants to store corn properly and their consequent insistence on eating spoiled flour.

A changed ideological framework had rendered out of date the fifteenth- and sixteenth-century notion that poor nutrition was an original and inevitable aspect of peasant existence, though the cultural consequences of this reacquired freedom of 'choice' were at best paradoxical. As is written in the *Dictionnaire de Trévoux*: 'The peasants are usually so stupid because they live only on coarse foods.'[46]

Among the foods most often denied the peasantry, meat held first place, and most European peasants and 'poor' people came to consider it a dream beyond their reach. Nor were there lacking those who claimed that privations of this sort were in fact good for one's health. Are peasants unable to eat meat? Good for them; who ever said that one had to eat meat? In 1776 Adam Smith wrote: 'It may indeed be doubted whether butchers meat is any where a necessary of life. Grain and other vegetables, . . . it is known from experience, can, without any butchers meat, afford the most plentiful, the most wholesome, the most nourishing, and the most invigorating diet. Decency no where requires that any man should eat butchers meat.'[47]

The meat controversy was the order of the day in eighteenth-century Europe. One writer even expressed a degree of irritation with the situation: Louis Lemery wrote at the beginning of the century that 'without entering into what seem to me to be fruitless debates, I believe one can say that the use of animal flesh can be advisable, provided it is in moderation',[48] words which echo a heated debate more ideological (or philosophical) in nature than scientific. Health and food hygiene – invoked in support of food choices that implied a particular social order and world-view – were just one aspect of the general discussion. The success of vegetarian doctrines, advocated by many Enlightenment thinkers and philosophers (most notably perhaps Rousseau)[49] represented the 'enlightened' revival of well-tested Christian images and motivations: vegetable food represented the food of peace and non-violence, the choice for a 'natural', simple and frugal life; vegetable food insured against bodily heaviness and so allowed the mind to work more freely (for spiritual uplift according to the Christian monks and hermits, for the operations of reason and intelligence according to the new ascetic philosophers). Nor were these images and motivations lacking ambiguity and contradiction, to which was also added a keenly political and social component: the choice in favour of a 'hygienic', 'light' and 'intelligent' dietary regime was also an alternative to the *ancien régime* and the food culture it had embodied. The battle against the excess, opulence and 'heaviness' of food was also a battle waged by the 'enlightened' nobility and bourgeoisie against old political, social and cultural forms. The strong flavours of wild game and a hearty appetite following a day on horseback were the food symbols of a feudal regime. In the eighteenth century new social groups, new ideologies and new fashions came to the fore and values of the latter sort were questioned; luxury became more delicate and refined, and milder, creamier sauces replaced earlier tartness and contrasting flavours. A vigorous appetite and an abundance of meat, once signs of strength, power and nobility, were no longer objects of universal social approval.[50]

These were of course problems and controversies of the elite and made sense only in the context of an opulent society like that of the aristocracy and upper bourgeoisie. When these themes began to find their way out of the social environment which created them, when exhortations for nutritional rationality and perhaps vegetarianism reached peasants or workers, the effect was grotesque if not ridiculous.

6

The Revolution

A Reversal of Trends

Until the middle decades of the nineteenth century, grains continued to dominate the European diet (except in the case of a small privileged elite). Economically, they might absorb as much as 90 per cent of a family's food budget; calorically their role was decisive as well, normally accounting for between two-thirds and three-quarters of the total, and in any case no less than half. These percentages had varied little from the fourteenth and fifteenth centuries (that is, from that point after which there exists documentation on which to base an estimate). They may, however, have increased slightly during the seventeenth and eighteenth centuries given the increased importance of corn, pasta and rice. In some cases they declined, but only in the presence of a competing product of similar nutritional 'significance', for example the potato, whose success in England and Holland coincided with a decrease in grain consumption in the eighteenth century. In Holland, grain consumption declined from about 900 g a day per capita at the beginning of the century to 475 g at its end; in England, the 600 g daily of 1770 fell to around 400 g by 1830. Daily rations of bread between 500 g and 800 g continued, however, to be the norm in many areas, as was a high level of rural polenta consumption in others.[1]

The bread eaten by the majority was, as always, dark: made primarily from rye, spelt, buckwheat, oats and barley in northern central Europe, while in the Mediterranean regions wheat might be mixed with lesser grains (rye, maize, barley).

Around the middle of the nineteenth century, a reversal of previous qualitative and quantitative trends took place. From a qualitative point of view, white bread captured a larger group of consumers as an improved food situation opened up new spaces to wheat production and sale. In addition, the introduction of new mills with iron cylinders (used for the first time in Hungary between 1840 and 1850) produced a whiter and drier flour than in the past. The new product was, however, less nutritious than traditional flour as the new system (perfected around 1870–80 with the introduction of porcelain cylinders) expelled the germ rather than crushing it together with the entire grain. However, the prestige and desirability of this whiteness – for centuries identified as a prerogative of wealthy consumers – were such that considerations of this sort took second place.[2] Efforts were also made to obtain the whitest possible rice; and sugar (now made from beet as well as cane) was refined to a similar end.

The greatest change, however, was quantitative: for the first time in many centuries the nutritional role of grains began to decline, while that of other foods, especially meat, increased.

Meat *Redux*

In 1847 the first English vegetarian society was founded in Manchester. The founding members constituted, as always in such cases, an elite group, and their motivations were not only the traditional condemnation of the violent slaughter of animals or the presumed healthiness and 'naturalness' of a vegetarian diet (in 1813 Shelley published a pamphlet entitled *Vindication of a Natural Diet*), but also new economic arguments which stressed the greater productivity of agriculture in comparison with animal husbandry. Moreover, there emerged a new 'humanitarian' concern for the lives of animals, as their normally public butchering came to inspire an ever stronger aversion. Nor is it difficult to detect behind these changing attitudes that process of 'civilization' (and thus distancing from 'nature') ably described by Norbert Elias. K. Thomas too has identified this phenomenon as typically urban and bourgeois, as characterizing a society separated from fields and animals and accustomed to regard the latter primarily as domestic companions. We might, however, add yet another consideration. Might the spread of the vegetarian movement, elitist to be sure but socially organized and 'institutionalized' for the first time, have been a function of the greater availability of meat, of the spread of greater nutritional well-being?[3]

The liveliness of the eighteenth-century debate over meat-eating versus vegetarianism (or 'Pythagorean diet'), inspired as we have suggested by ideological opposition to the food values of the *ancien régime*, may also have disguised a search for new models in a society where meat had become accessible to larger segments of population, at least within the bourgeoisie. Similar considerations should apply with still greater force to the bourgeois society of the nineteenth century; nor can it be an accident that the new vegetarian movement originated in Manchester, one of the capitals of English industry and thus a centre of labour and wealth. It is true that meat remained the privilege of only a few social strata, but these strata (and in particular that of the bourgeois businessman) were rapidly expanding. And while the workers continued to dine exclusively on tea and bread – Engels's description of their pitiful condition was not simply the fruit of impassioned political and social commitment – the 'average' level of urban consumption was increasing and required ever more in the way of imported good-quality foodstuffs. We have already mentioned the meat and butter imported by English landlords from Ireland.

Yet the logic of industrial production itself could not long exclude the poorer classes from the enjoyment of food resources. In order to function, industry needs consumers, and from the moment the economic function of agriculture began to change from simple food production to the supply of the raw materials of the food industry, the social expansion of the market became necessary. In addition to tea, which had replaced wine and beer as items of daily general consumption, the English working class came to be offered sugar, cocoa and a growing variety of products at ever more accessible prices. Ultimately, this variety came to include meat as well.

It was above all the increased consumption of meat that represented a break with the past; historical minima had been reached in the first decades of the nineteenth century when average annual per capita consumption seems to have varied between 14 and 20 kg in countries such as Germany and France that were relatively rich in livestock.[4] This change was due both to more advanced and scientific zootechnical practices (selection and crossing of breeds, specialization of livestock-raising for milk production or meat) and to other technological progress which brought about a radical change in the systems of meat transportation and conservation. The researches of Nicolas Appert and Louis Pasteur opened the way to the hermetic packaging of meat, vegetables and soups, while new refrigeration and freezing techniques made possible the importation of low-priced meat from distant countries where vast spaces were available for the raising of livestock, countries such as Argentina, the United States and New Zealand.[5] At the same time, the steam engine revolutionized transport, and the railroad made the movement of large and heavy loads by land practicable for the first time. Until the middle of the nineteenth century, animals for butchering continued to be shipped live to where they would be consumed, and long trips tired them out and lowered the quality and weight of their meat. After 1850, the transportation of well-preserved carcasses, ready for sale, began and the production sites were suddenly close to the markets: the slaughterhouse of London could be said to have moved to Aberdeen, 800 km from the capital, from which, wrote Wynte, 'in the course of a year, mountains of beef, mutton, pork, and veal arrive the night after it is slaughtered in perfect condition.'[6]

Unscrupulous producers and merchants did not hesitate to take advantage of the situation, endangering the health of consumers by the use of all sorts of fraud and adulteration. Frederick Accum's *Treatise on Adulterations of Food and Culinary Poisons*

(1820) was the first of a series of denunciations which led Parliament to appoint a commission for the study of alimentary fraud (1834). Inquiry continued during the following decades, blocked by producers (Accum himself was forced to leave England) and supported by a violent newspaper campaign. An 1855 vignette from *Punch* on the topic has earned a degree of fame: A little girl says to the grocer, 'If you please, sir, mother says, will you let her have a quarter of a pound of your best tea to kill the rats with, and an ounce of chocolate as would get rid of the black beadles?'[7] In 1860 the first law against food fraud was passed, the *British Food and Drugs Act*.[8]

During the early decades of industrialization, and accompanied by numerous contradictions and high social costs, a radical (and at the same time slow and progressive) change took place in both dietary regime and the *ideology* of food. The profit motive argued for the discarding of traditional distinctions and social symbols, namely the practice of exclusion and well-worn habits of considering certain foods as destined for a precisely defined group of consumers. Subsequently, differences would be more in quality than in kind, and foods might be of top, second or lowest quality, or perhaps imitations. But no one in capitalist industrial Europe could deny freedom of choice and the fact that all might (and indeed should) maintain a high level of consumption which included something of everything. The matured port drunk by workers, for example, would not be the same as that served in the most exclusive clubs (Accum in fact showed that much of the 'crusted old port' sold by the London merchants was new port 'crusted' with supertartrate of potash). Nevertheless, the idea of universal or 'democratic' consumption had cultural as well as economic importance.

All the World's a City

The European revolution in diet was gradual and varied both with respect to timing and character from region to region. To study it in detail would require going over the basic steps of the Industrial Revolution to which it was closely linked, and so we shall limit ourselves to a few general observations. Even in those countries that were the first to industrialize (England and France), it was only at the end of the nineteenth century that a significant change in the general standard of living of the population became apparent and that a dietary regime based on grains gave way to one in which protein and fat were supplied to a notable degree by animal foods. As for the more slowly developing countries such as Italy and Spain, this transition would not be complete until the mid-twentieth century, and in certain territorially and culturally limited areas, archaic (or we might call them pre-industrial) situations persisted none the less. It is clearly difficult to speak of an abstract and generic 'Europe' in this context. Food and economic systems are structurally linked to political choices that in fact split the continent in two; nor has the process of integration and reconciliation initiated in the last years of the twentieth century generalized the system characteristic of what we have come to describe as western Europe (itself marked by significant contrasts). Even so, I shall attempt to trace a general outline.

First of all, the 'delocalization' (to use the expression of Pelto and Pelto),[9] of the food system eased the links between territory, seasonal variations and food, and overcame the perennial hunger of the Europeans. The basic factors were the revolution in transport and the development of techniques for the transformation and conservation of food discussed above. Military and political power did the rest, effectively directing the economic choices made in many regions of the world in order to benefit the wealthy countries. In the service of these markets (which in addition to Europe include above all the United States) every sort of resource was mobilized, and often to the deteriment of local interests. For while the perfection of a global network of commercial distribution has eliminated famine in the industrialized world, it has often aggravated the living conditions in other countries. 'A major feature of food delocalization in the nineteenth and twentieth centuries has been the transformation of food systems in non-industrialized areas as they have become involved in supplying some of the food needs of Euro-American communities.'[10] For example, in many parts of Latin America the production of beef increased enormously as a function of the market for hamburgers and, in general, the high levels of meat consumption in wealthy countries; at the same time local meat consumption in these countries declined. In Guatemala (one example out of many) beef production doubled between 1960 and 1972 while internal per capita consumption declined by 20 per cent.[11] The complex web of relationships created by the global delocalization of food production and distribution threatens in particular those producer populations that depend on the sale of one or a few products (crops or livestock); this situation constitutes the most dramatic, though not the only, contradiction of a system that has succeeded for the first time in history in conquering famine. Even that accomplishment applies only in times of peace; war has witnessed the re-emergence not only of famine but also of forms of supply and consumption seemingly forgotten.

Secondly, delocalization, by weakening the economic and cultural links between food and territory, has imposed greater uniformity upon the dietary models of the industrialized world, a process furthered by the interests of large producers and the suggestion of advertisement. Other factors have also played a role: the expansion of general familiarity with the rest of the world as determined by greater social mobility (whether for work or tourism); the attenuation of seasonal restrictions (to which we shall return below); and the progressive decline of food rituals and the periodic variation of diet (weekly or annually) linked to religious festivities: Carnival and Lent, and the days or periods of lean or fatty diets.[12] Many products have effectively lost their cultural significance, the door has been opened to every sort of gastronomic combination and experiment, and all foods have been brought into a single unlimited 'dossier'. Symbolic of this latter development is the combination of meat and fish (traditionally mutually exclusive) in meals served at present-day restaurants.

Thirdly, the European food system has taken on a strong and increasingly *urban* character, not just in the obvious sense, namely that industrial society is highly urbanized and a large and growing number of people live in the cities, but above all because urban dietary *models* (with all the changes that have come to define them) constitute the norm and *can* be imitated by anyone. 'The tendency of rural populations to follow "urban" models . . . has never been stronger or more sought after.'[13] It represents the realization of a centuries-old dream, the elimination of a barrier which has long oppressed European food culture. The envy of luxury goods and protected markets felt by the peasantry and the jealously guarded privileges of the city-dwellers are now social, economic and psychological realities of the past. If anything, a reverse seems to have taken place. The negative aspects of a more uniform, homogeneous food system (which has also brought unquestioned advantages), divorced from its own region, has produced a new sort of 'nostalgia for the country' – though it is not difficult to find precedents in earlier periods of European history – and required a rethinking of rural values, even a renewed rural self-consciousness. None the less, these are *urban* values: the happy countryside is an urban image and one which manifests itself in rural environments only as a reflection (and only if the country-dwellers are themselves immersed in urban culture). What could be more urban than the present-day revival of lesser grains and dark breads? Only a wealthy society can afford to appreciate poverty.

A Food for All Seasons

The traditionally seasonal nature of foods and the existence of a harmonious relationship between man the consumer and nature the producer, both profoundly altered by modern systems of supply and distribution, constitute one of the most tenacious myths attached to the culture of food. The rediscovery of this lost dimension of our relationship with food has raised the concern of historians, anthropologists and sociologists, and is the basis of both the entreaties of dietitians and the proposals of leading restaurateurs. A brief reflection is in order.

The high-handedness of the food industry has unquestionably upset many of the traditional rhythms and habits of life, and created, together with many benefits, both health concerns and considerable cultural disorientation. Strawberries at Christmas and peaches for New Year's Day are a pleasant luxury but also a source of alienation and confusion, above all because we are unlikely to know where the products come from. Just at the moment when food has become plentiful thanks to an incredible assortment of products and unprecedented purchasing power, our relationship with it paradoxically has become more distant. We know not whence it comes (only for a few foods does law require this information), nor when or how it has been made.

In the past the regional nature of food was taken for granted and inevitable; it was part of the natural order of things, of the daily realities of production and consumption. Even those few who could afford products brought across great distances were well aware of the origin and particular qualities of their foods. An infinite number of authors and personages could be cited attesting to the fact that place of origin was always a factor in the appreciation of food, from the fourth-century BC gastronomic guide of Archestratus of Gela, in which the author precisely lists the types of fish that could be caught in the Mediterranean and where they were best, to Ortensio Lando, who describes the gastronomic and enological specialities of various cities and regions in his 'Commentary on the Most Notable and Monstruous Things in Italy and Elsewhere' (1548); and it is this cultural dimension above all that risks being lost today in the sea of interregional and international markets, and even on a local level, given the distancing of the mass of consumers from the processes of production. We need, however, to keep in mind that men have always *desired* to break these restrictions of place. Consider, for example, the words of Cassiodorus, minister to Theodoric, king of the Goths (sixth century AD), who in a letter ordered the finest products from every region for his sovereign, maintaining that power is also measured by the foods which a lord is able to offer his guests and that only a commoner limits himself to 'that which is available locally'.[14] The presence of exotic foods on our own tables then is not representative of a new culture; it is simply the case that many can today enjoy what was previously the prerogative of a privileged few. This achievement has created difficult problems, legislative and otherwise, regarding the control and knowledge of food. We might even question the importance of such an achievement, but only after recognizing that it constitutes a true conquest. Now we must seek to manage it, above all culturally.

The question of seasonality merits similar consideration. While the revolution of transportation and commercial organization (and also the massive role now played by chemistry in productive systems) may make us forget that food is irrevocably tied to the variations of season and climate, we still cannot ignore the fact that exactly this freedom from seasonal and climatic vicissitudes was for centuries a great desideratum and the purpose of much food system organization. Symbiosis with nature and dependence upon her rhythms was once practically complete, but this is not to say that such a state of affairs was desirable; indeed, at times it was identified as a form of slavery. It is true that, from Hippocrates on, physicians have insisted upon the need to adapt one's diet (and all other aspects of daily life: sleep, sexual activity, work and exercise) to natural and seasonal rhythms for the sake of good health;[15] and the *regimina mensium*, manuals which describe the principle hygienic and nutritional norms to follow in each month of the year, make up an important part of western medical literature (agronomic and botanical treatises also attribute considerable importance to the argument). These are all, however, texts and instructions directed at an elite public, one able to choose and vary its dietary regime; as for the rest (already according to Hippocrates), they must make do as best they can.

For most, making do meant relying upon dependable and conservable foods. Indeed, the large role historically played in the popular diet by grains, legumes and chestnuts must in large part have been due to their very conservability. Likewise, the decisive role played by salt for millennia in the food system (at least until the spread of modern refrigeration techniques) is largely attributable to its ability to preserve meat, fish and other foods for long periods of time. The key concept is *conservation*: to conquer the seasons, accumulate stock, fill up the storerooms, and escape from the uncertainty and fickleness of nature in order to maintain a constant and uniform standard of consumption. Even the terrestrial paradise, the ideal world, seems to be a place without seasons where food is always available and always the same. In Chrétien de Troyes' magic garden in *Erec et Enide*, 'there are flowers and ripe fruit all summer and all winter'.[16] Indeed, perhaps only vegetable gardens, well fertilized and carefully tended, could approach this ideal of continuous production; according to Isidore of Seville the garden (*ortus*) owed its name to the fact that something was always growing there (*oriatur*).[17] Hence the special importance (qualitative even more than quantitative) of gardens to peasant nutrition, at least for those settled on a plot of land where they could work a piece for themselves.

Techniques of food conservation (to which the food cultures of the past dedicated special and particular attention) were the 'poor' method for beating the seasons. On the other hand, the use of fresh and perishable foods (fruit, vegetables, meat and fish) was always a luxury reserved for the few. And so the desire to overcome the seasonality of products and the dependence upon nature and region was if anything more acute, though the methods for doing so were expensive (and prestigious); they required wealth and power. Recall the words of Cassiodorus or the example of the 'miserable refinement' of Gallienus, the third-century Roman emperor whose biographer records that he 'kept grapes for three years and ate melons in the dead of winter' and 'taught how to conserve grape juice for the whole year and always enjoyed offering green figs and fruit just picked from the tree *out of season*'.[18] In the mid-eighteenth century similar accusations were made by the Abbot Pietro Chiari against the extravagant tastes of the nobility: 'The foods used by the common people are immediately rejected: low-priced meat, seasonal fruit and vegetables . . . Only rare and foreign products are desirable, strawberries in January, grapes in April and artichokes in September.' Our abbot goes on to note that neither are the natural flavours of foods appreciated; indeed it would seem that foods were not even fit to be served 'unless they lose in the preparation both their original appearance and their name. All sorts of tree barks and spices that have been imported since the discovery of America are used for their alteration.' *For their alteration*: gastronomic artifice, the camouflage of form and flavour and the use of 'a thousand ingredients for every dish so that in the end it tastes of none of them', and so that 'no one can say exactly what it is' would seem to be just one more way to cheat nature.[19] Meldini has written that '*ancien régime* cuisine was universalist. The total disregard for natural flavors . . . entirely dominated questions of place and season.'[20] As we have seen, it was at the beginning of the eighteenth century that 'enlightened' cooks and gastronomes attacked these practices and espoused a simple and 'natural' cuisine; this approach was new and revolutionary, and imposed itself upon the dominant culture with difficulty. Perhaps it has really taken hold only of late.

It is doubtful whether we can attribute either a happy symbiosis with nature or an enthusiastic love for the seasonality of food to the 'traditional' food culture, whether working-class or bourgeois-aristocratic. Certainly we can find evidence of these attitudes, and the very morality that condemned exotic tastes in food was based on a widespread 'seasonal' culture. Yet the opposite tendency was equally widespread and in some ways dominant. It was noted by Bartolomeo Stefani, chef to the Gonzaga court in the seventeenth century and author of an

important treatise on food, that foods can never logically be 'out
of season'. Do not marvel, he writes, if 'in these my discourses I
sometimes order things, for example asparagus, artichokes or
peas . . . in the months of January and February, and others that
seem at first to be out of season'; do not marvel if at a banquet
held in honour of Queen Christina of Sweden on 27 November
1655 I ordered as a first course (on 27 November!) strawberries
with white wine. Italy (and today we would say the world) is so
rich in good things that it is a pity not to serve them at the
tables of gourmets. In the face of such abundance – and Stefani
at this point includes a list of regional specialities – why restrict
one's horizon by sticking to 'home-town bread'? Given 'good
horses and a good purse' (that is to say, a rapid transportation
system and wealth) one can find in all seasons 'all those ingredients I call for'.[21]

Today, in this fortunate part of the world many have a 'good
purse' (at least for food); and as for 'good horses', transportation
companies offer, if anything, too many. The dream has been
realized and the land of Cuccagna conquered: finally we can live
for the moment (just like Adam and Eve before the Fall) without
worrying about conserving or stockpiling. Fresh seasonal food is
a luxury which only now – and not 'once upon a time' – can be
served at the tables of many. It represents not the restoration of
a lost dimension, but the difficult conquest of a right previously
reserved for the privileged few; it is a perspective which looks
more to the future than to the past as the indifferent flavours of
industrial foods and the depressing uniformity of fast foods
reproduce more faithfully than 'seasonal aromas and flavours'
the food culture from which most of us come. The precooked
foods offered by the food industry are certainly not a novelty but
simply the perfection of a technique tested over millennia: cooking
in stages (preliminary boiling for better preservation – especially of
meat – followed by final preparation at the appropriate time)
has long been one of the most standard and widespread culinary
techniques. Canned, vacuum-packed and frozen foods are precisely the solutions which our ancestors sought.

Pleasure, Health and Beauty

'If I were king, I would drink nothing but fat.' This phrase, spoken by a French peasant in a seventeenth-century text, reveals a basic, perhaps the principal, deficiency of the 'popular' diet of the past. We have spoken at length of oil, butter and lard, and considered the profound cultural values (in addition to economic and nutritional) which underlay these basic items of food preparation. The availability of fats, though, was often uncertain. Butter and olive oil were expensive, and the peasant diet depended above all on fats derived from swine (lard in its various forms) and, in some regions, on walnut oil. When these were lacking, other animal fats might be used (cow or sheep) or else low-quality vegetable oils (rape seed, linseed, hemp seed and others). These latter, however, had always to be bought, something which the peasantry never did with great enthusiasm. As for animal fats, they became ever less frequent in the peasant diet as grains came to occupy a dominant and often solo role. As a result, the basic cooking medium was often simply water.[22]

This scarcity – more or less severe or chronic according to time and place – engendered both physiological and psychological hardship. If we consider, for example, that a deficiency of vitamin D, found above all in animal and vegetable fats, can cause rickets and congenital deformity, then perhaps we have uncovered one more reason for the overwhelming presence of cripples and lame people in so many visual and literary images. As for the *want* of fat, in the double sense of both lack and desire, we can find abundant textual testimony of a sort which contrasts strikingly with our present-day food culture. The exquisite cheese offered to Charlemagne by a French bishop in order to win his favour was 'white and fatty'.[23] The fava and millet soup that an eighth-century Italian will instructed should be distributed to the poor three times a week was to be 'thick and well dressed with oil or lard'.[24] According to the

German version collected by the Grimm brothers, 100 cartloads of fat are pulled by a goat in the land of Cuccagna.[25] To describe cuisine as 'fatty' was to call it wealthy: Matteo Bandello wrote of Milan that it was 'the most opulent and abundant city of Italy, and the one where the greatest attention is paid to a fatty and well-supplied table'; the epithet 'fatty' was certainly not applied to Bologna pejoratively.

A corresponding aesthetic ideal derived from this situation: to be fat was beautiful, a sign of wealth and nutritional well-being, both in a general quantitive sense (eating plentifully) and also in a more specific qualitive one (consuming a large amount of fat). A fifteenth-century Italian novella is particularly significant in this regard: in it, a peasant is jealous of his fat neighbour, and being persuaded that only castration can allow attainment of a similar girth, acts accordingly. 'Fat' then carried eminently positive connotations; it could be used to define the highest level of Florentine aristocracy (the *popolo grasso*) at the moment of its political and social emergence. Franco Sacchetti described one of his characters as 'typical of his family, fat with an angelic and beautiful visage'. As for the preferences of women, consider the words of the female protagonist of one of Goldoni's plays: 'If you are to be mine, you must be handsome, fat and sturdy.'[26]

There are, however, contrary indications as well, and leaness or slenderness might also be virtues. The great eaters of carnival-esque epics, for example, were not necessarily stout; on the contrary, their value and strength was measured by their ability to *burn* all the caloric energy ingested. We can even read of slimming diets, pursued not for reasons of health (a topic already dealt with by Galen in a treatise written for the purpose)[27] but of aesthetics. The latter were, however, marginal and culturally censured instances. Olivier, for example, in his 1617 treatise on the 'imperfections and evils of women' considers among the typical vices of that sex the singular dietary sin, not of gluttony but of excessive delicacy in eating, the desire to deprive oneself, not out of a spirit of penitence but for the purpose of corporeal beauty. 'If they become too swollen with fat, they will plunge into a Lenten fast not for the glory of God nor for health, but in order to reacquire their just proportions.'[28] Moreover, painting and sculpture reveal that ideas about these 'proportions' were considerably different in the past from today.

The values of slimness, together with speed, productivity and efficiency, seem to have been proposed as a new aesthetic and cultural model only in the course of the eighteenth century, and by those social groups – primarily but not exclusively bourgeois – opposed to the 'old order' and intent upon advocating new ideological and political points of view. We have already noted in this context the value attributed to coffee, represented as the drink of intelligence and efficiency in contrast to traditional aristocratic idleness and dullness. A parallel contrast was that between fat and lean, nor is it a coincidence that this 'subvers-ive' beverage was defined by physicians of the time as 'dry' (according to the Galenic classification) and therefore dehydrat-ing. Moreover, using it as a substitute for beer or wine, 'hot' beverages rich (we would say) in calories, implied the subver-sion of widespread aesthetic canons.[29] On the other hand, nine-teenth-century puritanism, which shared obvious traits with traditional Christian penitence, relaunched the image of a lean, slender and productive body: the bourgeois body which 'sacri-fices itself' to the production of goods and wealth.

There is yet another side to the question. As we have already described, privilege in food tended gradually to fade in the course of the nineteenth century as a progressive 'democratiza-tion' of consumption was imposed by the logic of industrializa-tion. This is not to say that the food orgies of the rich – *nouveau* and established – were on the decline: certain pages of Thomas Mann on the 'fat' German bourgeoisie of the late nineteenth century expertly describe the vengeance with which the new ruling classes pursued the traditional models of power and ostentation.[30] None the less, something was changing since, as Braudel has taught us, pleasures too widely shared quickly lose their allure;[31] and it is no surprise that the food revolution suggested new models of behaviour for the elites, while the custom of heavy eating and ostentation, traditionally characteristic of the upper classes, came instead to be identified as 'popular' practices (first of the middle and lower bourgeoisie and then of the worker and peasant classes). It was in fact just in the middle of the nineteenth century that the Milanese Giovanni Rajberti published a treatise on 'good manners' intended – for the first time in Italy – not for the nobility but for the middle class: 'The Art of Entertaining Explained to the People'. According to this author, the 'people' in particular lacked such instruction while the lords, taught by much experience with banquets, already knew how to comport themselves. The 'people' on the other hand needed to be taught, especially with regard to measure and balance:

> The principal fault of popular banquets lies in not respecting the excellent maxim *ne quid nimis* [nothing in excess], applicable even with regard to the finest things. The fear of not doing oneself sufficient honour tends to dominate, and so in a sort of frenzy all notions of measure and restraint, the first elements of beauty in all the arts, are abandoned. Hence a flood of overdressed and over-flavored dishes, and too much emphasis on hot and over-stimulating foods.

Too often at these feasts 'the meal is so oppressively long and there is so much food that they seem designed to satisfy an elephant or a whale'.[32]

Meat, naturally, was at the centre of these discussions: a huge amount of it in satisfaction of an atavistic hunger and desire. Ever more meat was consumed in the twentieth century, in particular (after 1950) as a component of popular diets; correspondingly the figure of the great, insatiable eater, once shared with the elites, became a predominantly working-class image.[33] Meanwhile, the new upper classes developed other forms of distinction: light eating, vegetarian diets – themes which we have already encountered and which accompanied both the great rise in meat consumption and the corresponding decline of its image. Between the two camps there exists, however, both a real and a symbolic contiguity. The privilege of eating copiously has normally gone together with that of eating meat; and the (unsatisfied) desire for fat has been above all a desire for meat. The coupling of these two terms may sound strange to those – like ourselves – who are accustomed to think of meat as a source of protein and, in some sense, as an *alternative* to 'fattening' foods. But if we allow ourselves to enter into the culture and language of past centuries, then we find that these two concepts are almost identical: the primary function of meat was as a source of fat, and the fattier meats were valued more (both economically and culturally) than those 'leaner' meats we prize today. Such was the case in the third century AD when Diocletian used this criterion for fixing the prices of meat;[34] the same attitude is revealed in the language of the Church, which classi-fied a meat-based diet as 'fatty' and the Lenten diet, charac-terized above all by the absence of meat, as 'lean'. Paintings and miniatures (consider the still-lifes of the sixteenth and seven-teenth centuries) also attest to the not only metaphorical exact-ness of this correspondence, as they represent, for example, the fatty part of hams as occupying more than half of the cut. Moreover, even the muscle fibre of meat is rich in fat, and this fact explains the preference in traditional cuisine, especially 'popular' cuisine, for boiling, a cooking technique which, as opposed to spitting or grilling, does not waste this richness but dissolves and concentrates the fat in a broth recognized for its invigorating virtues, which can either be consumed as it is or reused for other purposes (sauces etc.).

The nutritional and aesthetic ideal of slimness, seconded by the usual prescriptions regarding health, became widespread in Europe in the first half of the twentieth century; though still in the 1950s the women depicted on billboards and advertise-ments tended to reveal the traditional preference for a full figure. Only in the last two or three decades of the century has the 'lean' ideology been truly triumphant, and in spite of vari-ous contradictions: 'dieting' today has become not so much a

daily habit as a daily topic of discussion, preferably at table. It
is in any case undeniable that, on a cultural level, our relationship with food has been overturned: the danger and fear of
plenty have replaced the danger and fear of famine. Consider the
changing meaning of the word 'diet': invented by the Greeks to
indicate the daily nutritional regime (but also more generally of
life) that each individual ought to *construct* according to his own
personal needs and characteristics, it has come to mean – in
common usage – the limitation or denial of food; it has taken on
a negative rather than positive meaning. It is a choice that our
consumerist society would seem to propose on the basis not of
the moral or penitential values with which religious culture has
traditionally invested such behaviour, but rather for aesthetic,
hygienic and utilitarian motives (as noted by Barthes, light
eating is a sign and tool of efficiency and therefore of power).[35]
None the less, it is difficult to avoid the impression that the
success of 'diets' in mass society *also* hides reticent penitential
values, a desire for denial and, we might say, self-punishment
linked to the abundance (or rather excess) of food available and
the frankly hedonistic images used in publicity and mass media
to encourage consumption (not only of food). Pleasure, it seems,
continues to frighten: the weight of a religious tradition that
teaches the association of pleasure with guilt and sin is too
heavy.[36] Nor have the confident declarations of a now self-
defined 'secular' culture sufficed to cancel these associations.
Even in the 1960s a French public opinion study revealed that
advertising based *openly* on the enjoyment of eating was destined
to fail as the potential consumers would have felt guilty. Today
the situation has changed, and yet there remains the anxiety to
search elsewhere – that is not in pleasure – for the justification
of gastronomic and dietary choices: food which 'is good for you'
undoubtedly inspires greater enthusiasm.

As for the abundance of food, it clearly creates new and
difficult problems – once it becomes a permanent and socially
widespread phenomenon – for a culture we know to be marked
by the fear of famine. This fear continues to form attitudes and

behaviour, though the traditional schizophrenia between privation and waste, between careful parsimony and wild indulgence,
is clearly incompatible with the new situation. The irresistible
allure of excess, impressed upon our bodies and minds by millennia of famine, has begun to shock us now that abundance has
become a daily reality. In wealthy countries, the diseases of
nutritional excess have come to replace those of nutritional
deficiency; and a new and unprecedented fear (the Americans
call it 'fear of obesity') has inverted the ancient fear of famine
and, like the latter, exerts a stronger influence on individual
psychology than the circumstances merit: studies show that
over half of those who go on diets because they consider themselves overweight in fact are not. One excess has been conquered
by another, and a friendly and intelligent relationship with food
seems still to be out of reach. Abundance, however, should allow
us to achieve it with greater calm than was possible in the past.

Notes

1 The Basis for a Common Language

1 This passage of Fulgentius comes from *Mythologies*, I; see Novati (1899, p. 114).

2 For a detailed list of the disasters and food crises that afflicted Italy from the fourth to sixth centuries, see Ruggini (1961, pp. 152–76, 466–89). For the European situation in general, see Doehaerd (1971).

3 On the demographic history of Europe, see, in addition to the classic works of Beloch (1908 and others), also Russell (1958), Reinhard and Armengaud (1961), Durand (1977), Biraben (1979) and the synthesizing work of McEvedy and Jones (1978). Particularly relevant to the themes addressed in the present work is Livi Bacci (1991).

4 Gregory of Tours, *Historia Francorum*, VII, 45 (ed. B. Krusch in *Monumenta Germaniae Historica, Scriptores rerum merovingicarum*, I, 1).

5 The passages of Procopius are taken from *De bello gothico*, II, 20 (ed. J. Haury, Leipzig, 1963).

6 On penitential books, see Vogel (1969); on the importance of these texts to the history of nutrition, see Muzzarelli (1982) and Bonassie (1989).

7 Paul the Deacon, *Historia Langobardorum*, II, 4 (ed. L. Bethmann and G. Waitz, Hanover, 1878).

8 For the topics addressed in this section, see Duby (1974, pp. 17–24) and Montanari (1988a, pp. 13–22).

9 On Roman nutrition, see André's (1981) fundamental work.

10 On the importance (though secondary and culturally marginal) of methods for extracting resources from the wild in Roman times, see Giardina (1981) and Traina (1986).

11 On hunting in the Greek world, see Longo (1989); on Roman hunting and its basically 'exotic' character, see Aymard (1951).

12 Ovid, *Metamorphoses*, XIII, vss. 652–4 (trans. F. J. Miller), London, 1929, vol. II, p. 275.

13 Plutarch, *Life of Alcibiades*, XV, 4 (trans. B. Perrin), London, 1959, vol. IV, p. 39.

14 On the centrality of shepherding to the Roman economy, see Gabba and Pasquinucci (1979).

15 On imperial distributions to the people of Rome, see Mazzarino (1951, pp. 217ff) and Corbier (1989, p. 121).

16 Caesar, *The Gallic War*, VI, 22 (trans. H. J. Edwards), London, 1958, p 347.

17 Tacitus, *Germania*, XXIII (*The Complete Works of Tacitus*, New York, Modern Library, 1942, p. 720).

18 Procopius, *De bello gothico*, II, 15.

19 From Jordanes I use *Getica*, LI, 267 for the lesser Goths, XXIV, 122–3 for the Huns, and III, 21 for the Lapps; see also Paul the Deacon, *Historia Langobardorum*, I, 5.

20 Procopius, *De bello vandalico*, IV, 2.

21 Braudel (1981, p. 107).

22 For *The Story of Mac Datho's Pig* (Scéla Mucce meic Dathó), see Sayers (1990, p. 93) as well as Grottanelli (1981, pp. 137–8).

23 The citations from Snorri's *Edda* (chs 38 and 6) are taken from the version of G. Chiesa Isnardi (Milano, 1975, pp. 114, 68). See Branston (1955, pp. 57–8).

24 Hesiod, *The Works and the Days*, vss. 106ff (*Hesiod*, trans. R. Lattimore, Ann Arbor, 1959, p. 31).

25 For Democritus and Dicaearchus, see Longo (1989, pp. 13, 17); for Plato, see Vattuone (1985, p. 188) (with reference to *Laws*, VI, 782bc); for Virgil, see *Georgics*, II, 815–21.

26 Varro, *De re rustica*, II, 11.

27 Pythagoras' statement is reported by Diogenes Laertius in the *Lives of Eminent Philosophers*, VIII, I, 35 (trans. R. D. Hicks), London, 1950, p. 351.

28 For the Epic of Gilgamesh, see *Gilgamesh* (trans. J. Gardner and J. Maier), New York, 1984. On the myth of the Golden Age, see Le Goff (1988, pp. 227ff). On vegetarian philosophies in the ancient world, see Haussleiter (1935). On taboos regarding the consumption of meat, see Simoons (1981).

29 The excerpts from the *Historia Augusta* are taken from the biographies of Didius Julianus, ch. III (author Elius Spartianus); of the three Gordians,

ch. XIX (Julius Capitolinus); of Septimius Severus, ch. XIX (Aelius Spartianus); of Clodius Albinus, ch. XI (Julius Capitolinus); of the two Gallieni, ch. XVI (Trebellius Pollio); of the two Maximini, ch. IV, XXVIII (Julius Capitolinus); of Firmus, ch. IV (Flavius Vopiscus). See *Scriptores Historiae Augustae*, ed. E. Hohl, Leipzig, 1965; in addition to the Italian translation of F. Roncoroni, *Storia Augusta*, Milan, 1972 (pp. 236, 579, 272, 313, 669, 524, 549, 874 for the excerpts cited), there is also that of P. Soverini, *Scrittori della Storia Augusta*, Turin, 1983.

30 In addition to Montanari (1988a, pp. 15–16), see also id. (1979) on the development after the fifth century of a new relationship (cultural as well as productive) between man and nature which took advantage of the vast possibilities offered by open spaces.

31 Plutarch, *Life of Coriolanus*, 3 (*The Lives of the Noble Grecians and Romans*, the Dryden translation, Chicago, 1952, p. 175).

32 Cornelius Celsus, *De medicina*, II, 18 (trans. W. G. Spencer), London, 1948, pp. 191–3.

33 For the treatise of Anthimus (*De observatione ciborum epistula ad Theuderi-cum regem Francorum*), see Montanari (1988a, pp. 207–8).

34 For the link between meat and the ideology of violence, see Montanari (1988a, pp. 24–5, 47).

35 The prescription of Lothair (*Concilium et capitulare de clericorum percussori-bus*, a. 814–27) is in *Capitularia regum francorum*, I, no. 176 (*Monumenta Germaniae Historica, Leges*, I).

36 On Christian food symbols, established following disagreements and alternatives during the first and second centuries, see Vogel (1976).

37 On Jewish rules of diet, see Soler (1973).

38 On Christian food symbols, see Montanari (1988a, pp. 14–15).

39 The eulogy of Ambrose is found in St Augustine, *Confessions*, V, 13 (trans. H. Chadwick), Oxford, 1991, p. 87.

40 *Patrologia Latina*, 46, col. 835.

41 Sermon LXVII of Peter Chrysologus in ibid., 52.

42 With regard to vineyard expansion in northern Europe, one should also take into account the apparently mild climate of the eighth to eleventh centuries; see Duby (1974, pp. 11–12) and especially Le Roy Ladurie (1971, pp. 254ff). This development does not, however, seem adequate to explain an essentially cultural and 'anthropic' change of this sort.

43 The *Vita Remigi* of Hincmar is found in the *Monumenta Germaniae Historica, Scriptores rerum merovingicarum*, III (the episode cited appears in ch. 19, p. 311). The biblical reference is to the first book of Kings 17:16.

44 The *Vita Carileffi* is found in *Monumenta Germaniae Historica, Scriptores rerum merovingicarum*, III, ch. 7.

45 From the *Vita Columbani* of Giona (ed. B. Krusch, Hanover and Leipzig, 1905) I have used, in sequence, ch. 27, 16, 17.

46 For the dispositions of the Council of Aix, see *Monumenta Germaniae Historica, Concilia*, II, p. 401.

47 *Rabani Mauri Vita altera*, in *Patrologia Latina*, 107, col. 73.

48 Henry II Plantagenet's refusal to drink wine is reported by Walter Map in *De nugis curialium* (*Courtiers' Trifles*), V, 2 (trans. and ed. M. R. James), Oxford, 1983, p. 409; details of Ilispon's table are included in the same work, IV, 15, p. 389.

49 On the merits of Hugh, see Gilo, *Vita Hugonis*, I, 5 (ed. E. H. J. Cowdrey, 'Memorials of Abbot Hugh of Cluny', *Studi Gregoriani*, XI, 1978, pp. 17–175).

50 On 'moderation' and 'excess' as cultural values, see Montanari (1989a, pp. xiv–xviii).

51 The biography of Severus Alexander (by Elius Lampridius) is found in the *Historia Augusta*; I have cited ch. XXXVII.

52 Plutarch, *Life of Demosthenes*, 16 (*The Lives of the Noble Grecians and Romans*, the Dryden translation, Chicago, 1952, p. 697).

53 From Xenophanes I have cited 'The Administration of the Home', VII, 6; for Suetonius, see *De vita Caesarum*, III, 42.

54 For the cultural image of the 'great eater', see Montanari (1979, pp. 457–64).

55 On the borrowing of animal names, see Fumagalli (1976, pp. 6–7).

56 This episode is recounted in chapter 46 of *Edda*, pp. 129–32.

57 The story of Adelchis is in G. C. Alessio, ed., *Cronaca di Novalesa*, III, 21, Turin, 1982, pp. 169–71.

58 The passage of Aristophanes is found in *The Acharnians*.

59 On Odo's frugality, see the *Vita Odonis* of Johannes Italicus in *Patrologia Latina*, 133, col. 51.

60 The episode regarding the Duke of Spoleto is taken from the *Antapodosis* (J. Becker, ed., *Liudprandi Opera*. Hanover and Leipzig, 1915, p. 18).

61 The judgements of Nicephorus Phocas and Otto of Saxony are found in the *Relatio de legatione constantinopolitana* (ibid., pp. 196–7).

62 For the 1059 synod, see *Monumenta Germaniae Historica, Concilia aevi karolini*, II, p. 401. See also Rouche (1984, pp. 278–9).

63 On monastic diet, see Montanari (1988a, pp. 63ff). (and pp. 20–1 on the greater strictness of northern as compared to Mediterranean regulations).

64 On the (peasant?) Utopia of the land of Cuccagna, see pp. 94–7 below.

65 The calculations of dietary rations are found in Rouche (1973, 1984).

66 Moulin (1978, p. 104).

67 The descriptions of Charlemagne's dietary habits are taken from Einhard, *Vita Karoli Magni*, chs 22, 24 (ed. G. H. Pertz, Hanover, 1863).

68 On the very different characteristics of environment and modes of production in the period from the sixth to the tenth century, see Montanari (1979; 1984, pp. 5ff).

69 On the multiple notion of famine, see Montanari (1984, pp. 191ff; 1988, pp. 36–7).

70 The two passages of Gregory of Tours are found in the *Historia Francorum*, X, 30; III, 37.

71 Andrea da Bergamo, *Historia*, in *Monumenta Germaniae Historica, Scriptores rerum italicarum et germanicarum saecc. VI–XI*, p. 229.

72 *Annales Fuldenses* in *Monumenta Germaniae Historica, Scriptores*, I, p. 387.

73 The inventory referred to is the *Breve de curte Milliarina* (Migliarina in Emilia, property of the monastery of Santa Giulia di Brescia), published in *Inventari altomedievali di terre, coloni e redditi*, Rome, 1979, pp. 203–4. The revised dating of the inventory (eighth century, as opposed to the tenth as traditionally believed) is the fruit of recent research done by Carboni.

74 Sidonius Apollinaris, *Carmina*, 24 in *Monumenta Germaniae Historica, Auctores antiquissimi*, VIII.

75 For the trout of Gregory of Tours, see *Liber in gloria martyrum*, 75 in *Monumenta Germaniae Historica, Scriptores rerum merovingicarum*, I, p. 539. For the other references, see Montanari (1979, pp. 293–5) and also the important work of Zug Tucci (1985).

76 On the wheat crisis and subsequent success of lesser grains, especially rye, see Montanari (1979, pp. 109ff).

77 Pliny, *Natural History*, XVIII, 40 (trans. H. Rackham), London, 1950, p. 279.

78 On the yields of different grains, see Montanari (1984, pp. 55ff).

79 On the typology and colour of bread, see Montanari (1990a, pp. 309–17); on the importance of *pulmenta* made from lesser grains, see ibid., pp. 304ff. See also Bautier (1984), especially p. 37 on the different evaluations of rye bread. Gregory of Tours writes of the bishop of Langres in *Vitae Patrum*, VII, 2 (*Monumenta Germaniae Historica, Scriptores rerum merovingicarum*, I, 2, p. 237). On the greater importance of wheat cultivation in southern Italy and that region's adherence to the Roman model, see Montanari (1988a, pp. 124ff).

80 Rabanus Maurus, *De Universo*, 22, 1 (*Patrologia Latina*, 111, col. 590).

81 On the importance of salt curing for the preservation of meat and fish, see Montanari (1988a, pp. 184–6). Isidore of Seville's description of salt is in *Etymologiae*, XVI, 2 (quoting Pliny, *Natural History*, XXXI, 9).

82 On the story of the Syrian hermit (*Vitae Patrum*, IV, IX in *Patrologia Latina*, 73, col. 822) and its cultural implications, see Montanari (1990, pp. 281ff).

83 On the forest as the 'desert' of the western ascetics, see Le Goff (1983).

84 On the 'mobility' of the wild–domestic border, see Montanari (1990a, pp. 297ff) and also André (1981, p. 49) for analogous observations regarding the Roman period.

85 On the culture of the 'garden', see Montanari (1979, pp. 309–71).

86 On the wild cow and domesticated deer, see Montanari (1979, p. 271).

87 On the similarity between pigs and boars, see Baruzzi and Montanari (1981).

88 On the marsh–fishpond connection, see Montanari (1979, p. 49).

89 Hildegard of Bingen, *Subtilitatum diversarum naturarum creaturarum libri novem*, I, *Praefatio* (in *Patrologia Latina*, 197, cols 1126–7).

90 On the differing points of view of the nobility and the monastic orders with regard to nature, see Montanari (1988b, esp. pp. 67–8).

91 *Vita Menelei*, in *Monumenta Germaniae Historica, Scriptores rerum merovingicarum*, V, pp. 150–1.

92 *Vita Leonardi*, ch. 8 in *Monumenta Germaniae Historica, Scriptores rerum merovingicarum*, III.

93 *Vita Iohannis abbatis Reomaensis*, in *Monumenta Germaniae Historica, Scriptores rerum merovingicarum*, III, p. 510.

94 On the conflicts between rural communities and the seigniory (at first especially the monasteries) over forestland, see Fumagalli (1978, pp. 87–8) and Montanari (1979, pp. 90–3).

95 On the extensive nature of 'medieval' agriculture (though it remained so until the eighteenth century), see pp. 38–43 below.

2 The Turning-Point

1 For the two Bobbio inventories, see Montanari (1979, p. 469) (with reference to Fumagalli 1966).

2 Braudel (1981, p. 104).

3 On the question of grain yields, see Montanari (1984, pp. 55–85) and the works there cited.

4 The idea of a forced choice with regard to medieval land reclamation has been described by Fumagalli (1970, p. 328).

5 On the extensive nature of medieval agriculture and the 'vicious circle' which was only broken by the introduction of artificial pasture in rotation with planted fields in the eighteenth and nineteenth centuries, see Montanari (1984, pp. 32ff, 156ff) and Slicher van Bath (1963, pp. 239ff).

6 For the distinction between the *fructuosa* and *infructuosa* forest, see Fumagalli (1976, p. 5) and Montanari (1979, pp. 471–2).

7 On the development of the fruit-bearing chestnut groves, especially from the eleventh and twelfth centuries, see Toubert (1973, I, pp. 191–2) and, for a more general discussion, Cherubini (1984, pp. 147–71).

8 For the chronology of European famine between 750 and 1100, I have used Bonnassie (1989, pp. 1043–4).

9 Braudel (1981, p. 74).

10 Radulfus Glaber, *Historiae*, IV, 10 (the latest edition of which was edited by M. Prou and appeared in 1886).

11 For the famines discussed below, and also ergotism in eleventh-century Europe, see Le Goff (1967, p. 32).

12 On the events which led to the appropriation from peasant communities of the right to use uncultivated nature by the powerful, see Montanari (1984, pp. 159ff, 174ff); and also Zug Tucci (1983).

13 On seigniorial violence in the eleventh century, see Fumagalli (1978, pp. 243–9).

14 Jones (1980, p. 214).

15 For the transition from the adjectival use to the noun use of *comune*, see Montanari (1988c, p. 122).

16 See Hilton (1973) for the tenth-century revolt in Normandy, as well as for those of 1381 and 1525; passages quoted are on pp. 71–2.

17 Abelard's 'rule' for Héloïse in Letter VIII. See P. Abelardo, *L'origine del monachesimo femminile e la Regola* (trans. S. Di Meglio), Padua, 1988, pp. 217–18.

18 *La Bataille de Caresme et Charnage* (ed. G. Lozinski), Paris, 1933 (vss. 38ff for the dislike of the poor for Lent). See *La battaglia di Quaresima e Carnevale* (ed. M. Lecco), Parma, 1990 for its introduction and bibliography; and Chevalier (1982, pp. 194–5) for the social and economic climate in which the text is set.

19 Isidore of Seville, *Etymologiae*, XX, II, 15.

20 On the economic and cultural obsession with bread, see Montanari (1984, pp. 157, 201ff).

21 On the famine of 843, see the *Annales Bertiniani* in *Monumenta German-iae Historica, Scriptores*, I, p. 439.

22 Radulfus Glaber, *Historiae*, IV, 12.

23 On the Swedish famine of 1099 and also the question of 'rational response', see Bonnassie (1989, p. 1045).

24 On the agronomic texts of Moorish Spain, see Bolens (1980) (pp. 470–1 for the passage cited here).

25 On the 779 harvest and the passage from the *Vita Benedicti Anianensis*, see Montanari (1979, p. 433).

26 Ibid., p. 438, n. 48.

27 On the economic and social significance of the 'reconversion to wheat', see Montanari (1984, p. 163).

28 Bonvesin de la Riva, *De magnalibus Mediolani*, IV, 14.

29 On the consumption of white bread in the Tuscan countryside, see Pinto (1982, pp. 129ff).

30 On the prevalence of wheat in southern Italian production, but not necessarily consumption, see Montanari (1988a, pp. 124ff.).

31 The poem of William of Aquitaine is entitled 'The Red Cat' in A. Roncaglia, ed., *Poesia dell'età cortese*, Milan, 1961, p. 287.

32 For Humbert of Romans, see 'Sermo XXX ad conversos', in *Maxima bibliotheca veterum patrum*, XXV, Lyon, 1677, p. 470.

33 For Giovanni Sercambi, see *Novelle*, CLII (G. Sinicropi, ed., Bari, 1972, II, p. 733).

34 Trans. note: The Italian *gola* means both throat and gluttony; the *double entendre* of the original title, 'La gola della città', is lost in trans-lation.

35 The passage from Cassiodorus is in *Variae*, VII, 29 (A. J. Fridh, ed., *Corpus Christianorum, Series latina*, XCVI, Turnhout, 1973).

36 On late Roman victualling policy, see especially Ruggini (1961).

37 On late medieval ruralization, which affected all aspects of civil life (economic, social, cultural, institutional), see Fumagalli (1976). See Bois (1989) for the thesis according to which the energy of the country-side was 'liberated' with the decline of oppressive urban regulation, and that this was the basis for the rebirth of the markets (first in the countryside, then in the cities) in the tenth and eleventh centuries.

38 On the victualling policy of medieval cities, see Montanari (1988c, pp. 113ff); and Montanari (1984, p. 163) for the similarities between 'public' statutes and 'private' contracts. See also Peyer (1950) and Pinto (1978, pp. 107ff).

39 The *Thesaurus rusticorum* of Paganino Bonafede can be found in L. Frati,

ed., *Rimatori bolognesi del trecento*, Bologna, 1915; cited here are vss. 169–70, p. 108.

40 For English agronomic texts of the thirteenth and fourteenth centuries, see D. Oschinsky, ed., *Walter of Henley and other Treatises on Estate Management and Accounting*, Oxford, 1971.

41 G. Fasoli and P. Sella, eds, *Statuti di Bologna dell'anno 1288*, I, Vatican City, 1937, p. 123.

42 For the markedly urban character of wheat consumption (in spite of the examples here cited), a status symbol sought after by *all* social classes, see de La Roncière (1982, pp. 430–1 and *passim*).

43 G. Manganelli, ed., *Il novellino*, Milan, 1957, novella LXXXV, pp. 96–7.

44 We shall take this topic up again in ch. 4.

45 This passage from Bonaventure occurs in the *Quod renunciationem*; see Mollat (1978, p. 131).

46 Ibid., p. 158.

47 For Riccobaldo da Ferrara (*Rerum Italicarum Scriptores*, IX, p. 128), see Montanari (1984, p. 166).

48 For Wernher der Gartenaere's *Helmbrecht*, See Martelotti (1984).

49 For the *Chanson de Guillaume*, see J. Frappier, *Les Chansons de geste du cycle de Guillaume d'Orange*, Paris, 1955–65, I, pp. 126–7.

50 A Martellotti and E. Durante, eds, *Libro di buone vivande. La cucina tedesca dell'età cortese*, Fasano, 1991, p. 20.

51 See ibid., pp. 21–2 for Chrétien de Troyes, as well as Le Goff (1982).

52 On the invention of 'good manners', Elias (1969) remains a fundamental work.

53 On the gastronomic initiation of Tirant lo Blanc, see Crous (1990) and Tudela and Castells (1990).

54 For Innocent III's *De contemptu mundi*, see *Patrologia Latina*, 217 (cols 723–4 for the excerpts cited).

55 On the spread of spices beginning in the centuries before 1000, see Laurioux (1983, 1989a).

56 On the freshness of meat and fish consumed and the debate over the use of spices, see Flandrin and Redon (1981, p. 402) and Rebora (1987, pp. 1520ff). For a general discussion of medieval gastronomy, see Henisch (1976) and Laurioux (1989b).

57 For the *Ordinaciones* of Peter III the Great of Aragon (to which we shall return), see Montanari (1990b) (the reference to 'bedroom spices' is in book II, ch. 2).

58 On the relationship between pharmacology and gastronomy, see Plouvier (1988).

59 Rebora (1987, p. 1523).
60 Ibid. pp. 1441, 1471 and *passim* for the differences between 'bourgeois' and 'courtly' cookery books.
61 For Bernard's reprimand of the Cluniacs, the *Statutes* of Peter the Venerable and Ulrich's *Consuetudines*, see Montanari (1988a, p. 90).
62 See Le Goff (1977) for the dream of the fabulous Orient.
63 Laurioux (1989a) (p. 206 for the citation of Joinville).
64 G. Sercambi, *Novelle*, CVIIII (G. Sinicropi, ed., Bari, 1972, I, p. 480) for the use of recipe books by professional cooks.
65 G. Sermini, *Le novelle* XXIX (ed. G. Vettori), Rome, 1968, p. 494.
66 Salimbene da Parma, *Cronica*, G. Scalia, Bari, 1966, I, p. 322.
67 Flandrin (1984, pp. 77–8).
68 Ibid., p. 81.
69 On the relation between the *urban* availability of ovens and the importance of 'cakes', see Rebora (1987, pp. 1513–18).
70 G. Sercambi, *Novelle*, LXXV, (I, p. 330) for the habit of city-dwellers of frequenting the cooks' shops.
71 For the relation between 'high' and common cuisine, see Rebora (1987, pp. 1518–19).
72 For the 'famine cakes' of 1246, see *Chronicon Parmense*, in *Rerum Italicarum Scriptores*, IX, p. 772.

3 To Each His Own

1 Le Goff (1967, p. 305).
2 On the European famines of the thirteenth century, see Mollat (1978, pp. 158–62).
3 On Italian famines in particular, see Pinto (1978).
4 For the descriptions found in the chronicles, see also Montanari (1984, pp. 202, 206–7).
5 On the controversial link between nutrition and disease, see Livi Bacci (1991).
6 Biraben (1975, p. 147).
7 Slicher van Bath (1963, pp. 89–90).
8 On the demographic impact of the plague, see Helleiner (1967, pp. 8–9); the estimate of 25 per cent made more than a century ago by J. F. Hecker is still held to be valid; there were, however, areas for which estimates run as high as 50–60 per cent and above.
9 Matteo Villani, *Historia*, I, 5 (see *Croniche storiche di Giovanni, Matteo, e Filippo Villani*, Milan, 1848).

10 Giovanni de Mussis, *Chronicon Placentinum* in *Rerum Italicarum Scriptores*, XVI, pp. 581–2; see also Rebora (1987, pp. 1502–4).

11 Braudel (1981, pp. 190ff) (p. 193 for the phrase quoted). For the examples cited below, see, in addition to this work, Dyer (1986), Wyczanski and Dembinska (1986), van der Wee (1963), Neveux (1973), Slicher van Bath (1963, pp. 84 and *passim*), Stouff (1969, 1970), Aymard and Bresc (1975), Guiffrida (1975), Chevalier (1958), Fiumi (1959, 1972) and Le Roy Ladurie (1974); see Bennassar and Goy 1975 for some general considerations.

12 See Abel (1937) (but also 1935) for the hypothesis regarding the evolution of meat consumption; these works also take into account previous studies of G. Schmoller. See Mandrou (1961, p. 967) for their evaluation.

13 On the increasing consumption of mutton in the second half of the fourteenth century as an alternative to traditional dietary patterns (and in particular pork consumption), the Florentine case as described by de La Roncière (1982, p. 707 and *passim*) is representative. See also Redon (1984, p. 123). Archaeological sources also confirm this tendency: see Tozzi (1981) and Beck Bossard (1984, p. 25) (and p. 20 for the *rural* connotations of pork consumption). On the increase of sheep-raising (and the practice of transhumance), especially in relation to the wool industry, see Slicher van Bath (1963, pp. 142–3, 165–8) and Wickham (1985). The citation regarding Forez is in Alexandre Bidon and Beck Bossard (1984, p. 69); that from Sermini is in *Novelle*, XII, p. 284).

14 On the medical distrust of penned animals, see Nada Patrone (1981a, pp. 281–2).

15 For the events of 1465 and 1494, see Montanari (1984, p. 183).

16 On meat abstinence as a central theme of Christian culture (and the relevant complex motivations), see Montanari (1988a, pp. 64ff).

17 On the slow and contested rise of fish as the principal and, ultimately, natural meat substitute, see above all Zug Tucci (1985, pp. 293–322). For the following references to Beda, the *Domesday Book*, Thietmar of Merseberg, Charlemagne's capitulary, Thomas de Cantimpré, Albertus Magnus, the *Vita* of Thomas Aquinas, and Giovanni Michiel, see ibid., pp. 303–5, 310–12, 316.

18 On the contrast between Carnival and Lent, see Chevalier (1982), Grinberg and Kinser (1983) and Lecco, *La battaglia di Quaresima e Carnevale*.

19 On the Florentine meat and fish sellers, see Redon (1984, p. 121).

20 See pp. 43–7 above.

21 On Beukelszoon's invention, see Braudel (1981, p. 215).

22 On herring and then cod fishing, see ibid., pp. 215–20.

23 On the sale of dried and salted sturgeon, see Messedaglia (1941–2) and Rebora (1987, pp. 1507–10); on salmon fishing, see Halard (1983).

24 For the Venetian decree of 1562, see Paccagnella (1983, pp. 44–6).

25 The Hippocratic text referred to is *Regimen*, III, 67–73 (see *Hippocrates*, trans. W. H. S. Jones, London, 1959, IV. pp. 367–95); see also Montanari (1989a, pp. 29–36).

26 For the Carolingian capitularies, the text of Alcuin and the *Vita* of Appianus, see Montanari (1979, pp. 457–8, 468).

27 Salimbene da Parma, *Cronica*, p. 409.

28 For the *Ordinaciones* of Peter (IV/8 for the relation between quantity of food and social status), see Montanari (1990b).

29 For the provisions regarding the poor (I/3, I/6, II/13, III/18–20, IV/29), see ibid.

30 For Sabadino degli Arienti's novella, see *Le Porretane*, Bari, 1914, pp. 227–30.

31 The death of Bertoldo is told by G. C. Croce in P. Camporesi, ed., *Le sottilissime astuzie di Bertoldo*, Turin, 1978, p. 74; see also Montanari (1991, pp. IX–XII).

32 For Piero de' Crescenzi, see *Trattato della agricoltura, traslato nella favella fiorentina, rivisto dallo 'Nferigno accademico della Crusca*, Bologna, 1784, I, p. 180.

33 For Albini, see Nada Patrone (1981b, pp. 439–40).

34 For the social distinctions of Michele Savonarola, see J. Nystedt, ed., *Libreto de tutte le cosse che se magnano; un'opera dietetica del sec. XV*, Stockholm, 1988, p. 14 (in which the editor attributes a 'realistic social awareness' to the author, an interpretation with which I evidently disagree).

35 On the four booklets of Sylvius, see Dupèbe (1982) (the quotation is from p. 52).

36 For the treatises on nobility, see Maravall (1979, pp. 54–8) and Jouanna (1977, pp. 21–30).

37 On infant nutrition, see Fontaine (1982) and Lazard (1982), as well as Alexandre Bidon and Closson (1985).

38 G. Cirelli's *Il villano smascherato* has been published by G. L. Masetti Zannini in *Rivista di storia dell' agricoltura*, 1967, 1; the passage quoted is from ch. 6.

39 For the scientific theories on the natural order of the world and the parallelism between natural 'society' and human society, I use Grieco

(1987, pp. 159ff). The quotations from Piero de' Crescenzi and Corniolo della Cornia on plant 'digestion' are taken respectively from *Trattato della agricoltura*, I, p. 50 and *La divina villa* (ed. L. Bonelli Conenna), Siena, 1982, p. 47.

40 The physician referred to is Castore Durante da Gualdo, author of a *Tesoro della sanità* published in 1565 in Latin and in 1586 in Italian; see the ed by E. Camillo (Milan, 1936); the quotation cited here is from p. 136.

41 Andreolli (1988, p. 64).

42 Matteo Bandello, *Novelle*, II, XVII (ed. G. Brognoligo), Bari, 1931, III, p. 42.

43 Landi's *Commentario delle più notabili e mostruose cose d'Italia e d'altri luoghi* was published in Venice in 1548. For the passage cited here, see Faccioli (1987, p. 279).

44 The passage from *Lazzarillo de Tormes* is from ch. 3 (in the Italian translation of G. Greco, Milan, 1990, p. 52).

45 See Grieco (1987, pp. 176ff).

46 The Bologna banquet of 1487 is described by C. Ghirardacci in *Historia di Bologna* (in *Rerum Italicarum Scriptores*, XXXIII/I, pp. 235–41); see also Montanari (1989a, pp. 483–8).

47 On the Utopia of Cuccagna, see Graf (1892), Cocchiara (1956, pp. 159–87), Cioranescu (1971), Camporesi (1978, pp. 77–125) (the passage cited is taken from p. 115) and also Fortunati and Zucchini (1989) (especially the contribution of Richter). For the *fabliau de Coquaigne*, see G. C. Belletti, ed., *Fabliaux. Racconti comici medievali* Ivrea, 1982, no. IX, pp. 95–105 (for the original version, E. Barbazan and D. M. Meon, *Fabliaux et contes des poètes français des XIe, XIIe, XIVe et XVe siècles, tirés des meilleurs auteurs*, Paris, 1808, IV, 175).

48 Boccaccio, *Decameron*, VIII, 3.

49 On Christmas in Naples, see J. W. von Goethe, *Italian Journey* (trans. R. Heitner), New York, 1989, pp. 268–9.

4 Europe and the World

1 The *Capitolo qual narra l'essere di un mondo novo trovato nel Mar Oceano* is published in Camporesi (1976, pp. 309–11).

2 The *Relazione d'alcune cose della Nuova Spagna* can be found in G. B. Ramusio, *Navigazioni e viaggi*, VI (ed. M. Milanesi), Turin, 1988 (see Montanari 1991, pp. 85–6).

3 For data on European demographic growth, see Livi Bacci (1991, p. 2) (with reference to Biraben 1979). For Castille, I use Slicher van Bath (1963, p. 195); ibid., pp. 199ff for a synthetic description of the sixteenth-century process of agricultural colonization.

4 Braudel (1981, p. 74).

5 For the booklets of Sylvius, see the references in ch. 3, p. 87.

6 For the treatise 'sopra la carestia', see Camporesi (1983a, pp. 45–7); id., 1980.

7 On the spread of buckwheat in Europe, see Slicher van Bath (1963, pp. 264–5).

8 On the 'first' introduction of corn into Europe, see Hémardinquer (1973), Slicher van Bath (1963, pp. 265–6) and Braudel (1981, pp. 164–6). In particular, for France see Hémardinquer (1963); for Italy, the classic and not yet surpassed Messedaglia (1927) as well as Coppola (1979); and for the Balkan peninsula, Stoianovich (1970).

9 On the timing and nature of the spread of the potato in Europe, see, in addition to the classic work of Salaman (1985), Slicher van Bath (1963, pp. 266ff) and Braudel (1981, pp. 167–71).

10 For the texts of 1550 and 1560, see Braudel (1981, pp. 194–5).

11 For the studies of Abel, see pp. 68–71 above.

12 For Geneva, see Piuz (1970), especially p. 143 on meat consumption.

13 Braudel (1981, p. 196).

14 For Italian data of the fourteenth and fifteenth centuries, see Mazzi (1980, pp. 84–5).

15 For general European data, see Neveux (1973).

16 Piuz (1970, pp. 130, 140–1).

17 Goubert (1966, p. 167).

18 Braudel (1981, p. 132).

19 Thuillier (1970, p. 156).

20 Piuz (1970, pp. 138–9).

21 Ibid., p. 140.

22 Braudel (1981, pp. 143–4).

23 Piuz (1970, p. 136).

24 Bloch (1970, p. 233).

25 On the image of the 'baker-king', see Kaplan (1976); see also Tannahill (1973, p. 316).

26 On 'bourgeois ferocity' and measures against the poor, see Braudel (1981, pp. 75–6); unfortunately, this expression is lost in the English version.

27 Ibid.

28 Pompeo Vizani, *I due ultimi libri delle historie della sua patria*. Bologna, 1608, pp. 138–9.

29 On the spread of pauperism in new and more serious forms in the sixteenth and seventeenth centuries, see Geremek (1980, 1986).

30 Braudel (1981, pp. 75–6).

31 Piuz (1970, pp. 134–5).

32 Martin Luther, *Luther's Works. 54: Table Talk* (trans. T. G. Tappert), Philadelphia, 1967, p. 207.

33 Tacitus, *Germania*, XXIII (trans. M. Hutton), London, 1958, p. 297.

34 For the theme of the drunken German, see Messedaglia (1974, I, pp. 37–8); see also Braudel (1981, pp. 233–4).

35 Redi is cited in Camporesi (1990, p. 147).

36 M. Montaigne, *The Diary of Montaigne's Journey to Italy in 1580 and 1581* (trans. E. J. Trechmann), New York, 1929, pp. 108, 216, 218–19.

37 On soldiers' diets, see Morineau (1970), especially pp. 110, 118–19.

38 Ibid., p. 111.

39 On the relation between demographic curves and wheat prices in England and France, see Livi Bacci (1991, pp. 55–9).

40 The *Brieve racconto di tutte le radici, di tutte l'erbe e di tutti i frutti, che crudi o cotti in Italia si mangiano* of Castelvetro (first published in London in 1614) can now be found in L. Firpo, ed., *Gastronomia del Rinascimento*, Turin, 1973, pp. 131–76; see also pp. 32–8 for a comment by the editor.

41 For Felici's 'letter' *Dell'insalata e piante che in qualunque modo vengono per cibo del 'homo* (addressed to Ulisse Aldrovandi), see C. Felici, *Scritti naturalistici*, I (ed. G. Arbizzoni), Urbino, 1986; Massonio's *Archidipno, overo dell'insalata, e dell'uso di essa* was published in 1627 in Venice.

42 Martin Luther, *Table Talk* (see *Discorsi a tavola*, ed. L. Perini, Turin, 1969, p. 11).

43 Paolo Zacchia, *Vitto quaresimale*, Rome, 1636.

44 I take the story of the Florentine inquisitor from Camporesi 1983a, pp. 192–3 (who in turn cites Imbert 1930, pp. 254–5).

45 On the impact of the Reformation on the European fishing industry, see Michell (1977, p. 175).

46 On the extension of beer consumption in the seventeenth century, see Braudel (1981, p. 238).

47 Flandrin (1984, p. 77).

48 On the concession regarding the use of *oleum lardinum*, see Walter Map's description in *De nugis curialium*, I, 24, p. 77.

49 The discussion of the use of fats in European cooking is taken primarily from Flandrin (1983); see. 108 for dispensations regarding the use of

butter (and also Hémardinquer 1970a, p. 260). See also Flandrin (1984).

50   The story of the Cardinal of Aragon is from Braudel (1981, p. 212); 'structures of taste' is Flandrin's expression.

51   The principal source used in this section, and that from which many of the documentary references are taken, is Flandrin (1983).

52   On the 'lean' character of sauces used until the sixteenth century, see also Flandrin and Redon (1981, pp. 401ff) and Laurioux (1989b, pp. 35ff)

53   On the differing uses of spices in European cuisine, a practice connected to the more or less marked luxury image they enjoyed in different areas, see Braudel (1981, p. 222). This process also took place on a smaller scale, as in the case of melegueta pepper which was abandoned in France as it became more common; see Laurioux (1989a, pp. 200ff).

54   On the increased use of sugar in the fourteenth and fifteenth centuries, see Laurioux (1989a, pp. 208ff).

55   For this German example, see *Libro di buone vivande. La cucina tedesca dell'età cortese*, p. 56.

56   The passage from Sacchi is in *De honesta voluptate et valetudine*, CLXXVIII; I use the recent Italian translation edited by E. Faccioli: *Il piacere onesto e la buona salute* Turin, 1985, p 141

57   For the Ortelius passage (*Theatrum orbis*), see Braudel (1981, p. 225).

58   On the history of sugar and of colonial plantation slavery, see Mintz (1985), Meyer (1989) and also the seminar proceedings of *La caña de azúcar en tiempos de los grandes descubrimientos, 1450–1550*, Motril, 1989.

59   On the high levels of wine consumption verified up to the seventeenth century, see Montanari (1979, pp. 381–4), Rouche (1973, pp. 308, 311), Pini (1989, pp. 122ff) and Bennassar and Goy (1975, pp. 408, 424).

60   The Swedish data are in Slicher van Bath (1963, p. 85). See also Braudel (1981, pp.234–5).

61   On the Hôtel-Dieu, see Hohl (1971, p. 187).

62   On the practice of mixing wine and water, see Montanari (1988a, pp. 88–9); on the the difficulty of obtaining potable water through the nineteenth century, see Bennassar and Goy (1975, p. 424), Roche (1984) and Goubert (1986).

63   There are many studies on the sacred use of wine in pagan religions; see, for example, Otto (1933) and the proceedings of the conference *L'imaginaire du vin* (Marseille, 1989), as well as Detienne (1986). For the use of wine as a euphoric drug, see, in addition to the classic de Félice (1936), Escohotado (1989).

64 On the invention and spread (first pharmacological then alimentary) of distilled alcohol, see Braudel (1981, pp. 241–7). See also Escohotado (1989, I, pp. 299–300). Brunello (1969) is also of some use.

65 On the history of coffee and its introduction to Europe, see Jacob (1935).

66 Schivelbusch (1980, p. 27).

67 Braudel (1981, pp. 256–60) (from which come the citations of Le Grand d'Aussy and L. S. Mercier, p. 258).

68 On tea, see Ukers (1936), Braudel (1981, pp. 250–6) (including some of the quotations used here) and Butel (1989). The late seventeenth-century Dutch figure is from Burema (1954), cited by Hémardinquer (1970b, p. 290). Ibid., p. 286 on English consumption (as derived from various authors including Drummond and Wilbraham 1937). The quotation of C. Bontekoe is in Jacob (1935, p. 81).

69 Jacob (1935, pp. 90–1).

70 Schivelbusch (1980, p. 83).

71 On the use of cocoa and choclate, see Braudel (1981, pp. 249–50). On the extravagant multiplicity of experimentation which characterized the use of cacao in the early eighteenth century (including every sort of error and abuse), see Camporesi (1990, pp. 115–16). On the social and ideological characterization of the new beverages as well as their cultural image (coffee as an intellectual and bourgeois drink, chocolate as an idle and aristocratic one), see also Schivelbusch (1980).

5 The Century of Hunger

1 On the European demography of the eighteenth century, see Livi Bacci (1991, p. 2) (with reference to Biraben 1979).

2 On the agricultural expansion of the eighteenth century, see Abel (1935) and Slicher van Bath (1963, pp. 239ff).

3 On the 'second' introduction of rice to European agriculture and its new status as a food for the poor, see, for example, the case of Auvergne (Poitrineau 1970, p. 151) and that of the area around Geneva (Piuz 1970, p. 144).

4 On buckwheat, see Slicher van Bath (1963, pp. 264–5). Holland provides an example of its introduction for the first time (Morineau 1970, p. 122, n. 4).

5 On corn and potato yields, see Stoianovich (1970, p. 283) and Slicher van Bath (1963, p. 93 and note).

6 The untranslated titles of these two works are: *Alimurgia, o sia modo di render meno gravi le carestie per sollievo de' poveri* and *Della ghianda e della quercia e di altre cose utili a cibo e coltura.*

7 See pp. 100–104 above.

8 Kula (1963, p. 261).

9 On the success of maize in northern Italy, see, in addition to Messedaglia (1927), Coppola (1979).

10 On the link between the expansion of the cultivation of maize and the development of agrarian capitalism, see Braudel (1981, p. 166).

11 Stoianovich (1970, p. 273).

12 Stoianovich (1970, p. 282); see this work in general for the case of maize in the Balkans.

13 G. Battarra, *Pratica agraria distribuita in vari dialoghi*, Cesena, 1782, pp. 104–5. See also Montanari (1991, pp. 341–3).

14 There are many studies on pellagra, including Messedaglia's classic works (1927, 1949–50, etc.); for a review, see Coppola (1979, pp. 189ff); among more recent works is De Bernardi (1984).

15 G. Strambio, *Cagioni, natura e sede della pellagra*, Milan, 1824, p. 2, n. 1.

16 Braudel (1981, p. 170).

17 On the spread of the potato in the eighteenth and nineteenth centuries, see Slicher van Bath (1963, pp. 267–9), Masefield (1967, pp. 344–6) Braudel (1981, pp. 169–70).

18 On Auvergne, see Poitrineau (1970, p. 150).

19 Stoianovich (1970, p. 272).

20 Thuillier (1970, p. 161).

21 Panjek (1976).

22 Ibid., p. 580.

23 Ibid., p. 585.

24 On the 'social rise' of the potato, see the brief observations of Bloch (1970, pp. 234–5).

25 Battarra, *Pratica Agraria*, pp. 131–4.

26 From a letter of G. Bonanome; see Panjek (1976, p. 585).

27 On the Irish famine of 1845–6, see Slicher van Bath (1963, p. 270), but especially Woodham-Smith (1962) and Salaman (1985, pp. 250ff).

28 Battarra, *Pratica Agraria*, pp. 131–4.

29 For consideration of the problems relative to the history of pasta, see the dossier 'Contre Marco Polo: une histoire comparée des pâtes alimentaires' in vols 16–17 (1989) of the journal *Médiévales. Langue, textes, histoire.* In particular, for Europe, see the contributions of O. Redon and B. Laurioux on the Italian cookery books of the fourteenth and fifteenth centuries;

M. Montanari on the state of scholarship on the question in Italy; J. L. Flandrin on Provençal gastronomy; see also F. Sabban-Serventi's essay on Chinese food culture and B. Rosenberger's on Arabic. The Arabic derivation of Italian pasta use is upheld by L. Sada (1982) (and see there also important references to previous research).

30 On the early history of pasta in Italy, see also Montanari (1988a, pp. 133, 167–8) and Rebora (1987, pp. 1497–500). For the Renaissance period, Messedaglia (1974, I, pp. 175ff) is a mine of information.

31 On terminology, see Alessio (1958).

32 On the use of millet and other grains to make pasta, see Messedaglia (1927, p. 231).

33 On the price of pasta in Sicily, see Aymard and Bresc (1975, p. 541).

34 On the seventeenth-century pasta revolution, see Sereni's fundamental work (1958) on which the discussion here is largely based (including reference to particular details such as the Neapolitan proclamation of 1509).

35 On the marginal role of pasta in parts of southern Italy in the nineteenth century, see Somogyi (1973, p. 848) and Sorcinelli (1983, p. 91).

36 The hypothesis of McKeown (1976, 1983) has been discussed by Livi Bacci (1991, pp. 19ff), and it is above all to the latter's work that I refer in the text. See in particular p. 114, on the need to distinguish between the medium and long run when evaluating the demographic effect of nutritional phenomena.

37 On the general impoverishment of the nutritional regime, both from a qualitative and quantitative–caloric point of view, and the untenability of McKeown's hypothesis, see Razzell (1974, pp. 8–9). Livi Bacci (1991, pp. 79–85, 95–9) has synthesized many studies on this argument (including Pugliese 1908; Perez Moreda 1980).

38 For the relative heights of European populations, I use again Livi Bacci (1991, pp. 107–10) (who incorporates the studies of Eveleth and Tanner 1976; Tanner 1981; Komlos 1985, 1986; Sandberg and Steckel 1980; Floud and Wachter 1982; and Würm 1982).

39 Thuillier (1970, pp. 166–7).

40 Poitrineau (1970, pp. 149ff).

41 Kula (1963, p. 413).

42 Battarra, *Pratica agraria*, pp. 133–4.

43 On the opposition between taste and necessity, see Flandrin (1983).

44 For Cirelli, see p. 88 above.

45 M. Lastri, *Regole per i padroni dei poderi verso i contadini, per proprio vantaggio e di loro. Aggiuntavi una raccolta di avvisi ai contadini sulla loro salute*. Venice, 1793, pp. 31–9 (see Montanari 1991, pp. 359–61).

46 See Braudel (1981, p. 78).
47 A. Smith, *An Inquiry into the Nature and Causes of the Wealth of Nations*, VI.ii.k, Oxford, 1976, p. 876.
48 Braudel (1981, p. 197).
49 On Rousseau's vegetarian philosophy, see Montanari (1991, p. xxiv).
50 On the contrast between the advocates of 'old' and 'new' cuisine, see Montanari (1991, pp. 284–5, 332–8) and especially Camporesi (1990).

6 The Revolution

1   On the economic and caloric importance of grains in Europe and the change occurring during the nineteenth and twentieth centuries, a large number of studies and statistical data might be cited; see in any case the general evaluations of Aymard (1975, p. 438) and Livi Bacci (1991, pp. 85–95); For France, see Toutain (1971); for Italy, Somogyi (1973). See also Dauphin and Pezerat (1975) and Sorcinelli (1983, p. 90). On English and Dutch potato consumption, see Razzell (1974, p. 8) and Vanderbroeke (1971, p. 35).
2   On the 'white bread revolution', see Braudel (1981, pp. 137–8); on the new milling techniques, Tannahill (1973, p. 374).
3   On the Manchester Vegetarian Society, see Mennell (1985, p. 307). Ibid., p. 306 for the new attitudes towards animals and against their public slaughter (with reference to Thomas 1983, pp. 182–3).
4   On levels of meat consumption at the beginning of the nineteenth century, see Abel (1935) and Toutain (1971, p. 1947).
5   On new conservation techniques and the world livestock market, see Tannahill (1973, pp. 352–63).
6   For Wynter's citation, see Tannahill (1973, pp. 348–9).
7   *Punch*, 4 August 1855, p. 47.
8   On food adulteration and and the accusations of Accum, see Tannahill (1973, pp. 343–6) and Nebbia and Menozzi Nebbia (1986, pp. 61–2) (this latter includes the *Punch* vignette).
9   Pelto and Pelto 1983, pp. 312ff.
10 Ibid., p. 323.
11 Ibid., p. 325.
12 On the psychological and cultural as well as economic importance of the traditional alternation of 'fat' and 'lean', see Claudian and Serville (1970b, p. 300) (which also includes reference to Jungian analyses).
13 Claudian and Serville (1970a, p. 174).

14 See the fragments of Archestratus of Gela in E. Degani, ed., *Poesia parodica greca*, Bologna, 1983, pp. 77–92. The passage from Cassiodorus is in *Variae*, XII, 4 (ed. A. J. Fridh in *Corpus Christianorum. Series latina*, XCVI. Turnhout, 1973, pp. 467–9). Both texts can be found in Montanari (1989a, pp. 37–41, 208–9).

15 On Hippocrates, see p. 84 above.

16 On the 'magic garden' in *Erec et Enide* (from which vss. 5696–7 are cited here), see Le Goff (1982).

17 Isidore's definition is in *Etymologiae*, XVII, 10.

18 For the biography of Gallienus (by Trebellius Pollio), see *Historia Augusta*, Life of the two Gallieni, XVI (p. 669).

19 For Chiari, see Montanari (1991, pp. 301–3); see also Camporesi (1990, pp. 104–5).

20 Meldini (1988, p. 429).

21 The citation of Stefani is found in *L'arte di ben cucinare*, Mantua, 1662, pp. 142–4; see also Montanari (1991, pp. 223–5).

22 The phrase of the French peasant (in P. Le Jeune, *Relation de ce qui arriva en Nouvelle France*, 1634) is reproduced in Hémardinquer (1970a, p. 271). See there also the discussion of water as the 'grand "fond de cuisson" rural'.

23 See Montanari (1989a, p. 241).

24 See Montanari (1979, p. 158).

25 For the Grimm brothers' description of the land of Cuccagna (Schlauraffenland), see *Grimm's Fairy Tales* (ed. J. Scharl), New York, 1944, pp. 660–1.

26 For the literary citations of Bandello, Sacchetti and Goldoni, I have used S. Battaglia, ed., *Grande dizionario della lingua italiana*, Turin, 1961 under the heading 'grasso'.

27 On Galen's slimming diet, see Montanari (1989a, pp. 161–2).

28 J. Olivier, *Alphabet de l'imperfection et malice des femmes*, Rouen, 1617, p. 412.

29 On the dehydrating and slimming values of coffee (contrasted to traditional alcoholic beverages), see Schivelbusch (1980).

30 I have in mind in particular the opening pages of Mann's *Buddenbrooks*.

31 Braudel (1981, p. 184).

32 The two volumes of Rajberti (*L'arte di convitare spiegata al popolo*) were published in Milan in 1850 and 1851. The passage cited is from Part I, chapter VI.

33 On the 'insatiable eaters' of popular epic, see Camporesi (1970, n. 1 and p. 46).

34 On meat prices (and the greater value of fatty meats) in Roman times, see Corbier (1989, pp. 129–30).
35 Barthes (1970, p. 314).
36 On the continued suspicion regarding 'pleasure' into the 1960s, see Barthes (1970, p. 308).

Bibliography

Abel, W. (1935) [1966] *Agrarkrisen und Agrarconjunktur in Mitteleuropa vom 13. bis zum 19. Jahrhudert*, Hamburg and Berlin.

—— (1937) 'Wandlungen des Fleischverbrauchs und der Fleischversorgung in Deutschland seit dem ausgehenden Mittelalter', *Berichte über Landwirtschaft. Zeitschrift für Agrarpolitik und Landwirtschaft*, vol. XII, no. 3, pp. 411–52.

Alessio, G. (1958) 'Storia linguistica di un antico cibo rituale: i maccheroni', *Atti dell'Accademia Pontaniana*, n.s., vol. VIII, pp. 261–80.

Alexandre Bidon, D. and Beck Bossard, C. (1984) 'La Préparation des repas et leur consommation en Forez au XVe siècle d'après les sources archéologiques', in *Manger et boire au Moyen Age*, Nice, II, pp. 59–71.

—— and Closson, M. (1985) *L'Enfant à l'ombre des cathédrales*, Lyon.

Amouretti, M. C. (1986) *Le Pain et l'huile dans la Grèce antique*, Paris.

André, J. (1981) *L'Alimentation et la cuisine à Rome*, Paris.

Andreolli, B. (1988) *Le cacce dei Pico. Pratiche venatorie, paesaggio e società a Mirandola tra Medioevo ed Età Moderna*, San Felice sul Panaro.

Aron, J. P. (1975) *The Art of Eating in France: Manners and Menus in the Nineteenth Century*, London.

Aymard, J. (1951) *Les Chasses romaines*, Paris.

Aymard, M. (1975) 'Pour l'histoire de l'alimentation: quelques remarques de méthode', *Annales ESC*, vol. XXX, nos. 2–3, pp. 431–44.

—— and Bresc, H. (1975) 'Nourritures et consommation en Sicile entre XIVe et XVIIIe siècle', *Mélanges de l'Ecole Française de Rome*, vol. 87, pp. 535–81.

Barthes, R. (1970) 'Pour une psycho-sociologie de l'alimentation contemporaine', in J. J. Hémardinquer, ed., *Pour une histoire de l'alimentation*, Paris, pp. 307–15 (also in *Annales ESC*, vol. XVI, 1961).

Baruzzi, M. and Montanari, M. (1981) *Porci e porcari nel Mediœvo. Paesaggio economia alimentazione*, Bologna.

Bautier, A. M. (1984) 'Pain et pâtisserie dans les textes médiévaux antérieurs au XIIIe siècle', in *Manger et boire au Moyen Age*, Nice, I, pp. 33–65.

Beck Bossard, C. (1984) 'Ostéologie et alimentation carnée', in H. Bresc, ed., *Matériaux pour l'histoire des cadres de vie dans l'Europe Occidentale (1050– 1250)*, Nice, pp. 17–30.

Beloch, K. J. (1908) 'La popolazione dell'Europa nell'Antichità, nel Medio Evo e nel Rinascimento', *Biblioteca dell'economista*, Turin.

Bennassar, B. and Goy, J. (1975) 'Contribution à l'histoire de la consommation alimentaire du XIVe au XIXe siècle', *Annales ESC*, vol. XXX, pp. 402–30.

Biraben, J. N. (1975) *Les Hommes et la peste en France et dans les pays européens et méditerranéens*, I. *La Peste dans l'histoire*, Paris.

—— (1979) 'Essai sur l'évolution du nombre des hommes', *Population*, vol. 34, pp. 13–25.

Bloch, M. (1970) 'Les Aliments de l'ancienne France', in J. J. Hémardinquer, ed., *Pour une histoire de l'alimentation*, Paris, pp. 231–35 (also in *Encyclopédie française*, vol. XIV, 1954, 40, 2–3).

Bois, G. (1989) *La Mutation de l'an mil*, Paris.

Bolens, L. (1980) 'Pain quotidien et pain de disette dans l'Espagne musulmane', *Annales ESC*, vol. XXXV, pp. 462–76 (also in appendix to id., *Agronomes andalous du Moyen-Age*, Geneva and Paris, 1981).

—— (1990) *La cuisine andalouse, un art de vivre. XIe–XIIIe siècle*, Paris.

Bonnassie, P. (1989) 'Consommation d'aliments immondes et cannibalisme de survie dans l'Occident du haut Moyen Age', *Annales ESC*, vol. XLIV, pp. 1035–56.

Branston, B. (1955) *Gods of the North*, New York.

Braudel, F. (1981) *Civilization and Capitalism*, vol. I. *The Structures of Everyday Life: The Limits of the Possible*. New York.

Brunello, F. (1969) *Storia dell'aquavite*, Vicenza.

Burema, L. (1954) *De Voeding in Nederland*, Assen.

Butel, P. (1989) *Histoire du thé*, Paris.

Camporesi, P. (1970) Introduction and notes to P. Artusi, *La scienza in cucina e l'arte di mangiar bene*. Turin.

—— (1976) *La maschera di Bertoldo. G. C. Croce e la letteratura carnevalesca*. Turin.

—— (1978) *Il paese della fame*, Bologna.

—— (1980) *Il pane selvaggio*. Bologna.

—— (1983a) *Alimentazione folclore società*, Parma.

—— (1983b) *La carne impossibile*, Milan.

—— (1990) *Il brodo indiano. Edonismo ed esotismo nel Settecento*, Milan.

Capatti, A. (1989) *Le Goût du nouveau. Origines de la modernité alimentaire*, Paris.

Cherubini, G. (1984) *L'Italia rurale del basso Mediœvo*, Rome and Bari.

Chevalier, B. (1958) 'Alimentation et niveau de vie à Tours à la fin du XVe siècle', *Bulletin philologique et historique*, pp. 143–57.

—— (1982) 'L'Alimentation carnée à la fin du XVe siècle: réalité et symboles', in *Pratiques et discours alimentaires à la Renaissance*, Paris, pp. 193–9.

Cioranescu, A. (1971). 'Utopia, Land of Cocaigne and Golden Age', *Diogenes*, vol. 75, pp. 85–121.

Claudian, J. and Serville, Y. (1970a) 'Aspects de l'évolution récente du comportement alimentaire en France: composition des repas et "urbanisation" ', in J. J. Hémardinquer, ed., *Pour une histoire de l'alimentation*, Paris, pp. 174–87.

—— (1970b) 'Les Aliments du dimanche et du vendredi. Etudes sur le comportement alimentaire actuel en France', in J. J. Hémardinquer, ed., *Pour une histoire de l'alimentation*, Paris, pp. 300–6.

Cocchiara, G. (1956) *Il paese di Cuccagna*, Turin.

Coppola, G. (1979) *Il mais nell'economia agricola lombarda*, Bologna.

Corbier, M. (1989) 'Le Statut ambigu de la viande à Rome', *Dialogues d'histoire ancienne*, vol. 15, no. 2, pp. 107–58.

Crous, J. (1990) 'L'alimentació com a llenguatge a partir dels llibres de cavalleria', contribution to *Coloquio de historia de la alimentación a la Corona de Aragón*, Lleida.

Curschmann, F. (1900) *Hungersnöte im Mittelalter*, Paris.

Dauphin, C. and Pezerat, P. (1975) 'Les Consommations populaires dans la seconde moitié du XIXe siècle à travers les monographies de l'école de Le Play', *Annales ESC*, vol. XXX, nos. 2–3, pp. 537–52.

De Bernardi, A. (1984) *Il mal della rosa. Denutrizione e pellagra nelle campagne italiane fra '800 e '900*, Milan.

De Félice, P. (1936) *Poisons sacrés. Ivresses divines*, Paris.

De La Roncière, C.-M. (1982) *Prix et salaires à Florence au XIVe siècle (1280–1380)*, Rome.

Desportes, F. (1987) *Le Pain au Moyen Age*, Paris.

Detienne, M. (1986) *Dionysos à ciel ouvert*, Paris.

Dion, R. (1959) [1990] *Histoire de la vigne et du vin en France des origines au XIXe siècle*, Paris.

Doehaerd, R. (1971) *Le Haut Moyen Age occidental: économies et sociétés*, Paris.

Drummond, J. and Wilbraham, A. (1937) [1955] *The Englishman's Food. A History of Five Centuries of English Diet*, London.

Duby, G. (1974) *The Early Growth of the European Economy: Warriors and Peasants from the Seventh to the Twelfth Century*, Ithaca.

Dupèbe, J. (1982) 'La Diététique et l'alimentation des pauvres selon Sylvius', in *Pratiques et discours alimentaires à la Renaissance*, Paris, pp. 41–56.

Durand, J. D. (1977) 'Historical estimates of world population: an evaluation', *Population and Development Review*, vol. 3, pp. 253–96.

Dyer, C. (1986) 'Changes in nutrition and standard of living in England, 1200–1550', in *Ninth Economic History Congress*, Berne.

Elias, N. (1969) *Über den Prozess der Zivilisation*, I. *Wandlungen des Verhaltens in den weltlichen Oberschichten des Abendlandes*, Frankfurt (with an introduction added to the original 1936 edn).

Escohotado, A. (1989) *Historia de las drogas*, Madrid.

Essen und Trinken (1987) *Essen und Trinken in Mittelalter und Neuzeit*, ed. I. Bitsch, T. Ehlert and X. von Ertzdorff, Sigmaringen.

European Food History (1992) *European Food History. A Research Review*, ed. H. J. Teuteberg, Leicester.

Eveleth, P. B. and Tanner, J. M. (1976) *Worldwide Variations in Human Growth*, Cambridge.

Faccioli, E., ed. (1987) *L'arte della cucina in Italia. Libri di ricette e trattati sulla civiltà della tavola dal XIV al XIX secolo*, Turin.

Finzi, R. (1976) *Un problema di storia sociale. L'alimentazione*, Bologna.

Fischler, C. (1990) *L'Homnivore*, Paris.

Fiumi, E. (1959) 'Economia e vita privata dei fiorentini nelle rilevazioni statistiche di Giovanni Villani', in C. M. Cipolla, ed., *Storia dell'economia italiana*, Turin, pp. 325–60.

—— (1972) 'Sulle condizioni alimentari di Prato nell'età comunale', *Archivio storico pratese*, vol. XLII, pp. 3–26.

Flandrin, J. L. (1983) 'Le Goût et la nécessité: réflexions sur l'usage des graisses dans les cuisines de l'Europe occidentale (XIVe–XVIIIe siècles)', *Annales ESC*, vol. XXXVIII, pp. 369–401.

—— (1984) 'Internationalisme, nationalisme et régionalisme dans la cuisine des XIVe et XVe siècles: le témoignage des livres de cuisine', in *Manger et boire au Moyen Age*, II, Nice, pp. 75–91.

—— (1989) 'Les Pâtes dans la cuisine provençale', *Médiévales. Langue, textes, histoire*, vols. 16–17, pp. 65–75.

—— (1992) *Chronique de Platine. Pour une gastronomie historique*, Paris.

—— and Redon, O. (1981) 'Les Livres de cuisine italiens des XIVe et XVe siècles', *Archeologia medievale*, vol. VIII, pp. 393–408.

Floud, R. and Wachter, R. (1982) 'Poverty and physical stature', *Social Science History*, vol. 6, no. 4, pp. 432–3.

Fontaine, M. M. (1982) 'L'Alimentation du jeune enfant au XVIe siècle', in *Pratiques et discours alimentaires à la Renaissance*, Paris, pp. 57–68.

Fortunati, V. and Zucchini, G., eds, (1989) *Paesi di Cuccagna e mondi alla rovescia*, Florence.

Fumagalli, V. (1966) 'Crisi del dominico e aumento del masserizio nei beni "infra valle" del monastero di S. Colombano di Bobbio dall '862 all '883', *Rivista di storia dell'agricoltura*, vol. VI, pp. 352–9.

Fumagalli, V. (1970) 'Colonizzazione e insediamenti agricoli nell'Occidente altomedievale: la Valle Padana', *Quaderni storici*, vol. 14, pp. 319–38.

—— (1976) *Terra e società nell'Italia padana. I secoli IX e X*, Turin.

—— (1978) *Il Regno italico*, Turin (*Storia d'Italia*, ed. G. Galasso, II).

Gabba, E. and Pasquinucci, M. (1979) *Strutture agrarie e allevamento transumante nell'Italia romana (III–I sec. a.C.)*, Pisa.

Geremek, B. (1980) *Inutiles au monde. Truands et misérables dans l'Europe moderne*, Paris.

—— (1986) *La pietà e la forca. Storia della miseria e della carità in Europa*, Rome and Bari (also exists in French: *La Potence ou la pitié: l'Europe et les pauvres du Moyen Age à nos jours*, Paris, 1987).

Giardina, A. (1981) 'Allevamento ed economia della selva in Italia meridionale: trasformazioni e continuità', in A. Giardina and A. Schiavone, eds, *Società romana e produzione shiavistica*, I. *L'Italia: insediamenti e forme economiche*, Rome and Bari, pp. 87–113.

Giuffrida, A. (1975) 'Considerazioni sul consumo della carne a Palermo nei secoli XIV e XV', *Mélanges de l'Ecole Française de Rome*, vol. 87, pp. 583–95.

Goody, J. (1982) *Cooking, Cuisine and Class. A Study in Comparative Sociology*, Cambridge.

Goubert, J. P. (1986) *La Conquête de l'eau*, Paris.

Goubert, P. (1966) *Louis XIV et vingt millions de Français*, Paris.

Graf, A. (1892) 'Il Paese di Cuccagna e i paradisi artificiali', in id., *Miti, leggende e superstizioni del Medio Evo*, Turin, I, pp. 229–38.

Grieco, A. (1987) *Classes sociales, nourriture et imaginaire alimentaire en Italie (XIVe–XVe siècle)*, thèse 3e cycle, Paris (EHESS).

Grinberg, M. and Kinser, S. (1983) 'Les Combats de Carnaval et Carême. Trajets d'une métaphore', *Annales ESC*, vol. XXXVIII, pp. 65–98.

Grottanelli, C. (1981) 'L'ideologia del banchetto e l'ospite ambiguo', *Dialoghi di archeologia*, vol. 3, pp. 122–54.

Halard, X. (1983) 'La Pêche du saumon en Normandie du XIe au XVe siècle', *Journal of Medieval History*, vol. 9, pp. 173–8.

Harris, M. (1985) *Good to Eat. Riddles of Food and Culture*, New York.

Haussleiter, J. (1935) *Der Vegetarismus in der Antike*, Berlin.

Helleiner, K. (1967) 'The population of Europe from the Black Death to the eve of the Vital Revolution', in *The Cambridge Economic History of Europe*, Cambridge, vol. pp. 1–95.

Hémardinquer, J. J. (1963) 'L'Introduction du maïs et la culture des sorghos dans l'ancienne France', *Bulletin philologique et historique*, vol. 1, pp. 429–59.

—— (1970a) 'Les Graisses de cuisine en France. Essai de cartes', in J. J. Hémardinquer, ed., *Pour une histoire de l'alimentation*, Paris, pp. 254–71.

—— (1970b) 'Le Thé à la conquête de l'Occident. Le cas maghrébin', in J. J. Hémardinquer, ed., *Pour une histoire de l'alimentation*, Paris, pp. 285–91.

—— (1973) 'Les Débuts du maïs en Méditerranée', in *Histoire économique du monde méditerranéen, 1450–1650. Mélanges en l'honneur de Fernand Braudel*, Toulouse, pp. 227–33.

Henisch, B. A. (1976) *Fast and Feast. Food in Medieval Society*, London.

Hilton, R. (1973) *Bond Men Made Free. Medieval Peasant Movements and the English Rising of 1381*, London.

Hohl, C. (1971) 'Alimentation et consommation à l'Hôtel-Dieu de Paris aux XVe et XVIe siècles', in *Actes du 93e Congrès des Sociétés Savantes, I, Les Problèmes de l'alimentation*, Paris, pp. 181–208.

Imbert, G. (1930) *Seicento fiorentino*, Milan.

Jacob, R. J. (1935) *Coffee. The Epic of a Commodity*, New York.

Jones, P. (1980) *Economia e società nell'Italia medievale*, Turin.

Jouanna, A. (1977) *Mythes et hiérarchies dans la France du XVIe siècle*, Paris.

Kahane, E. (1978) *Parmentier ou la dignité de la pomme de terre. Essai sur la famine*, Paris.

Kaplan, S. (1976) *Bread, Politics and Political Economy in the Reign of Louis XV*, The Hague.

Ketcham Wheaton, B. (1983) *Savoring the Past: The French Kitchen and Table from 1300 to 1789*, Philadelphia.

Komlos, J. (1985) 'Patterns of children's growth in the Habsburg monarchy: the standards of living and economic development in the eighteenth century', *American Historical Review*, vol. 90, no. 3.

—— (1986) 'Patterns of children's growth in east-central Europe in the Eighteenth century', *Annals of Human Biology*, vol. 13, no. 1, pp. 33–48.

Kula W. (1963) *Problemy i metody historii gospodarczej*, Warsaw (citation from Italian version: *Problemi e metodi di storia economica*, Milan, 1972).

Lachiver, M. (1988) *Vins, vignes et vignerons. Histoire du vignoble français*, Paris.

Laurioux, B. (1983) 'De l'usage des épices dans l'alimentation médiévale', *Médiévales. Langue, textes, histoire*, vol. 5, pp. 15–31.

—— (1989a) 'Modes culinaires et mutations du goût à la fin du Moyen Age', in *Artes mechanicae en Europe médiévale*, Brussels, pp. 199–222.

—— (1989b) *Le Moyen Age à table*, Paris.

Lazard, M. (1982) 'Nourrices et nourrissons d'après le traité de Vallambert (1565) et la Paedotrophia de Scevole de Sainte Marthe (1584)', in *Pratiques et discours alimentaires à la Renaissance*, Paris, pp. 69–83.

Le Goff, J. (1967) *Il Basso Medioevo*, Milan (translation of *Das Hochmittelalter*, Frankfurt a. M., 1965).

Le Goff, J. (1977) 'L'Occident médiévale et l'océan Indien: un horizon onirique', in *Pour un autre Moyen Age*, Paris, pp. 230–98.

—— (1982) 'Quelques remarques sur les codes vestimentaire et alimentaire dans "Erec et Enide" ', in *Mélanges René Louis*, Argenteuil, pp. 1243–58.

—— (1983) 'Il deserto-foresta nell'Occidente medievale' in id., *Il meraviglioso e il quotidiano nell'Occidente medievale*, Rome and Bari, pp. 25–44.

—— (1988) 'Età mitiche', in id., *Storia e memoria*, Turin.

Le Roy Ladurie, E. (1971) *Times of Feast, Times of Famine: A History of Climate since the Year 1000*, New York.

—— (1974) *The Peasants of Languedoc*, Urbana.

Livi Bacci, M. (1991) *Population and Nutrition: An Essay on European Demographic History*, Cambridge.

Longo, O. (1989) *Le forme della predazione. Cacciatori e pescatori della Grecia antica*, Naples, 1989.

McEvedy, C. and Jones, R. (1978) *Atlas of World Population History*, London.

McKeown, T. (1976) *The Modern Rise of Population*, London.

—— (1983) 'Food, infection and population', *Journal of Interdisciplinary History*, vol. 14, no. 2, pp. 227–47.

Mandrou, R. (1961) 'Théorie ou hypothèse de travail?' *Annales ESC*, vol. XVI, pp. 965–71.

Manger et boire (1984) *Manger et boire au Moyen Age*, I–II, Nice.

Maravall, J. (1979) *Poder, honor y élites en el siglo XVII*, Madrid.

Martelotti, A. (1984) 'Cibo dei signori e cibo dei contadini in una novella in versi del basso medioevo tedesco', *Annali della Facoltà di Lingue e Letterature Straniere dell'Università di Bari*, serie III, 5, pp. 279–98.

Masefield, G. B. (1967) 'Crops and livestock', in E. E. Rich and C. H. Wilson, *The Cambridge Economic History of Europe*, IV. *The Economy of Expanding Europe in the Sixteenth and Seventeenth Centuries*, Cambridge, pp. 275–301.

Maurizio, A. (1932) *Histoire de l'alimentation végétale depuis le préhistoire jusqu'à nos jours*, Paris.

Mazzarino, S. (1951) *Aspetti sociali del quarto secolo. Ricerche di storia tardoromana*, Rome.

Mazzi, M. S. (1980) 'Note per una storia dell'alimentazione nell'Italia medievale', in *Studi di storia medievale e moderna per Ernesto Sestan*, Florence, pp. 57–102.

Meldini, P. (1988) 'A tavola e in cucina', in P. Melograni, ed., *La famiglia italiana dall '800 ad oggi*, Rome and Bari, pp. 417–82.

Mennell, S. (1985) *All Manners of Food. Eating and Taste in England and France from the Middle Ages to the Present*, Oxford and New York.

Messedaglia, L. (1927) *Il mais e la vita rurale italiana. Saggio di storia agraria*, Piacenza.

—— (1941–2) 'Schienale e morona. Storia di due vocaboli e contributo allo studio degli usi alimentari e dei traffici veneti con il Levante', *Atti del Reale Istituto Veneto di scienze, lettere ed arti*, vol. CI, no. II, pp. 1–58.

—— (1949–50) 'Granoturco e pellagra. Scipione Maffei e Volfgango Goethe in guerra contro il granoturco', *Annali dell'Accademia di Agricoltura di Torino*, vol. XCII, pp. 27–43.

—— (1974) *Vita e costumi della Rinascenza in Merlin Cocai*, Padua.

Meyer, J (1989) *Histoire du sucre*, Paris

Michell, A. R. (1977) 'The European Fisheries in Early Modern Europe', in E. E. Rich and C. H. Wilson, *The Cambridge Economic History of Europe*, V *The Economic Organization of Early Modern Europe*, Cambridge, pp. 133–85.

Mintz, S. W. (1985) *Sweetness and Power. The Place of Sugar in Modern History*, New York.

Mollat, M. (1978) *Les Pauvres au Moyen Age. Etude sociale*, Paris.

Montanari, M. (1979) *L'alimentazione contadina nell'alto Medioevo*, Naples.

—— (1984) *Campagne medievali. Strutture produttive, rapporti di lavoro, sistemi alimentari*, Turin.

—— (1988a) *Alimentazione e cultura nel Medioevo*, Rome and Bari.

—— (1988b) 'Uomini e orsi nelle fonti agiografiche dell'alto Medioevo' in B. Andreolli and M. Montanari, eds, *Il bosco nel Medioevo*, Bologna, pp. 55–72.

—— (1988c) *Contadini e città fra 'Langobardia' e 'Romania'*, Florence.

—— (1989a) *Convivio. Storia e cultura dei piaceri della tavola dall'Antichità al Medioevo*, Rome and Bari.

—— (1989b) 'Notes sur l'histoire des pâtes en Italie', *Médiévales. Langue, textes, histoire*, vols. 16–17, pp. 61–4.

—— (1990a) 'Vegetazione e alimentazione', in *L'ambiente vegetale nell'alto Medioevo*, Spoleto, vol. I, pp. 281–322.

—— (1990b) 'Alimentazione, cultura, società nel Medioevo', contribution to *Coloquio de historia de la alimentación a la Corona de Aragón*, Lleida.

—— (1991) *Nuovo convivio. Storia e cultura dei piaceri della tavola nell'età moderna*, Rome and Bari.

—— (1992) *Convivio oggi. Storia e cultura dei piaceri della tavola nell'età contemporanea*, Rome and Bari.

Morineau, M. (1970) 'Rations militaires et rations moyennes', in J. J. Hémardinquer, ed., *Pour une histoire de l'alimentation*, Paris, pp. 107–25.

Moulin, L. (1975) *L'Europe à table*, Brussels.

—— (1978) *La Vie quotidienne des religieux au Moyen Age, Xe–XVe siècle*, Paris.

Muzzarelli, M. G. (1982) 'Norme di comportamento alimentare nei libri penitenziali', *Quaderni medievali*, vol. 13, pp. 45–80.

Nada Patrone, A. M. (1981a) 'Trattati medici, diete e regimi alimentari in ambito pedemontano alla fine del Medioevo', *Archeologia Medievale*, vol. VIII, pp. 369–92.

—— (1981b) *Il cibo del ricco ed il cibo del povero. Contributo alla storia qualitativa dell'alimentazione. L'area pedemontana negli ultimi secoli del Medio Evo*, Turin.

Nebbia, G. and Menozzi Nebbia, G. (1986) 'Breve storia delle frodi alimentari', in S. Canepari, C. Maltoni and F. Saccani, eds, *Alimentazione e salute*, Bologna, pp. 59–68.

Neveux, H. (1973) 'L'Alimentation du XIVe au XVIIIe siècle', *Revue d'histoire économique et sociale*, vol. LI, pp. 336–79.

Novati, F. (1899) *L'influsso del pensiero latino sopra la civiltà italiana del Medio Evo*, Milan.

Otto, W. F. (1933) *Dionysos*, Frankfurt a. M.

Paccagnella, I. (1983) 'Cucina e ideologia alimentare nella Venezia del Rinascimento', in *Civiltà della tavola dal Medioevo al Rinascimento*, Venice, pp. 37–67.

Panjek, G. (1976) 'In margine alla storia dell'alimentazione: un dibattito settecentesco sull'introduzione della patata nel Veneto', in *Raccolta di scritti per il cinquantesimo anniversario* [della Facoltà di Economia e Commercio dell'Università degli Studi di Trieste], Udine, pp. 573–87.

Pelner Cosman, M. (1976) *Fabulous Feasts. Medieval Cookery and Ceremony*. New York.

Pelto, G. H. and Pelto, P. J. (1983) 'Diet and Delocalization: Dietary Changes since 1750', in R. I. Rotberg and T. K. Rabb, eds, *Hunger and History*, Cambridge, pp. 309–30.

Perez Moreda, V. (1980) *Las crisis de mortalidad en la España interior, siglos XVI–XIX*, Madrid.

Peyer, H. C. (1950) *Zur Getreidepolitik oberitalienischen Städte im 13. Jahrhundert*, Vienna.

Pini, A. I. (1989) *Vite e vino nel Medioevo*, Bologna.

Pinto, G. (1978) *Il libro del biadaiolo. Carestie e annona a Firenze dalla metà del '200 al 1348*, Florence.

—— (1982) *La Toscana nel tardo Medioevo. Ambiente, economia rurale, società*, Florence.

Piuz, A. M. (1970) 'Alimentation populaire et sous-alimentation au XVIIe siècle. Le cas de Genève et de sa région', in J. J. Hémardinquer, ed., *Pour une histoire de l'alimentation*, Paris, pp. 129–45.

Plouvier, L. (1988) 'La Confiserie européenne au Moyen Age', *Medium Aevum Quotidianum*, news. 13 (Krems 1988), pp. 28–47.

Poitrineau, A. (1970) 'L'Alimentation populaire en Auvergne au XVIIIe siècle', in J. J. Hémardinquer, ed., *Pour une histoire de l'alimentation*, Paris, pp. 146–53.

Pratiques et discours (1982) J. C. Margolin and R. Sauzet, eds, *Pratiques et discours alimentaires à la Renaissance*, Paris.

Pugliese, S. (1908) *Due secoli di vita agricola*, Turin.

Razzell, P. E. (1974) 'An Interpretation of "The Modern Rise of Population in Europe". A Critique', *Population Studies*, vol. 28, no. 1.

Rebora, G. (1987) 'La cucina medievale italiana tra Oriente e Occidente', *Miscellanea storica ligure*, vol. XIX, no. 1–2, pp. 1431–579.

Redon, O. (1984) 'Les Usages de la viande en Toscane au XIVe siècle', in *Manger et boire au Moyen Age*, Nice, II, pp. 121–30.

—— and Laurioux, B. (1989) 'La Constitution d'une nouvelle catégorie culinaire? Les pâtes dans les livres de cuisine italiens de la fin du Moyen Age', *Médiévales. Langue, textes, histoire*, vols. 16–17, pp. 51–60.

—— Sabban, F. and Serventi, S. (1992) *La Gastronomie au Moyen Age*, Paris.

Reinhard, M. R. and Armengaud, A. (1961) *Histoire générale de la population mondiale*, Paris.

Richter, D. (1989) 'Il paese di Cuccagna nella cultura popolare: una topografia storica', in V. Fortunati and G. Zucchini, eds, *Pæsi di Cuccagna e mondi alla rovescia*, Florence, pp. 113–24.

Roche, D. (1984) 'Le Temps de l'eau rare du Moyen Age à l'Epoque Moderne', *Annales ESC*, vol. XXXIX, pp. 383–99.

Rosenberger, B. (1989) 'Les Pâtes dans le monde musulman', *Médiévales. Langue, textes, histoire*, vols. 16–17, pp. 77–98.

Rouche, M. (1973) 'La Faim à l'époque carolingienne: essai sur quelques types de rations alimentaires', *Revue historique*, CCL, pp. 295–320.

—— (1984) 'Les Repas de fête à l'époque carolingienne', in *Manger et boire au Moyen Age*, Nice, pp. 265–96.

Ruggini, L. (1961) *Economia e società nell' "Italia Annonaria". Rapporti fra agricoltura e commercio dal IV al VI secolo d.C.*, Milan.

Russell, J. C. (1958) 'Late Ancient and Medieval population', *Transactions of the American Philosophical Society*, Philadelphia.

Sabban-Serventi, F. (1989) 'Ravioli cristallins et tagliatelle rouges: les pâtes chinoises entre XIIe et XIVe siècle', *Médiévales. Langue, textes, histoire*, vols. 16–17, pp. 29–50.

Sada, L. (1982) *Spaghetti e compagni*, Bari.

Salaman, R. N. (1985) *The History and Social Influence of the Potato*, Cambridge (1948 original revised by J. G. Hawkes).

Sandberg, L. G. and Steckel, R. (1980) 'Soldier, soldier, what made you grow so tall?' *Economy and History*, vol. 23, no. 2, pp. 91–105.

Sayers, W. (1990) 'A cut above: ration and station in an Irish king's hall', *Food and Foodways*, pp. 89–110.

Schivelbusch, W. (1980) *Das Paradies, der Geschmack und die Vernunft*, Munich and Vienna.

Sentieri, M. and Zazzu, G. N. (1992) *I semi dell'Eldorado. L'alimentazione in Europa dopo la scoperta dell'America*, Bari.

Sereni, E. (1958) 'Note di storia dell'alimentazione nel Mezzogiorno: i Napoletani da "mangiafoglia" a "mangiamaccheroni" ', *Cronache meridionali*, IV–V–VI (also in id., *Terra nuova e buoi rossi*, Turin, 1981, pp. 292–371).

Simoons, F. J. (1981) *Eat Not This Flesh. Food Avoidances in the Old World*, Westport.

Slicher van Bath, B. H. (1963) *The Agrarian History of Western Europe*, London.

Soler, J. (1973) 'Sémiotique de la nourriture dans la Bible', *Annales ESC*, vol. XXVIII, pp. 943–55.

Somogyi, S. (1973) 'L'alimentazione nell'Italia unita', in *Storia d'Italia, V. I documenti*, Turin, I, pp. 839–87.

Sorcinelli, P. (1983) 'Note sull'alimentazione nell'Italia giolittiana', *Italia contemporanea*, vol. 150, pp. 89–94.

—— (1992) *Gli italiani e il cibo. Appetiti, digiuni e rinunce dalla realtà contadina alla società del benessere*, Bologna.

Stoianovich, T. (1970) 'Le Maïs dans les Balkans', in J. J. Hémardinquer, ed., *Pour une histoire de l'alimentation*, Paris, pp. 272–84.

Stouff, L. (1969) 'La Viande. Ravitaillement et consommation à Carpentras au XVe siècle', *Annales ESC*, vol. XXIV, pp. 1431–48.

—— (1970) *Ravitaillement et alimentation en Provence aux XIVe et XVe siècles*, Paris and The Hague.

Tannahill, R. (1973) *Food in History*, New York.

Tanner, J. M. (1981) *A History of the Study of Human Growth*, Cambridge.

Thomas, K. (1983) *Man and the Natural World: Changing Attitudes in England, 1500–1800*, London.

Thuillier, G. (1970) 'L'Alimentation en Nivernais au XIXe siècle', in J. J. Hémardinquer, ed., *Pour une histoire de l'alimentation*, Paris, pp. 154–73.

Toubert, P. (1973) *Les Structures du Latium médiéval. Le Latium méridional et la Sabine du IXe siècle à la fin du XIIe siècle*, Rome.

Toussaint-Samat, M. (1987) *Histoire naturelle et morale de la nourriture*, Paris.

Toutain, J. C. (1971) 'La Consommation alimentaire en France de 1789 à 1964', *Economie et Societé*, Cahiers de l'ISEA, vol. A, no. 11, Geneva.

Tozzi, C. (1981) 'L'alimentazione nella Maremma medievale. Due esempi di scavi', *Archeologia medievale*, vol. VIII, pp. 299–303.

Traina, G. (1986) 'Pæsaggio e "decadenza". La palude nella trasformazione del mondo antico', in A. Giardina, ed., *Società romana e impero tardoantico*, III, *Le merci, gli insediamenti*, Rome and Bari, pp. 711–30.

Tudela, L. and Castells, F. (1990) 'Sistemes alimentaris i usos de taula al "Tirant lo blanc", contribution to *Coloquio de historia de la alimentación a la Corona de Aragón*, Lleida.

Ukers, W. H. (1936) *The Romance of Tea*, New York.

Van der Wee, H. (1963) 'Typologie des crises et changements de structures aux Pays-Bas (XVe–XVIe siècles)', *Annales ESC*, vol. XVIII.

Vanderbroeke, C. (1971) 'Cultivation and consumption of the potato in the 17th and 18th centuries', *Acta Historiæ Neerlandicæ*, vol. 5.

Vattuone, R. (1985) 'Aspetti dell'alimentazione nel mondo greco', in *L'alimentazione nell'anitichità*, Parma, pp. 185–207.

Vogel, C. (1969) *Le Pécheur et la pénitence dans l'Eglise au Moyen Age*, Paris.

—— (1976) 'Symboles culturels chrétiens. Les aliments sacrés: poisson et refrigeria', in *Simboli e simbologia nell'alto Mediævo*, Spoleto, I, pp. 197–252.

Wickham, C. (1985) 'Pastoralism and Underdevelopment in the Early Middle Ages', in *L'uomo di fronte al mondo animale nell'alto Mediævo*, Spoleto, I, pp. 401–51.

Woodham-Smith, C. (1962) *The Great Hunger. Ireland 1845–1849*, New York.

Würm, H. (1982) 'Über die Schwankungen der durchschnittlichen Körpehöhe', *Homo*, vol. 33, no. 1, p. 297.

Wyczanski, A. and Demninska, M. (1986) 'La Nourriture en Europe centrale au début de l'Age Moderne', in *Ninth Economic History Congress*, Berne.

Zug Tucci, H. (1983) 'La caccia da bene comune a privilegio', in *Storia d'Italia. Annali*, VI. *Economia naturale, economia monetaria*, Turin, pp. 397–445.

—— (1985) 'Il mondo medievale dei pesci tra realtà e immaginazione', in *L'uomo di fronte al mondo animale nell'alto Mediævo*, Spoleto, pp. 291–360.

Index